MW01489849

Transformative Theological Perspectives

Karen L. Bloomquist, Editor

on behalf of
The Lutheran World Federation – A Communion of Churches

Lutheran University Press
Minneapolis, Minnesota

Theology in the Life of the Church series

Being the Church in the Midst of Empire. Trinitarian Reflections, Karen L. Bloomquist (ed.)
Deepening Faith, Hope and Love in Relations with Neighbors of Other Faiths, Simone Sinn (ed.)
Identity, Survival Witness. Reconfiguring Theological Agendas, Karen L. Bloomquist (ed.)
Lutherans Respond to Pentecostalism, Karen L. Bloomquist (ed.)
Theological Practices that Matter, Karen L. Bloomquist (ed.)
Transformative Theological Perspectives, Karen L. Bloomquist (ed.)

Transformative Theological Perspectives

Theology in the Life of the Church, vol. 6
Karen L. Bloomquist, Editor
on behalf of the Lutheran World Federation

Editorial assistance and layout: LWF/Department for Theology and Studies
Design: LWF/Office of Communication Services
Artwork on cover: LWF/Office of Communication Services.
Photo © LWF/D.-M. Grötzsch

Published by Lutheran University Press under the auspices of:
The Lutheran World Federation—A Communion of Churches
150, rte de Ferney, P O Box 2100
CH-1211 Geneva 2, Switzerland

This book is also available in certain European bookstores using ISBN 978-3-905676-90-7

Library of Congress Cataloging-in-Publication Data

Transformative theological perspectives / Karen L. Bloomquist, editor, on behalf of The Lutheran World Federation.
    p. cm. -- (Theology in the life of the church)
ISBN-13: 978-1-932688-44-3 (alk. paper)
ISBN-10: 1-932688-44-7 (alk. paper)
    1. Lutheran Church--Doctrines--Congresses. I. Bloomquist, Karen L., 1948- II. Lutheran World Federation.
BX8065.3.T73 2009
230'.41--dc22
                2009049559

Lutheran University Press, PO Box 390759, Minneapolis, MN 55439
Printed in the United States of America

Contents

Introduction

Karen L. Bloomquist

This final volume in the Theology in the Life of the Church series, is the second book of articles based on papers that were presented and discussed at the March 2009 global theological consultation, "Transformative Perspectives and Practices Today" in Augsburg, Germany (hereafter, Augsburg 2009). Whereas the previous volume focused on theological practices that matter in various contexts around the world, this volume presents various constructive hermeneutical and theological proposals intended to further the development of Lutheran theological insights that are transformative in relation to new contexts and challenges today.

"Transformative" implies first how a theological legacy is continually changing, rather than remaining static. Second, it suggests that through our interaction with those who are different from us, or foreign to our context, we ourselves are decisively changed through the transformative power of the gospel. Third, this leads to injustice, exclusion, suffering and meaninglessness being transformed, in both church and society.

The transformative theological perspectives developed here challenge the assumption that Lutheran theology is inevitably European (especially Germanic) in its logic, conceptualization and tradition, which others can participate in on terms that remain foreign to them and their contexts. How then can others participate in a set of assumptions, ways of being, anthropology or worldview that are not their own and in some ways continue to feel "foreign"? With the ongoing, postmodern decentering of universals, especially of European discourses, we begin to discern a grammar or code that "transcends" the particularity of its founding context. There are central dynamics in Lutheran theology that are continually upsetting, challenging and provoking us to think beyond certain categories and our tendency to domesticate the faith. At the same time, we realize that in the Bible those who are marginalized or "different" often become the very means through which God's purpose is glimpsed.

The articles in this book develop constructive theological responses to at least three pervasive concerns today: (1) the growing awareness of differences or diversity, which sometimes are feared to threaten unity; (2) the problem of Christian exclusiveness in the face of religious pluralism; and (3) the tendency to separate redemption from creation, or humans from the rest of creation.

Hans-Peter Grosshans underlines how essential theology is in the life of the church—by being creative, constructive and critical. While acknowledging that theology is inevitably contextual, he reminds us, based on the example of German theology in the 1930s, that every context requires critical evaluation. He maintains that "while there is not 'one' Lutheran perspective—Lutheran theology is concrete and therefore related to the concrete Christian life of people—there is one theological endeavor that holds Lutherans together all over the world. This endeavor is based on some common theological principles and methodologies,"[1] which he enumerates. Grosshans recently served in the Department for Theology and Studies, and currently teaches systematic theology at the University of Münster, Germany.

Guillermo Hansen, an Argentinean who currently teaches systematic theology at Luther Seminary in St. Paul, USA, posits that Lutheran theology's attractiveness "is not grounded in the 'authority' given to its Confessions, or those who presume to be custodians of it, but in the compelling and flexible quality of the web of belief that is formed by the codes that once were unraveled by Luther."[2] This is a web that many today claim but no one owns. Using a cultural–linguistic approach in which cross, justification and God's two-fold rule figure prominently, Hansen contends that "Lutheran theology is alive and well today, precisely because it is plural, chaotic and messy."[3]

Turning to the Bible, Barbara Rossing, who teaches New Testament at the Lutheran School of Theology in Chicago, USA, insists that diversity in the Bible is not a problem but a blessing. For example, she exegetes 1 Corinthians 12:12 as "*because* we are many, we are one."[4] In relation to what can be significant differences over matters such as sexuality, she maintains that "faithful diversity is not communion dividing," but leads toward "recognizing God's grace in the other,"[5] that is, those whose interpretations may be different from ours. The goal is not agreement but *koinonia* in Christ.

---

[1] Hans-Peter Grosshans, "A Common Theological Perspective in a Diverse Global Communion?," in this publication, pp. 17–18.

[2] Guillermo Hansen, "Resistance, Adaptation or Challenge: The Versatility of the Lutheran Code," in this publication, p. 25.

[3] Ibid., p.37.

[4] Barbara Rossing, "Diversity in the Bible as a Model for Lutheran Hermeneutics," in this publication, p. 40, author's own italics.

[5] Ibid., p. 48.

Monica Jyotsna Melanchthon teaches Old Testament and Women's Studies at Gurukul Lutheran Theological College and Research Institute in Chennai, India. She emphasizes that those at the bottom of caste, class and gender hierarchies, which render them extremely vulnerable and oppressed—such as Dalits in India—are those whose marginalized voices need to be heard, if theology is to be transformative. Marginal readings of Scripture "attempt to undo the power of dominant readings that represent themselves as universal. Above all, they emphasize the need for the proclamation of liberty to those enslaved by systems of oppression."[6] Such readings are consistent with a Lutheran hermeneutic, which requires "interpretative humility and charity"[7] so that God's work of reconciliation can be fostered within the life of the communion.

Dean Zweck, who teaches church history and theology at Australian Lutheran College in Adelaide, Australia, draws on his teaching experience in Papua New Guinea and among Aboriginal Australians to emphasize how a transformative gospel lies at the heart of the biblical narrative: in and through Christ, all things are being made new. Our unity consists of our diversity because that diversity is held together in Christ. At the time of the Reformation, Luther's transformative, evangelical perspective—especially justification—resulted in transformative practices that promoted the gospel, which renewed the life of the church then and continues to do so today.

Girma Mohammed, an Ethiopian who recently completed his doctorate in philosophy at the Free International University of Amsterdam, Netherlands, analyzes the complex "wax and gold" tradition that permeates Ethiopian history and culture. Formulating such an hermeneutic, which claims to be unconditioned by human experiences, as a way of repressing others in the name of dogma, unity and even scientific neutrality is objectionable, he insists. Biblical interpretation must account for changing political, economic and cultural situations, overcome ideologies that reduce the richness of biblical teachings to single, social and political principles, and, in the process, overcome hatred, contempt and social fragmentation.

Duane Priebe focuses on the interplay of text and context: what God has done in Christ can only be understood in the context of the entire history of the world and its cultures. He examines select New Testament and Old Testament passages that show how, through this interplay between a text

---

[6] Monica Jyotsna Melanchthon, "Marginal Readings: Implications for a Lutheran Hermeneutic and Communion," in this publication, p. 65.

[7] Ibid., p. 67.

and its surrounding context, receive meanings that they would not have on their own. The strange horizons of the world of the texts and of our world engage each other in transformative ways. He provides examples of how this can apply in religiously plural situations, such as India. Priebe teaches systematic theology at Wartburg Theological Seminary, Dubuque, USA.

J. Paul Rajashekar, who teaches systematic theology and serves as dean at Lutheran Theological Seminary at Philadelphia, USA, addresses the challenge of religious pluralism through Lutheran theological categories. While acknowledging that the well-known *solas* (Scripture, Christ, faith) have made Christian engagement with others problematic because of their exclusive claims, he proposes that the *simuls* affirm God's inclusive love for the world, and free us to affirm the reality of God's grace and truth in the world, wherever they may be found. Thus, "the dialectic of the *solas* and the *simuls* calls us to be vulnerable before others in order to be loyal to Christ!"[8] Originally from India, Rajashekar previously staffed the Lutheran World Federation's Office for the Church and People of Other Faiths.

Because of how difficult it is to share the gospel in Japan without connecting with traditional ancestral rites, Motoo Ishii, who teaches theology at Japan Lutheran College and Seminary in Tokyo, considers how Luther's understanding of the communion of saints might address this, and, in turn, how Japanese spirituality challenges traditional Western theological thought. He proposes a comprehensive understanding of the salvation of the whole world, including nature, and proposes that through the *communio sanctorum*, Japanese Christians can pray more positively for the salvation of their non-Christian ancestors.

Continuing in the same vein, Kristin Johnston Largen, who teaches systematic theology at the Lutheran Theological Seminary in Gettysburg, USA, explores the relationship between creation and salvation, and the implications for Christian eschatological thought, especially as this pertains to people of other faiths. Emphasizing the ongoing relationship of love that the indwelling God has with all of creation, she advocates using a greater range of metaphors for God, de-emphasizing the concept of hell, and including brothers and sisters of other faiths in God's economy of salvation.

Ecclesiology is the framework through which Eva Harasta, who teaches theology at the University of Bamberg, Germany, approaches the challenges of religious pluralism. Drawing in nuanced ways upon insights of Luther and

---

[8] J. Paul Rajashekar, "Rethinking Lutheran Engagement with Religious Plurality," in this publication, p. 116.

Bonhoeffer, she interprets the all-encompassing claim of Christ's revelation in ways that allow for a "pluriformity" of this one truth, without compromising its binding character. She focuses on the particular, contextual unity and apostolicity of the church in ways that respect the proclamation of other faiths (without denying the church's own identity), and the sanctity of the church through Luther's *simul iustus et peccator* and Bonhoeffer's emphasis on the church's confession of guilt. Interacting with those of other faiths is not about being right but trusting Christ and being God's witnesses.

Allen G. Jorgensen, who teaches systematic theology at Waterloo Lutheran Seminary, Canada, takes up the Lutheran task of distinguishing the first (civil) use from the second (theological) use of the law, and thus of the law/gospel dialectic. For him, this is key for bridging redemption and creation, and, in turn, for affirming a dynamic view of creation and of diverse cultures. We are as dependent upon God in creation as we are in redemption. Creation, a locus of the self-giving God, is itself sustained by the promise of salvation.

The divine *logos* has assumed not only humanity, but also the depths of materiality, contends Niels-Henrik Gregersen, who teaches systematic theology at Copenhagen University, Denmark. In becoming "flesh" in Jesus, God's eternal *logos*—as "deep incarnation"—entered into all dimensions of God's creation. Such a biophysical interpretation of incarnation has significant consequences for understanding the crucial relation between God and the material world at large, especially amid heightened concerns for the environment. By attending to the full dimension of the gospel of the Word becoming flesh, the mystery of salvation stretches into the depths of our planet's conditions for life.

Vítor Westhelle, a Brazilian who teaches systematic theology at the Lutheran School of Theology in Chicago, USA, reflects on the significance of what happened overall at Augsburg 2009, including among participants beyond these authors, viewing it as an apex that built upon previous theological developments in the Lutheran World Federation. Theology as inspired by the Reformation is a process of "re-forming" the church. With reference to Galatians 2, he describes communion as the event that takes place in the actual interface between the teachings of the church (its dogmatic function) and its mission (its receptive function) and calls for the conversations that began at Augsburg to continue.

A Common Theological Perspective in a Diverse Global Communion?

Hans-Peter Grosshans

How important is theology and what is its role in the life of the Lutheran churches? If theology is literally the study of God, then it is essential for Lutheran churches. Churches are congregations of people, living in the presence of the Triune God and reconciled with God and with one another. Because the members of the church need to understand emotionally and intellectually what is going on in the church and what it means to live in the presence of God, theology is indispensable for the church. Lutherans follow Anselm of Canterbury's well-known motto: faith seeks understanding because the Triune God lives in an intentionally filled relationship with people. In their relationship to the Triune God, Christians do not understand themselves as mere puppets, but as full partners and cooperators with all their physical, emotional and intellectual capacities and abilities.

The church is primarily about communicating the Triune God among Christians and with non-Christians. In order to find words, signs, expressions or gestures for this communication, it needs theology. This implies three distinct characteristics: (1) theology needs to be creative in order to find new parables for the presence of the Triune God in our world; (2) theology needs to be constructive in order to relate the Word of God to the minds, hearts and bodies of people and their cultures; and (3) theology needs to be critical because in the permanent twilight of our world there is confusion about God, even within the churches. Theology must continue the critical discussion on doctrines and teachings in relation to the Triune God and to God's presence in our world and lives, in order to give space to God's liberating, renewing and transforming work. Every worship should include these three elements. Biblical texts need to be interpreted and applied in the lives of the listeners; the same applies to all other areas of the church's life.

Theology clearly has a serving role within the churches. The church's life is the basis for theology. We can observe this already in an historical setting, which we might refer to as the foundation of Christian theology: the dispute between the apostles Paul and Peter, which Paul reports in Galatians 2. The concrete issue at stake was whether new members in the Christian communities, whose ethnic origin was not Jewish, should accept the old Jewish ritual laws and therefore be circumcised and eat only kosher food, or whether they could become Christians without acknowledging these laws. Peter's own life was ambiguous: he ate with non-Jews, which was against Jewish law, while demanding that all new members should live according Jewish law. Unlike Peter and some others, who wanted unity between the new Christian faith and Jewish faith and piety, Paul insists on a new formation according to the "truth of the gospel" (Gal 2:5, 14). Therefore, for Paul, one could become a Christian and be a member of the Christian community without accepting all the obligations resulting from God's covenant with the Jewish people. This reflection marks the birth of Christian theology: Paul tried to clarify a concrete problem in the life of the church by reflecting the new insight in God's relationship to humankind, as given in Jesus Christ.

Theology helps the church to clarify its problems based on what Paul calls the "truth of the gospel," and not only pragmatically on the basis of cultural, ethnic or traditional specificities. Theology can never replace the church's spiritual and diaconal life, where the real dynamics of the Christian faith are lived out. Theology can only serve by being creative, constructive and critical. However, if the life of the church needs theology, as illustrated by the conflict between Peter and Paul, one dimension of the church's life, where theology is much needed, is the relationship and communication between Christians and different traditions, cultures and confessions.

We could add a fourth characteristic, which becomes relevant for communicating between Christians of different traditions, cultures and origins. Theology needs to be argumentative in order to reach consensus despite the many significant differences in our lives. Nowadays, we are very much aware of the various geographical, cultural, social and religious contexts in our globalized world. Nevertheless, as Christians we have a strong sense of a reconciled life—in the first instance with God, but also with one another. Such a reconciled life needs certain forms with which to express itself in our world. The churches in the Lutheran tradition do not express their unity as a reconciled people through a common hierarchy. They are a communion of churches (plural). Therefore, they have to work toward this community through communicating about the common faith in various situations. Theology is the main means whereby Lutheran churches work toward unity; it is responsible for the church's unity in the world.

Over the last years, efforts have been under way within the Lutheran World Federation (LWF) to define the role and relevance of theology in the life of the church. What do the churches—be it their governing bodies, pastors and teachers or parishioners in their congregations—expect of theology? What do they contribute to theology? How far do they understand their Christian life—in the various aspects of church life—as participating in theology? What can theology contribute to the life of the church? What kind of theology do we have in mind when we ask these questions? What kind of theology is helpful and enriching for the life of the church?

In looking at the rich variety in Lutheran churches and Lutheran theology, we have to ask, Is a common Lutheran theological perspective possible worldwide on the basis of the very diverse cultural, political, economic and religious contexts?[1]

The relevance of Lutheran theology

Nowadays, it is common for our theology to be contextual. At least this is the case if theology aims to understand Christian faith in light of today's world. Especially in dogmatics, ethics and pastoral theology, it is vital that the contexts of churches and theologians, as well as that of their audience are taken into consideration. Pastoral theology is concerned with finding the best way of presenting the gospel today in the various places in the world and organizing the church in such a way that it is most true to the gospel and fits best into society. This is so because dogmatics and ethics are not about the repetition of old doctrines, but about the endeavor to discuss the old Christian doctrines in light of people's worldview and the problems and challenges facing them today. Take for example the doctrine of justification: because of Jesus Christ's redeeming and saving work, the Triune God justifies the sinner through faith alone. Nevertheless, to understand this truth and to explain it to our contemporaries and ourselves we have to delve into our respective cultural heritages and use our societies' and cultures' symbolic resources. As a result, in former centuries, theologians produced numerous theological books, all of which tried to make intellectual sense of the Christian faith and to interpret it for their contemporaries. We therefore need more new theological books and articles in all parts of the world, which bring the

---

[1] The discussion at Augsburg showed that there is a common theological perspective among Lutheran theologians despite their coming from very different cultural, political and economic contexts. The discussion revealed a stronger difference within contemporary Lutheran theology than the differences between the various contexts: the methodological difference between a Lutheran theology related almost exclusively to the Lutheran Confessions or Luther's theology and between a Lutheran theology related almost exclusively to the principle of today's contextuality.

Christian faith into discussion with the various cultures, intellectual trends and political and economic problems people face today.

Contextual theology in Europe

All over the world, Lutheran theology needs to decide how it deals with the various conditions and challenges of its respective context. In some parts of Europe, Lutheran theology has long been aware of its own contextuality—and not always for the better. Nationalistic European theologies justified themselves with specific contextual arguments. As a German, I am very aware of the negative implications of a Protestant theology that emphasizes too strongly its specific cultural, ethnic, political and historical context. The history of the German Protestant churches and theology between 1920 and 1945 clearly shows that this ends in a type of new paganism. Moreover, only those theologians who resisted the influence of the contextual conditions on their theology and insisted on the sole orientation of theology on Jesus Christ, preserved their critical mind during the political turmoil of the time. This is not an argument against taking the various contexts into consideration, but rather a warning that contextualization as such is rather ambiguous and that every context needs critical evaluation. On this basis, there is today in Germany and all over Europe considerable interaction between Protestant theology and the European context. In fact, European Protestant theologians are working hard to relate Protestant theology to their cultural, intellectual, political and economic environments, and are in intensive discussion and cooperation with philosophers, social scientists and natural scientists. They are attempting to keep the teaching of Christian doctrine or pastoral theology up-to-date by taking into account the intellectual and social theories of our time, because they want the gospel to be heard and European cultures to be influenced by the Christian faith.

Protestant theologians in Europe are well aware of the fact that there is not one theology for all places in the world and for all times in history. European theology is the result of European history and related to certain constellations and challenges Christian theology and churches face in Europe.[2] Already one hundred years ago, the German theologian Ernst

---

[2] The Community of Protestant Churches in Europe (CPCE) carried out a study project on the question of how far Europe had been a subject of reflection within European Protestant theology. See, Martin Friedrich, Hans Jürgen Luibl and Christine-Ruth Müller (eds), *Theology for Europe. Perspectives of Protestant Churches* (Frankfurt am Main: Verlag Otto Lembeck, 2006).

Troeltsch used the word "Europeanism." Europeanism is "the historical context of theology where 'European' theology is understood only as one, and no longer the universally valid case for the formation of the church and Christianity in the future, where others attempt to give themselves their own form in relation to this."[3]

Attention was directed to the particular character of European theology that characterized it beyond and independently of the universalizing European culture. According to Lutheran theologian Trutz Rendtorff, European theology refers to how "its principles, capacities and orientations" and thus its academic scholarly style became located in the universities where it was pursued in relation to reason. Rendtorff identifies individualization as another mark of European theology, of which the historical relativization of "European" theology is already in itself an indicator. The formation of contextual theologies can therefore be seen as a fruit of European Protestant theology. The universal extension of a European Christian culture (understood as Protestantism) does not aim at a worldwide cultural unification, but at different cultures shaped by the Christian faith.

Taking local and regional cultures and societies seriously is typical of European Protestant theology. Therefore, in Germany, Protestant theology is involved in intensive discussions with all the other academic disciplines, and the Protestant churches contribute to public debates on the major questions and challenges facing society.[4]

Moving beyond postcolonialism in the global South

In the southern hemisphere, the contextual conditions for theological work are very different from those in Europe. In my opinion, Lutheran theologians in the South and East should take their contexts as seriously as Europeans take their own context. In our theological work, we must seriously consider our cultures while remaining critical of some elements of our own contexts. This should include seeking to overcome postcolonialism.

[3] Trutz Rendtorff, "Europäismus als geschichtlicher Kontext der Theologie. Bemerkungen zur heutigen Kritik an 'europäischer' Theologie im Lichte von Ernst Troeltsch," in Trutz Rendtorff (ed.), *Europäische Theologie. Versuche einer Ortsbestimmung* (Gütersloh: Gütersloher Verlagshaus Mohn, 1980), pp. 165–79, here p. 175.

[4] At the University of Münster, in the northern part of Germany, I am part of a large research project on religion and politics, where I collaborate with fellow professors and colleagues from the faculties of history, politics, law, philosophy, the social sciences and Catholic theology. Such cooperation with researchers from other disciplines is part of the European context.

Postcolonial theology is still oriented toward a theology from somewhere else, be it from Europe or North America.

Instead, we have to enter into a period of post-postcolonialism. Here I do not want to suggest that we avoid the still necessary discussion about the injustices caused by colonialism. Rather, I would propose that a theology in the South and East develops in discourse with the particular cultures, societies and people rather than depending on theologies from elsewhere—the Holy Scriptures are the only given "from somewhere else." To a certain extent, postcolonial theology has remained tied to colonialism, and nowadays Lutheran theology should move beyond this. On the basis of the biblical witness and the theological insights of Reformation theology, theologians everywhere should develop a Lutheran theology that reflects the questions, problems and challenges that the Christian faith in the Triune God faces in the various countries and regions of the world. Each and every theologian—wherever she or he lives—is responsible for reflecting on the Christian faith in light of today's realities.

The role of contexts in Lutheran theology

What exactly do we mean when we say that theology must be contextual? Theology is in the first instance about God. Drawing on Martin Luther, we can put this more precisely: theology is about the guilty and lost human being and the justifying and saving God.[5] Theology is about God relating to human beings. God is justifying and saving all over the world. God's activities are not limited to certain contexts. As Christians, we believe that it is the same God, who acts in the same way in all contexts. Everywhere in the world, Christians believe Jesus Christ to be their Savior and the Savior of humankind and creation.

When Luther speaks of the guilty and lost human being, we presuppose that in all contexts human beings are similar with respect to their relationship to God. What this means and how it is expressed in concrete life situations varies from context to context and culture to culture. It is part of theology to find words, expressions, images and concepts to express the universal truth about human beings: in relation to God, every human being is lost and guilty.

---

[5] "*... proprie sit subiectum Theologiae homo reus et perditus et deus iustificans vel salvator.*" Martin Luther, "Enarratio des 51. Psalmes, 1532," in *WA* 40/II, 328, 1f. Cf. Jaroslav Pelikan (ed.), *Luther's Works*, vol. 12 (Saint Louis: Concordia Publishing House, 1955), p. 311.

Similarly, it is part of theology to find words, expressions, images and concepts for the universal truth that God relates to human beings in such a way that the almighty God justifies, redeems and saves human beings. This is revealed in Jesus Christ. What this means might be conceived and expressed in various ways, depending on the respective cultural environment.

The context is the concrete situation in which the living Triune God acts in concrete ways to save and redeem a guilty and lost humanity and to redeem a suffering creation. It is the same God we believe in who acts everywhere and at all times. But the living God is sensitive to concrete life; this is the deepest reason why theology is contextual.

Do the various contexts reveal God? Can we learn something about God from the cultural, religious and political contexts we live in?

We find traces of the God known from the Old and New Testaments in our own contexts, just as we can find traces of the Triune God in our individual lives. But the context itself does not reveal God. We only see God at work in the cultures, societies and people we belong to, the God revealed in the history of the Jewish people and in Jesus Christ and to whom the Holy Scriptures bear witness. For Lutherans, the only source and norm for Christian knowledge of God is the witness of the Holy Scripture.

Were we to take the various contexts as a source and norm for our knowledge of God we would end up with a number of gods, because the differences between the contexts are too significant. In each context, culture, tradition and society, we could create our own God, which sums up people's present experience as well as the values they strive for. In fact, because of the social differences within a society, we would necessarily end up with polytheism within each society: the God of the powerful, rich and successful would be different from the God of the powerless, poor and unsuccessful; the God of one ethnic group would be different from the God of the others. But it is the one God revealed in Jesus Christ who, despite our many differences, is the God of all of us.

While every culture and context has specific questions and challenges for Lutheran theology as well as some common ones, there are not necessarily common answers. What then holds Lutheran theology and theologians all over the world together despite the great diversity in culture, history, language, religion, politics and the economy? Is a common Lutheran theological perspective possible in view of this diversity?

I would like to argue that while there is not "one" Lutheran perspective—Lutheran theology is concrete and therefore related to people's concrete Christian life—there is one theological endeavor that holds Lutherans together all over the world. This endeavor is based on some common theological principles and methodologies. There is a common way of dealing theologically with problems and encounters with the respective cultures.

Common Lutheran theological principles, attitudes and methods

First, since the Reformation, Lutheran theology has been strictly related to the witness of the Holy Scriptures, which are the only source and norm for all theological knowledge.[6] Because of this reference to the normative witness of the Holy Scriptures, Lutheran theology is critical. To be critical means not being satisfied with the obvious and with what seems to be true, but to put one's own life, the life of one's own congregation and one's own church and all that surrounds us into the light of the gospel—and to judge everything in this light.

In other words, Lutheran theology is committed to the truth. This applies at least in two respects: first, to our knowledge in general and our veracity in particular, and second to our personal qualities. In the first instance, this concerns our dealing with the natural and social world. As Jesus advised the disciples, when he sent them out: "[. . .] be wise as serpents and innocent as doves" (Mt 10:16). Lutheran theologians strive to know as much as possible, not only in the field of theology, but also in other fields, be it their own traditions and cultures, or the latest findings of the social and natural sciences. Lutheran theology strives to be informed at the highest level. Therefore, a solid theological and general education is necessary for Lutheran theologians. Informed theology is the contrary of ideological theology, which ignores reality. Therefore, Lutheran theology seeks to be highly informed at the intellectual level and prepared for dialogue in academia as well as society with experts from different disciplines.

"Be wise as serpents" and "innocent as doves." The second part of Jesus' advice to his disciples is also essential. Purity of heart should characterize Lutheran theologians. No other intention than to do theology for the glory

---

[6] As is said at the beginning of the "Epitome of the Formula of Concord": "We believe, teach, and confess that the sole rule and standard according to which all dogmas together with [all] teachers should be estimated and judged are the prophetic and apostolic Scriptures of the Old and of the New Testament alone, as it is written Ps. 119:105: 'Thy Word is a lamp unto my feet and a light unto my path'. And St. Paul: 'Though an angel from heaven preach any other gospel unto you, let him be accursed', Gal. 1:8." *The Book of Concord. The Confessions of the Lutheran Church,* at **www.bookofconcord.org/fc-ep.php#**, Comprehensive Summary, Rule and Norm.

of God and in the service of our neighbor should direct our theological work. Thus, Lutheran theologians are reliable partners for all those who are also of good intent. Lutherans cannot compromise on the truth; lies cannot be tolerated. "Be wise as serpents and innocent as doves" should be a motto for the work of every Lutheran theologian.

Second, Lutheran theology emphasizes the life renewing and justifying power of God's Word. Lutheran theology is about the life renewing and creative God who acts through God's Word. Lutheran theology does not rehash time and again the same old teaching material. Rather, it uses old theological material creatively in order to be relevant for the present time. In fact, the Word of God is the inspiring power for all theological work. Not only Christians' spiritual life but also their theological work has to reflect this in a world that is in a permanent crisis and lacks inspiration and thus does not find new solutions for its problems. Lutheran theologians should reflect God's creativity by doing creative theology.

This characteristic of Lutheran theology can be exemplified by looking at my own European context, where Protestant theologians are struggling with a church that has become weary. It is almost as if the churches were hibernating. Instead of actively proclaiming the gospel of God, the churches seem only anxious to preserve their present status. They have little spiritual and missionary force. Protestantism's critical and sobering approach to worldly success has apparently completely defeated its faith in God and led to a spiritual pessimism. But if the Triune God is no longer trusted, where can faith, hope and love come from? In this way, Christian life loses its future, becomes self-satisfied and wants only to cope with the present. Accordingly, churches and theology are provincial and self-satisfied. But after hibernation comes a period of awakening, and Protestant theologians in Europe are working hard to contribute to this awakening.[7]

Third, Lutheran theology is related to experience. Theology will develop as long as the story of God's relationship with human beings continues. It is an ongoing process of exploration. Theology arises out of a vivid faith, which is tested time and again. According to Luther's understanding, it is essential that an individual's faith should be challenged if they are to be a theologian. In the introduction to "The Freedom of a Christian" Luther

---

[7] Cf. Hans-Peter Grosshans, "Making the Gospel Attractive. The German-language Protestant Churches and their Contribution to the Unity and Freedom of Europe," in Martin Friedrich, Hans Jürgen Luibl and Christine-Ruth Müller (eds), *Theology for Europe—Perspectives of Protestant Churches, mandated by the Executive Committee of the Community of Protestant Churches in Europe—Leuenberg Church Fellowship* (Frankfurt a. Main: Verlag Otto Lembeck, 2006), pp. 280–90.

writes, "It is impossible to write well about it or to understand what has been written about it unless one has at one time or another experienced the courage which faith gives a man when trials oppress him."[8]

For Luther, no one can be a theologian who is not existentially related to God, and whose faith has not been tested by their experiences in the world. When persons, in a concrete situation, find themselves unable to trust in the gospel and God's promises, Luther considers this to be a trial for their faith and their relationship to God. The same happens when God's love and grace remain hidden. Then God may be experienced as being distant or even as rejecting them. For Luther, such trials are necessary on the journey of faith. They will continue throughout one's life, and doubts and uncertainties are bound to occur. The only way out is to turn to God, to argue with and complain to God and to remind God of the promises given in God's Word. In particular, remembering Jesus Christ's fear of death in Gethsemane (Mk 14:32–42), which was the great trial for the Son of God, will help us to avoid lapsing into despair. According to Luther's understanding, trials are part of a living relationship with God, which cause people to argue with God and so to intensify their relationship with God.

Fourth, Lutheran theology is open-minded with respect to everything going on in the world. Lutheran theologians are curious; they want to learn and to understand. Lutheran theology is devoted to the world and its well-being. It knows about the Christian responsibility to improve the world and to resist evil and injustice.

Lutheran theology does not restrict itself to the sacred as a separate religious space in the world, because according to Lutheran understanding the old difference between the "sacred" (or holy) and "profane" is irrelevant for living out Christian faith. The Triune God alone is sacred. Within our world, there are no sacred places, times or activities, as distinct from profane places, times or activities. According to Lutheran understanding, Christian life is situated in the (profane) world. This is also relevant for the church that sees its place not outside the world, in a separate sacred place, but within the world, as part of the world. This is so for individual Christians, who serve God in their daily businesses and occupations. Our shaping of the world has a religious dimension, because Christians want to change life in the world with love. In individual ethics, we can best

---

[8] Martin Luther, "The Freedom of a Christian, 1520," in Helmut T. Lehmann, *Luther's Works*, vol. 31 (Philadelphia: Muhlenberg Press, 1957), p. 343.

observe the consequences. Because Lutherans seek their self-fulfillment in loving service of the neighbor, they are often characterized by an ascetic and rationally organized life.

To exist and live in the world does not mean assimilating. Instead, it means working to change the world so that humankind can live reconciled with God and with one another. This critical dimension of Protestant faith in relation to the world is preserved by its reference to Jesus Christ. Rather than being a form of escapism, this deepens our relation to and our involvement in the world, including striving to understand it better, as well as seeking the reconciliation of all human beings with God and with one another, as is already realized in Christ. Therefore, for the sake of the world and all human beings, Lutheran theology witnesses to Jesus Christ as the Savior, Redeemer and Reconciler of all and as the one human symbol for a reconciled life of all human beings in love, peace, justice and freedom.

Fifth, Lutheran theology emphasizes reason. Lutheran theology has a twofold attitude to reason: distrusting it regarding divine or spiritual matters, but praising it with regard to earthly affairs and realizing human responsibility in the world.[9] Luther had a surprisingly modern and inspired understanding of reason and its role in public and private life. He considered reason as the God-given means to explore the psychological, social and physical realities and to shape the natural, social and moral world.

For Luther, reason is a faculty of the human soul and therefore a part of nature. It is bound to the created world, time and space. When it respects its own limitations, it fulfills its God-given vocation. Yet, when it overextends itself beyond the empirical world, reason gets it wrong. Reason is woefully inadequate, even stubbornly sinful, in religious and spiritual matters. For Luther, when deployed in religion, reason always misses the true God and ends up constructing idols of its own fabrication. Luther's sharp criticism of reason as it relates to true religion and the true God lies behind his condemnation of reason as a "whore,"[10] who sells herself to anyone and to every religious endeavor that pays well. Because of this critique, Luther's praise of reason as God's best gift for ordering life on earth has often been overlooked.

---

[9] For Luther's concept of reason, see Hans-Peter Grosshans, "Luther on Faith and Reason. The Light of Reason at the Twilight of the World," in Christine Helmer, *The Global Luther. A Theologian for Modern Times* (Minneapolis, Fortress Press, 2009), pp. 173–85.

[10] In his last sermon in Wittenberg (17 January 1546) Luther said: "But since the Devil's bride, reason, that pretty whore, comes in and thinks she is wise, and what she says, what she thinks, is from the Holy Spirit, who can help us, then? Not judges, not doctors, no king or emperor, because [reason] is the Devil's greatest whore." *WA* 51, 126, 7ff.

In the history of Europe, reason became more important when, after the Reformation, Europe suffered from numerous wars, injustices and devastating diseases. Reason was called on to establish peace among previously warring religious and political groups, and it did so by providing ways to articulate the universal common good in the midst of competing interests. But, the first and probably best example of reason's potential to establish truthful consensus was Socrates in Greek antiquity. Socrates dedicated his life to striving for the good of society based on reason, and his vision contained an implicit critique of his own culture and morality, which led to his death.

Today's intellectual currents are similar to those in Socrates's own time. The local is favored when it comes to solve cultural, religious, political and legal differences; the particular, not the universal, dictates the rules according to which people should live their lives. Current problems tend to be solved by referring to traditional answers from the past. Looking at the past may be safer in terms of preserving group identity, yet the result is that communication between different groups is not fostered. By placing various cultures, traditions and contexts alongside but not in interaction with each other, power stand-offs result. Lutheran theology is convinced that societies should not be organized by power alone, but by the most rational arguments that further the common good.

How then should we proceed when past traditions and ways of life do not provide solutions to today's problems? This question is particularly pertinent in today's context of radical global change. Lutheran theology and churches are in a universal network, through which there can be theological communication globally about the problems we face in our various contexts. It is through theological discourse and by listening to one another that Lutheran theologians seek to go beyond their respective cultures and in a common effort to work toward improving our common world.

Resistance, Adaptation or Challenge: The Versatility of the Lutheran Code

Guillermo Hansen

What is the shape of Lutheran theology in a post-confessional, post-secular, post-foundational, postcolonial and post-patriarchal environment? Lutheran theology in its many locations and expressions has been deeply touched and reshaped by many of these currents.

There was a marked methodological and epistemological shift in Lutheran theology after the spirited debate around the doctrine of justification at the 1963 Assembly of the Lutheran World Federation (LWF) in Helsinki, where the normative vision emerging from the German–Scandinavian axis was challenged for the first time.[1] After that, the notion of a uniform "center" was confronted, and methodological questions permeated the search for new and better ways to describe contexts where the text could be meaningfully decoded. The church's praxis, mission and context became focal points in this. In turn, the increasing acceptance of the methodological shifts, as exemplified by liberation and feminist theologies, radically shaped the way in which theological matters began to be discussed.

The emergence of contextual and constructive Lutheran theologies has been an epochal event. In the wake of the modern decoupling of the social or cultural from specific religious views, and the globalization of churches and confessions,[2] new vistas were opened for contemporary theology, and universalistic and essentialist pretensions unmasked. Furthermore, these theologies revealed the shortcomings as well as the potential of the law/gospel methodology in terms of a new set of "grievances." This reshaped the concrete content and structures of the law, and concomitantly gave a new spin to the promise of the gospel. Thus, the marks of the dominant

---

[1] The 1963 Assembly in Helsinki attempted to reexamine, reformulate and restate the doctrine of justification vis-à-vis the new reality signified by the experience of "modern man" in a secularized world. See Jens Holger Schjørring (ed.), *From Federation to Communion: The History of the Lutheran World Federation* (Minneapolis: Fortress Press, 1997), p. 377.

[2] Cf. Slavoj Žižek, *The Puppet and the Dwarf: The Perverse Core of Christianity* (Cambridge, Mass: MIT Press, 2003), p. 3.

script were slowly, but steadily, exposed as a prison enclosing the peoples
from the global South (as well as those marginalized in the North) in a
controlling logic of identity, where hierarchy was assumed, multiplicity
and difference denied and transformation considered contrary to nature
and doctrine. These were "anomalies" that classical interpretive schemes
could not surmount.

In the ongoing process of LWF theological reflection[3] after Helsinki,
the traditional "sages" of Western academia, with their particular understanding of the human experience and the "Lutheran code," while not
entirely displaced, began to be considered as one among many voices. The
notion of a "center" generating the normative theological discourse has
faded, and a univocal normative understanding has been replaced by plural
voices, ambiguity, fragmentariness and openness. From attempting to prove
God's existence and the "rightness" of the Lutheran tradition, contextual
theologies have moved into the poetics and politics of God's relation
to the world, borrowing new scripts (critical theory, deconstructionism,
postcolonial studies, popular religiosity, etc.) whose primary concern is to
promote new healing ways of living.[4]

This decentering can be seen as a celebration of late modern plurality,
as liberation from the chains of a colonial and patriarchal past. Yet, others
see this as a descent into night, where everything is dark, or the emergence
of new essentialisms of tribal, class or gender identities. While there are
those who celebrate and embrace new discursive shifts, others seek to guard
an ancient code. All of us inhabit the tension between these two dramatic
forces, where we are being continually undone and remade, decentered and
centered, disarticulated and redeployed, affirmed and denied. In the midst
of such forces, theologically, what can maintain a common identity without
canceling these creative forces? Are there any images that can translate the
apparent cacophony into polyphony?

The question today is what makes this plurality "Lutheran"? To unravel
this conundrum, I consider that Lutheran theology has to do with identity formation. We are socialized through religious narratives, which are
constantly intertwined with other narratives. While roles are defined by

---

[3] Cf. Vitor Westhelle, "And the Walls Come Tumbling Down: Globalization and Fragmentation in the
LWF," in *Dialog: A Journal of Theology* 36/1 (Winter 1997). This pluralization of voices was not a theological
whim; it followed in the wake of the cracks of the Western liberal consensus. See Immanuel Wallerstein,
The Uncertainties of Knowledge (Philadelphia: Temple University Press, 2004), p. 77; Eric Hobsbawm, *The
Age of Extremes: A History of the World, 1914–1991* (New York: Vintage Books, 1994), p. 343.

[4] Cf. Rebecca Chopp and Mark Taylor, *Reconstructing Christian Theology* (Minneapolis: Fortress, 1994),
pp. 1–24.

norms that are structured by institutions and organizations, identities are "sources of meaning for the actors themselves, and by themselves, constructed through a process of individuation."[5] Identities involve social actors, who have thoroughly internalized meanings through the symbolic construction of certain types of skins, barriers and borders, from which the difference between "self and others," or between "we and they," are enacted.

In what he terms "the information age," Manuel Castells proposes that two major forces shape our lives today: the restructuring of capital and labor under globalization, along with the information and communications technology revolution, and the surge of powerful expressions of collective identities.[6] This reclaiming and/or creating of identities can be either proactive, such as feminism and environmentalism that seek to transform human relationships at a fundamental level, or reactive, entrenched resistance "on behalf of God, nation, ethnicity, family, locality or any other category of millennial existence now perceived to be threatened."[7] Most contemporary identities structured around religion, Castells argues, fall into this latter category.

In the wake of this, what type of identity does Lutheranism signify today? How can a theological and ecclesiological tradition, born almost five hundred years ago in a declining empire, shaped by a Germanic culture that was unappealing to the rest of the world, and carried around the globe by displaced and uprooted peasants and/or nonconformists, or by pietist missionaries who found "unconditional grace" to be as strange as the cultures they met—how can this Lutheran theological tradition serve as a code for structuring identities today?

I argue that the attractiveness of Lutheran theology is not grounded in the "authority" given to its Confessions, or those who presume to be custodians of it, but in the compelling and flexible quality of the web of belief that is formed by the codes that once were unraveled by Luther. In a way, much of Lutheran theology seems to be alive and well precisely because it does not look "Lutheran" from a classical perspective. Many anomalies and grievances have given new and different faces to the scripts of the Lutheran churches. Yet, amazingly, these anomalies and grievances have not challenged the basic structure of the Lutheran grammar, but

---

[5] Manuel Castells, *The Power of Identity. The Information Age: Economy, Society and Culture*, vol. II (Malden, MA: Blackwell, 2004), p. 7.

[6] Ibid., p. 2.

[7] Ibid.

have expanded and strengthened it. It seems that the Lutheran "code" is versatile enough to connect the scriptural narrative with the narratives of our own lives, forging a "culture" that can only stay alive insofar as new and diverse environments are integrated into the web of belief that forms and builds a "tradition."

We are now able to visualize a common terrain emerging amid the forces that both enclose and open up the code. Contextual and constructivist efforts, by and large, have not disparaged the classical Lutheran themes, but have recoded and rewired them within new semantic fields. Even more important, new networks of engaged actors have emerged and expanded the code. A plurality of interpretations has resulted, yet the network itself continues to be sustained by common codes, claimed by all, but owned by no one. Centers of ownership have faded. We all become custodians of a code that paradoxically can shine only as it changes in relation to the most pressing tensions that every culture faces—such as individuality vs collectivity, changing gender roles, etc. In sum, normative truths coexist with prophetic critique and hermeneutical suspicion. Together this forms a circularity essential for the organizational flow of a (cultural) system that constantly seeks new semiotic inputs from its environment.

Lutheranism as a cultural sign system

My first thesis is that Lutheranism is the discrete religious software of the church's mind. It is a sign system, a culture with an historically transmitted pattern of meanings, encoded in symbols and embodied in a social organism, the church. As it brings forth a world through its discursive and non-discursive practices (mission), it shows its resilience as it engages the variables that bodies encoded by this mind have to confront.

If religion is a cultural sign language, promising a benefit in life by corresponding to an ultimate reality, then we should consider Lutheranism not simply as an historical artifact, but a complex cultural sign system through which a significant number of human beings inhabit the world. Second, Lutheran theology and its codes can never be abstracted from the actual sign systems that are embodied in and through their concrete social embodiments, the churches. They constitute the primary locus of the theological enterprise, for they embody this complex of myth, ritual and practices in which "codes" are embedded and motifs raised up. Third, because churches—and theologians—are living organisms interacting with very specific and changing natural, social, economic and cultural environments, the original code or semiotic array is always under stress. This calls for innovation, change, reaction or resistance. Here is where the deep sense of dialectics sets in, for even though the religious code opens up a space that we inhabit religiously, this very space also impinges upon the code that opens up this space(s) in the first place. Fourth, only a religious code which is able to integrate new semiotic and/or structural innovations can continue to reproduce the code; otherwise, it is dead. Therefore, it can only carry on a religious identity by constantly negotiating with other types of identities.

We must ask ourselves to what extent Lutheranism—as a particular cultural linguistic system—creates an environment of stimuli that can bring forth and increasingly illuminate an habitable world. In other words, what are the symbols and codes that shape its ever novel semiotic field by evoking the power of a hidden reality that becomes visible, and, therefore, habitable? The task of theology, situated within a particular cultural se-miotic construct, is to disclose the hidden connections with regard to the intra-systematic truth that a particular corpus reveals, as well as the world within which this truth is enacted.

Doctrines as "hinges" between texts and contexts

My second thesis is that doctrines function as rules within a larger semiotic tapestry mediated by a social body, the church. More specifically, doctrines function as "hinges" or connectors between a particular reading of foun-dational texts and the context in which the social bodies are immersed. Within this interplay between text and context, a theologically inflected world is brought forth.

George Lindbeck made an important breakthrough with regard to understanding how doctrines and theology operate.[8] Religion, he states, is a cultural/linguistic framework or medium shaping the entirety of life and thought. It is not primarily an array of beliefs and ideas about the true and the good (although they always contain these), or a set of symbols that express attitudes, feelings or sentiments (although these are certainly always present). Like a culture, it is a communal phenomenon that shapes

---

[8] See George Lindbeck, *The Nature of Doctrine: Religion and Theology in a Postliberal Age* (Philadelphia: The Westminster Press, 1984), pp. 32ff.

the subjectivities of individuals rather than being primarily a manifestation of those subjectivities. It contains a vocabulary of discursive and non-discursive symbols, together with a logic or grammar through which this vocabulary is meaningfully deployed.

Lindbeck is also helpful in understanding religious and theological change and innovation.[9] These do not result from new experiences or insights, but from the active interaction of cultural linguistic systems with changing situations. When religious interpretative schemes—embodied in practice and beliefs—develop anomalies in new and different contexts, then the system as a whole enters into a crisis. Sometimes, minor adjustments or reformulations here and there will stabilize it for a while. Most often, however, practices, beliefs and theories are gradually or suddenly abandoned because they prove unfruitful for new and different questions that intersect with the life of believer.

But what types of anomalies should be considered? How are they detected and from where do they come? The distinction between vocabulary and grammar seems critical here. As Lindbeck himself seems to assume, the cultural linguistic system is often taken either as a totality or as constituting an autonomous world. In this sense, to speak in a "Lutheran" mode would not only mean being guided by a set of rules, but with a common vocabulary that may be largely outdated and/or unintelligible. But what happens if the rules are seen as flexible enough to accommodate a wider vocabulary?

From the perspectives of linguistics, if grammar and vocabulary are considered an indivisible whole, not much stress can be accommodated. Grievances and anomalies slip in but without being able to assimilate new semantics. The rule is too tied up with an old lexicon and therefore unable to operate in new settings. Believers continue to go on with their lives in two separate semantic fields.

Here I want to point to doctrines as regulative principles embedded in a grammar, which shows its versatility only when it is able to encompass new semantic arrays through the engagement with different contexts. In his recent study of contextual Christologies,[10] Volker Küster revamped Paulo Freire's conception of generative themes in an intriguing and suggestive way. Every community lives within a network of generative themes, which

---

[9] See Ibid., pp. 39f.

[10] See Volker Küster, *The Many Faces of Jesus Christ: Intercultural Christology* (Maryknoll, NY: Orbis Books, 2001), pp. 33–35.

disclose the whole linguistic and thematic universe of a location in space and time. Slum, rain, land, water, housing, HIV and AIDS, food, banks, hospital, soldiers, etc., compose generative words which, once interlocked, reveal another dimension, in principle hidden to the participants. These are generative themes. Freire called this power of interlocking "hinged themes," that is, this dimension of culture that creates a mapping of a territory allowing for a new exploration (action) within familiar yet alien landscapes.

In the case of Christian communities, another hinged theme appears, not displacing the above, but interlocking them at a new level. Here the importance of theology emerges, bringing together two very different generative themes: that of the context and that of the text. Theology opens up the code for inhabiting new spaces that formerly were hidden from the religious imagination.

The Lutheran code is invaluable for a proactive identity that seeks to transform human relationships at the most fundamental level, and thus to provide a dynamic mapping for life. This identity is not based on being socialized into an ecclesiastical organization, but on the dynamic of law and gospel, and the new possibility this opens up to live truly and kenoti- cally in the here and now. The Lutheran code has proven to be resilient, not because it is entrenched in a safer past, but because its code has an in- ner flexibility that allows us to confront and engage the anomalies of new contexts, and to assimilate them into a wider cultural linguistic universe. These new anomalies seem to cohere well with the grammatical code, even though lexically they may be far from classical Lutheran language.

Codes do morph, but they do so expansively in order to continue their appropriate task. As they are reproduced, circulated and transmitted, they are enriched and expanded by being embodied in local identities. New semiotic fields may subvert them, but they may also unlock reservoirs of meaning that previously were neglected, repressed or ignored. I propose that the latter is what is happening in and through the Lutheran code today.

The structuring codes of Lutheranism

My third thesis is that Lutheranism consists of three structuring codes or rules: cross as (dis)location, justification as relation and God's twofold "con- testing" governances. These codes operate through the law/gospel meta-code, with an energy that is simultaneously decentering (law) and re-centering (gospel). This transversal code also ensures that four sociocultural variables are theologically hinged: power–distance; individuality–collectivity; gender roles; and uncertainty–avoidance.

The question here is how codes and rules work hermeneutically within a system—interlocking a text with a context, and vice versa. Here the content of a rule is manifested, that is, the peculiar doctrinal import of a code. We should note that what is referred to here is not the propositional value of such a code, but how it functions within a semiotic field creating a difference that makes a difference. In sum, these codes—doctrines—hinge on an intra-systematic ordering of texts by constantly exposing them to the hermeneutics of a "con-text."

As an example of how a doctrinal code can function as the hinged theme between "text" and "con-textual" generative themes, we can look at how the Lutheran code may function attending to both the stories presented in the biblical texts as well as the stories that map our present life. A reminder: codes establish a relationship that is at once intra-systematic as well as contextual, opening up spaces for living truly. In other words, they guide our attention by gathering impressions into a coherent whole, and linking those with actions by "pulling" the sacred into the profane.

The Lutheran codes, of course, are embedded within the larger scriptural and Christian tradition, and therefore they presuppose a structural congruence with God who is known through Jesus the Christ. This highlights that Christian discourse in general, and Lutheran discourse in particular, is bound to a specific body (Jesus) related to God and catalyzes a new set of structural couplings through the Holy Spirit. The Lutheran code does not deny the gap between Creator and creature, but within that, has an unconditionally salvific bent. In a sense, the Lutheran discourse is centered on a God who "falls" through this gap into the world, which, contrary to Gnostic views, is a "fall" that is salvific.[11]

The cross as a Lutheran theme is the decisive code for deciphering the type of God Christians meet. From early on, it has been a code or rule for making distinctions in situations that are devoid of any hope or filled with alienating hopes. It is a subversive code that challenges all cultural and religious notions of what is considered transcendent or successful in life. The cross as a code situates what is considered most important: God is available to us in what seems to be a gap devoid of any god. Although tied up with the lexicon of patristic and medieval theories of atonement, as a

---

[11] Cf. Žižek, op. cit. (note 2), p. 87.

code, it always undermines these. And because it is a rule, it also expands beyond Luther's own understanding in order to incorporate our contemporary semiotic and social fields. This innovation brought by the code not only provides us with a better grasp of the tenor of biblical texts, but also with a hinge to draw into the text our present histories of living in this gap. The cross is the point where our current epistemes are questioned and destabilized,[12] making room for what is truly new and different.

In this sense, the most substantial Christian promise for the world—communion or kingdom of God—is heard in the struggle that occurs in space, devoid of God's luminosity and filled with an alien, imperial presence. This draws our attention to an "impotent" God who has fallen into our world, challenging our notions of power. In the midst of this tension between imperial potency and divine impotency, between the law and the end of the law, the cross appears as the center of a new gospel—sites of failure in history become the places where God abides. In this encoding, our attention is drawn to the cross as a sociopolitical event.

The law, as imperial sovereignty, does not exist without the negation of an "other." The cross is a verdict denouncing that something is fundamentally wrong with how the world is structured,[13] and how it attempts to fill in the gaps. Golgotha is the mirror image of the *Ara Pacis Augustae*, the critical reflection of Octavian's imperial realized eschatology, the unmasking of Rome as the benefactor of all humanity.[14] This God on a cross totally reverses values: God justifies the victims of public, legal and official imperial power, through the man Jesus, friend of sinners and prostitutes.[15] A mysterious power of attraction is revealed in our midst: God "falls" for the victims of a law that constantly saps honor, self-esteem and lives. But the vindication of that cursed Jew reveals a God to whom impotent creatures are attracted. In Jesus the Christ, we see not just a novel adaptation of the creature to God, but also of God to the creature. It functions as a script for living truly, challenging those scripts that bring forth sinners, miserable ones, fools and the weak of this world as scapegoats of the perverse

---

[12] See Vitor Westhelle, *The Scandalous God: The Use and Abuse of the Cross* (Minneapolis: Fortress Press, 2006), p. 84.

[13] Cf. John Dominic Crossan, *The Birth of Christianity: Discovering what Happened in the Years Immediately after the Execution of Jesus* (San Francisco: HarperSanFranscisco, 1998), p. 258.

[14] See Helmut Koester, "Jesus the Victim," in *Journal of Biblical Literature* 111/1 (1992), pp. 3–15.

[15] See John Dominic Crossan, "The Resurrection of Jesus in its Jewish Context," in *Neotestamentica* 37/1 (2003), pp. 29–57.

dynamics of exclusion. They become the preferential "attractors" of divine mercy and grace.

The cross, therefore, is a code that locates a God who transcends into our world not to condone sacrifice, but as the very Savior from the sacrifices that are always being exacted from us. Faith implies a mutation leading to new life. For that reason, this faith will determine the flow and ebb of behavior, emotion and imagination by means of which a human group interlocks with its environment and its final meaning.

Speaking this Word of God declares a reversal—justification—in the midst of all conditionalities that entrap us in life denying fields. The code is not only a verbal declaration (forensic) but also makes accessible to us the energies of life that are truly eternal. It grants permission to live truly, leaning toward an inexhaustible promise. As creatures, we lean away from God, holding our breath, conserving energy for ourselves, living without a horizon or boundaries. In justification, the "event horizon" of our lives is opened by a blast of the Spirit. God comes into the lives of persons sucked in by the margins—psychologically, spiritually, socially, economically. It radically redraws the boundaries of God's domain in order to include those who hitherto were considered far away.

Justification implies not only being present at the many boundaries that divide humanity, but also discerning which ones need to be crossed, which ones dismantled and which ones simply named and made visible. The gospel narratives in which this crossing occurs are a vindication of the bodies that have been broken by the curse of the law in dark holes of debt, torture, imprisonment, despair and abandonment. Christians are called to participate in these "crossing movements," in and out of the same love that has first crossed over to them. Nobody really is an insider; we live by grace, recognizing that we are all part of a *koinonia* of outsiders and marginalized.

Jesus' proclamation of a kingdom for the nobodies and undesirables touched on the most pressing issues of the time: debt, daily bread, shame and impurity. Exorcisms and the healing of bodies and spirits broke the spell that bound and burdened colonized and "undesirable" people. When Jesus broke bread, he adopted the "degraded" position of women: he served, he was the hostess. With this practice, he witnessed to the righteousness God wills for creation, and communicated an egalitarian and un-brokered sharing of God's goodness and mercy. In the same vein, Jesus' crossing of different frontiers allowed individuals and groups to enter into an imme-diate physical and spiritual contact with God's justice, and thus with one another. As the gospels emphasize, Jesus crossed the traditional boundaries of family, honor and dishonor, Jews and Gentiles, men and women, sick and healthy, pure and impure, country and city, poor and rich. Bearing witness to the Father's mercy and coming reign, Jesus embodies a new space: the space of the Spirit. His body and his presence become the locus of a new narrative that is not only about God, but also about how God crosses over into the bodies and minds of those who never expected to be considered "somebodies." To draw frontiers is an act of disenfranchising power; to trespass is an act of divine imagination and love.[16]

This code, when unhinged from its forensic trappings, is the hinge for a new set of semantic fields. Liberation and political theologies, for example, have taught us to take a new look at the way in which the generative theme of sin operates.[17] Sin is a power bent upon itself. It is always constructed by a set of polarities between perpetrators and victims, healthy and sick, rich and poor, men and women, righteous and unrighteous. Energies of life are sucked in, as in a vacuum, extracting from one pole to feed the other. Feminist theologians[18] have taught us to see the self in relation to the patriarchal, cultural and linguistic frameworks that encrypt women's self as a prideful sinner, when in fact many women have been deprived of being able to experience a true sense of self. Overabundant male pride comes at the expense of that which feeds male egos. In both cases, there is a depiction of sin as the shattering of the self that is enacted by these relational fields—all worlds that have been brought forth by "somebodies" in power.

To be undone by the law in order to receive a new center of graced identity always involves decentering that which entraps the self in a diabolical dance. Justification unravels those scripts. The language of justification expresses a strategy of including the destitute, the marginal and the excluded into a new community in which social, spiritual and material goods are redistributed.[19] This is what theologies stemming from India (Dalit), Africa

[16] See Guillermo Hansen, "On Boundaries and Bridges: Lutheran Communio and Catholicity," in Wolfgang Greive (ed.), *Between Vision and Reality: Lutheran Churches in Transition,* LWF Documentation 47/2001 (Geneva: The Lutheran World Federation, 2001), pp. 87f.

[17] Cf. Juan Luis Segundo, *El hombre de hoy ante Jesús de Nazaret,* vol. II/1, *Sinopticos y Pablo* (Madrid: Cristiandad, 1982), pp. 129ff; Jürgen Moltmann, *The Spirit of Life: A Universal Affirmation* (Minneapolis: Fortress Press, 1992), p. 125.

[18] See Serene Jones, *Feminist Theory and Christian Theology: Cartographies of Grace* (Minneapolis: Fortress Press, 2000), pp. 62ff.

[19] See this concept developed in Martin Luther, "Sermon on the Blessed Sacrament of the Holy and True Body of Christ and the Brotherhoods, 1519," in Helmut T. Lehman (ed.), *Luther's Works,* vol. 35 (Philadelphia: Muhlenberg Press, 1960), pp. 45ff.

(*ubuntu*) and Latin America (liberation) have pressed upon the Lutheran code, ringing the same tones that we hear among feminist and critical theologies in the North.

Precisely because it allows us to live truly, we are able to engage the multiplicity of life's conflicting demands and identities. We do so with the hope that every aspect of life can be de- or recoded with a surplus of meaning that critiques as well as promises real fulfillment. Luther's understanding of God's twofold rule, which has often been applied with less than happy consequences, nonetheless continues to be a regulating code in the Lutheran grammar; it provides the plasticity to incorporate new sociocultural semiotic fields. Through this code, Lutheran theology manifests itself as a public theology, and, therefore, always in "con-tens[t]ion" within any con-text.

Since the social construction of identity always takes place in a context marked by power relationships, the power in defining codes and unleashing the clout of symbols always has political and social effects. For individuals or communities, there may be a plurality of identities that become a source of stress and contradiction. Which ones will dominate? Which ones will catalyze others? I contend that Lutheranism possesses a grammar that can weave its religious code with a wide array of social and cultural forces that are not only secular marks of identity, but also places where the holy and a sense of whole-ness is lived out. The basis for that is Luther's identification of "orders" within society as sacred places, where the specific religious code is not in competition, but acts as both a critique and an affirmation of these different fields.

Luther spoke of these orders as church, family/economy and secular authority.[20] Admittedly, he did so in a patriarchal tone that is unpalatable for us today. He also took for granted an hierarchical structuring of society that contemporary democratic sensitivities find objectionable. He fell short of affecting the codes of justification and cross in more explicitly transversal ways. He spoke of institutions and orders of what today we call civil society, which in a postmodern world do not have the power for constructing iden-tity as they once had. But these problems are Luther's, not ours. The code, I believe, is still valid, because it relates the reality of Christian identity with those different areas of life that make claims through other rules and codes for structuring who we are. In short, he made secular borders transparent to the inflecting claim of the gospel without cancelling their provisional and necessary existence.

---

[20] See Martin Luther, "Confession Concerning Christ's Supper" (1528), Part III, in Timothy Lull (ed.), *Martin Luther's Basic Theological Writings*, 2ⁿᵈ edition (Minneapolis: Fortress Press, 2005), pp. 64f.

In this sense, the dynamic Trinitarian concept of God and the twofold or multiple ruling of this God encourage a public and political theology. While grounded in an unconditional and absolute claim that comes from beyond us, this also recognizes the desirability and necessity of living within certain boundaries. In the worst case, these boundaries lose the malleability proper to any historical and cultural construction, as they did for many intelligent, "respectable" German theologians during the Nazi era. But in other cases, this can also lead to a deeper appreciation of the irreducible plurality that is an expression of a creative God who opens up spaces to live in. Feminism, indigenous movements, gays and lesbians, ecologists, Zapatistas, Barrios de pie, Dalits—all are expressing a desire to bring forth worlds in which they can live, and in so doing, are expressing what the First Article professes.

For this code to be publicly relevant, its metaphors must be woven with generative themes proper to other cultural linguistic fields. The Rousseauian concept of *volonté générale*, Montesquieu's and Locke's division of powers, Madison's constitutional check and balances, Marx's concept of social democracy, Foucault's microphysics of power, Lacan's conception of the repressed, as well as a myriad of local and non-Western traditions, all coalesce in a postmodern notion of radical democracy that grows as the living alternative through the networks spawned by empire. It is a new form of sovereignty based on communication, relationships and different ways of living that nonetheless have something in common. Democratic demands—although always imbued with particular and local interests—can be seen as the means through which the living God is continually creating. This fluid communication—rather than an hierarchical *Ordnung*— reflects the dynamism of a Trinitarian God.

And yet, as we weave these networks together, as we voice our demands, as we reach beyond our borders, we know that the Lutheran code contains a cautionary tone. The unconditional promise of the gospel is receiving in the midst of different kinds of (secular) identities. While the claiming of identities is essential for survival, for life, for societies, these claims always involve the distinction between a self and another, a "we" and "they" distinction, that limits our egos and super-egos. On the one hand, the reclaiming of identities is a cry for justice, for subverting a "new order" that satisfies very few; this is good and necessary, for without those boundaries life would continue to be siphoned off. On the other, identities can readily run afoul or become reactive, claiming to embody essential attributes accessible to none but themselves.

To be encrypted by a Lutheran code is to be aware that in the multiple worlds we bring forth, we live not only from the gospel. Yet, we cannot exercise a power that is incongruent with the values of this same gospel. Rather than falling into new dualisms, this Lutheran caution is the basis for critiquing any essentialist enthusiasms, or any form of power, which attempt to hide the violence of its demands under a putative *evangelium* of peace, progress or free market.

This is why the "two governances" code always implies a "con-ten[t]sion" with any and all forms of secular claims. The God of the crucified is always crossing the boundaries erected to dispossess others, and is always in "con-ten[t]sion" with those structures, systems and dynamics that promise self-gain at the expense of others. But, in the midst of this tension, another gap opens up—the gap that God inhabits as the crucified and risen One. It is still a gap, between God and God, between human and other humans, between humans and nature, and between human beings and their final fulfillment. To live truly is to learn how to carry this tension in ourselves.

A proactive identity

My fourth thesis is that the grammar signified by the Lutheran code points to a proactive rather than a reactive identity. This identity weaves together the diversity of our local frameworks, and is at odds with fundamentalisms, essentialisms and archaic confessionalisms of any type.

What are we here for? We are here to play—in the sense of performance. Our theologies play with codes, as instances of a performative dance. It is not that this playfulness suddenly changes our natures, but they display an identity as we perform in "dresses" that are not ours by right, but are given as a gift. Even the old forensic notion of imputed grace has its place here; after all, we are playing with the clothing and an identity that was given to us—an alien righteousness. We are all "drag queens," wearing clothes that transform us with a new radiance that comes from beyond ourselves, making us truly alive. The fabric seems to become one with our flesh. Finnish Luther research had it right all along: we do not only partake, but we are partaken; we receive not only a favor, but are made participants in who God is.[21]

---

[21] See Tuomo Mannermaa, "Why is Luther so Fascinating? Modern Finnish Luther Research," in Carl Braaten and Robert Jenson (eds), *Union with Christ* (Grand Rapids: Eerdmans, 1998), pp. 1–20.

I believe that a cultural linguistic approach offers us the possibility of going beyond the 1963 Helsinki scenario with its push and pull between those who celebrated and embraced new discursive shifts, and those who saw themselves as guardians of an ancient code. Our generation has dwelt within the tension of these two dramatic forces, and it has learned to differentiate what belongs to a colonial project, and what are the codes that liberate. In this learning process, we are used to being continually undone and remade, disarticulated and redeployed, affirmed and denied. We no longer revere the ancient orthodox lexicon but we have not given up the code. We are very much aware that it is the task of theology to be situated within a particular cultural semiotic construct to disclose the hinge that holds our religious identity together with the generative themes of our environments. Theology is like alchemy, it imagines gold where other semiotic fields find only rust. Theology encrypts in order to irradiate, binds in order to free.

I also believe that the understanding of our tradition as a cultural linguistic system that we share helps us to realize the profound meaning of doing theology not only in the context of our particular churches, but of a global communion. We have come a long way since Budapest 1984. One of the outcomes of this ecclesiological shift—whose consequences are still looming on the horizon—is that we are gradually being "networked." Belonging to a tradition that has been networked has led to this acute sense of plurality in the communion, yet we are also more aware of the versatility of our codes as they are inflected and therefore enriched through new contextual generative themes.

Lutheran theology is alive and well today, precisely because it is plural, chaotic and messy—different strategies of "structural couplings" with our diverse environments. This is the best indicator that our identity is not static, but always in a state of flux. Our web of belief is enriched when we have to deal with reverence for ancestors, speaking in tongues, healing practices, HIV and AIDS, sexuality or empire. To be networked in such a web implies that through these new demands under the law, we gain new and additional insights into the gospel.

Participation in this Lutheran web makes all of us not only custodians, but receivers. To be Lutheran is not only to "give" Lutheranism but to receive it also from those corners from where we least expect it. Perhaps we can all learn that in this world we are all marginal in some way. The Lutheran code, recognizable as it flows through the nodes of the network, always comes back to us in surprisingly new formulations, intertwined with new local identities. We must learn to code, to give, but also to decode, to receive. This is where the consensus emerges as to what "Lutheran" is, with the task of always discerning what belongs to a colonial and patriarchal past, and what are the codes that liberate and ground our future.

This network is not limited to space, but also expands in time. This is the other side of being networked, where our forebears also join in an unending conversation and we discuss with them our issues as friends. And even when we are stuck, when the alleys are dark, when we may be a little lost, they appear as kind of psychopomps—not to correct our theologies, nor to deny them, but to give us this gentle push that reminds us not to fear as we face the gap.

Diversity in the Bible as a Model for Lutheran Hermeneutics

Barbara R. Rossing

The question of how to interpret the Scriptures is one of the most important questions within our Lutheran communion today. When we study the Bible across different cultural contexts, we can be enriched by one another's perspectives and come to deeper understandings of the Word of God. But, as Christian history shows, the Bible can also be used as a weapon to attack one another, to foster intolerance and to silence those with whom we disagree. Our different biblical interpretations can sometimes clash, both within and between contexts.[1]

My church, the Evangelical Lutheran Church in America (ELCA), is involved in an initiative called the "Book of Faith: Lutherans Read the Bible," which seeks to deepen biblical literacy and biblical fluency among members of our church. Goals for the initiative include introducing Lutheran hermeneutics, encouraging Bible reading among parishioners and helping to deepen contextual readings of the Bible.[2]

I hope we will also seek ways to help people see and value the great diversity of perspectives within the Bible itself. Appreciation of that biblical diversity can be a resource for our churches today, as we address challenging issues and witness faithfully in our pluralistic contexts.

The Bible is God's living Word for us. As Luther says, the Bible is the cradle within which Jesus, the Word of God, is laid. But the Bible is not a single, monolithic book dropped from heaven. It is a library of voices. It is God's Word spoken differently, through different Christian and Jewish communities and different authors, in different contexts. Various com-

---

[1] See for example the essays in Reinhard Boettcher (ed.), *Witnessing to God's Faithfulness: Issues of Biblical Authority*, LWF Studies 2/2006 (Geneva: Lutheran World Federation, 2006); David Ratke (ed.), *Hearing the World: Lutheran Hermeneutics—A Vision of Life Under the Gospel* (Minneapolis: Lutheran University Press, 2006); and the biblical essays in Musimbi Kanyoro (ed.), *In Search of a Round Table: Gender, Theology and Church Leadership* (Geneva: WCC Publications, 1997).

[2] See Diane Jacobson, Mark Allan Powell and Stanley N. Olson, *Opening the Book of Faith: Lutheran Insights for Bible Study* (Minneapolis: Augsburg Fortress, 2009), and *The Lutheran Study Bible* (Minneapolis: Augsburg Fortress, 2009).

munities in the biblical conversation understood God's Word in different, even competing, ways.

A lively conversation among different voices is represented within the Bible itself. This is a fundamental insight of biblical scholarship. Both the Old and New Testament represent diverse communities and diverse authors, with different theologies and views, all seeking to be faithful to God, even while sometimes understanding God's Word quite differently. The early church in its wisdom decided to include many voices in the canon, canonizing not just one view but a range of views.

Some in our churches argue that we should protect lay Christians from insights of biblical scholarship about diversity in the Bible. In their view, to begin to acknowledge diversity within the Bible would be too confusing for lay people. They believe it could lead the church down the slippery slope towards relativism and confusion. I would counter that diversity in the Bible is a great treasure that the church very much needs for mission and ministry today.

The questions I want to address in this essay are these: What is "faithful diversity" when it comes to biblical interpretation?[3] How, in a positive way, can we theologians bring into our churches and into the Lutheran World Federation (LWF) one of the most important results of biblical scholarship—namely the appreciation of multiple voices and diversity within the Bible? How can studying the Bible teach us to view diversity in our churches as a blessing, rather than as something that leads to division? How can this appreciation help us to grapple with some of the issues we face in our churches today, such as sexuality and other issues that some claim are church dividing?

Faithful diversity in 1 Corinthians 12:12: "Because we are many we are one"[4]

To support the argument for the importance of faithful diversity in church life today I begin by considering the apostle Paul's discussion of the body of Christ with many different members in 1 Corinthians 12:12, a difficult phrase to translate. The question is how we should understand Paul's phrase, "being many," grammatically a Greek circumstantial participle. I

---

[3] The conference of bishops of the ELCA issued a pastoral letter regarding the proposed sexuality statement in March 2009, which they employ the term "faithful diversity." See "A Pastoral Word to the Evangelical Lutheran Church in America from the Conference of Bishops," March 10, 2009, at **www.elca.org/ELCA/Search.aspx?q=conference+of+bishops+pastoral+letter+march+2009**, accessed November 2009.

[4] Author's own translation.

propose to translate the Greek phrase *polla onta hen esmen* as, "Because we are many, we are one." As far as I know, this is not a translation ever given in any published translation.

The Greek is literally, "Being many, we are one." The King James Version leaves it simply "being many"—the most literal translation possible. This is perhaps also the best translation, since it leaves ambiguity.

Unfortunately, in seeking to resolve the ambiguity of "being many," translators frequently add the word "though," even though "though" is not in the text. To be sure, the concessive translation of the participle as "although" is one possible option for a circumstantial participle: "though many, are one body." That is the decision of the Revised Standard Version and the New Revised Standard Version and many translations in other languages as well. (I invite you to look up this verse in the Bible in your first language, to see whether the word "though" or "although" is used.)

Another option is to translate the participle temporally, probably the most common use of the Greek circumstantial participle, "When we are many we are one." The option I suggest is the causal translation, also a very common meaning for circumstantial participles, "Because we are many, we are one."

Paul may intend more than one meaning. Maybe he even intends all three. That is the genius of Greek participles, that they can hold together multiple, even contradictory meanings. The simple translation "Being many, we are one," perhaps is most faithful to that openness and ambiguity.

If we want to try to understand Paul's meaning more precisely we must look at Paul's argument in context. That leads to a key question for both Pauline churches and our churches today: What is the relationship of our many-ness to our one-ness? Is Paul saying that many-ness constitutes a problem in Corinth, something that must be overcome? That is what the concessive translation of the participle as "although" would seem to imply. Or, is Paul saying that many-ness is a blessing, a resource that can help the Corinthians discover their deeper unity in Christ? The sense of many-ness as a blessing is what the translation "because" would imply.

The letter of 1 Corinthians is strongly concerned with the unity of the body of Christ in the face of differences among church members on a number of issues. The question is what role diversity plays in that larger unity that Paul envisions. Romans 12:5 is the closest parallel passage, another discussion of the metaphor of the body with many members. Here, Paul does not use the participle at all, so there is less ambiguity. He simple writes, "we, who are many, are one body in Christ." Nonetheless, the Revised Standard Version (mistakenly, in my view) inserts the word "though" in Romans 12:5—"we, though many, are one body in Christ"—as if to imply that many-ness is a problem, a concession, that must be overcome in order to find one-ness. But Paul does not say that. With his image of the body and its diverse members, Paul is saying that diversity is a gift from God, a vital asset for mission.

Therefore, I want to propose the "causal" translation of the participle in 1 Corinthians 12:12 as Paul's most likely meaning, "Because we are many, we are one."

Conversations within the Bible: A community of diverse views

That perspective of "many-ness" as a blessing in 1 Corinthians is consonant with the diversity we find within the Bible itself. Both Testaments contain diverse, even competing, perspectives. The Bible is a library of documents, written over many centuries. Even the New Testament, while written over a much shorter span of time than the Old Testament, includes a diversity of theologies and perspectives, reflecting the considerable diversity of early Christianity. That very diversity of voices can be a blessing for our churches today.

This idea of diversity within the New Testament is not new. That is why it is perhaps surprising that we do not draw on it more often and more explicitly in our church life and in the Lutheran communion. Already in 1951, Ernst Kasemann proposed in his famous essay, "The Canon of the New Testament and the Unity of the Church," that churches engaged in ecumenism must consider the great diversity and plurality of New Testament theologies.[5] That the Bible contains a diversity of perspectives and theologies is an insight largely shared among Lutheran biblical scholars in the global communion. We teach it to our students in seminary Bible courses. Yet, too often, pastors are afraid to share the insights of critical scholarship once they leave seminary, out of fear of confusion or of being perceived as undercutting the authority of the Bible. We scholars have apparently not been persuasive enough in making the case that canonical diversity can be a blessing for people in local congregations.

This perception of confusion is exacerbated by the challenge of fundamentalisms and literalism in many local Lutheran contexts today. Pastors and teachers who seek to employ the insights of critical scholarship can be

---

[5] Ernst Kasemann, "The Canon of the New Testament and the Unity of the Church," in Ernst Kasemann, *Essays on New Testament Themes* (London: SCM, 1964). The essay was first delivered as a lecture in Göttingen in 1951.

accused of appearing weak in comparison with fundamentalist neighbors or family members who make sweeping claims about what "Bible believing" Christians believe. Tensions between the Missouri Synod affiliated International Lutheran Council (ILC) and the LWF also play out in debates about the Bible in some LWF member churches.

It has been my experience as a pastor that parishioners are more ready to learn about biblical scholarship, including the multiple authors and perspectives, than we sometimes assume. Several years into my first pastorate in the 1980s, for example, I tentatively introduced the idea that Genesis 1–3 includes the voices of the Yahwist and the Priestly writer, and that the perspectives on the creation in Genesis 1 differs from that of Genesis 2–3. While I was expecting my parishioners to be shocked, instead they were relieved. Their faith was enriched, not shaken, through learning more about the multiple contexts and perspectives of the different authors of biblical texts. Many lay people in our churches are interested in the idea that the books of the Bible do not all say the same thing, and that the unity of the biblical canon also includes great diversity of perspectives and voices.

To be sure, critical biblical scholarship has not always served the church as well as it should have. Historical-critical scholarship has made important contributions by opening up the complex layers of biblical history, including the textual history of biblical manuscripts. But one shortcoming of the historical-critical method of interpretation was a tendency to assert that only the history behind the text mattered. Newer, critical methods, such as narrative and rhetorical criticism, can help us discover not just the world behind the text but to the rich worlds within and in front of the text. The perspectives of liberation, post-colonial and feminist/womanist interpretations can help us expose dynamics of power and imperialism reflected in biblical texts as well as in interpretations.

My point is that the critical methods and insights of biblical scholarship today can contribute to helping the church see the remarkable diversity of perspectives within the Bible that together make up the Word of God. The challenge is to open up that rich history and diversity of voices while also articulating the authority of the Bible with confidence.

Different types of biblical diversity

Some of the diversity is between various authors in the Bible, for example on issues of ecclesiology and church structure. While some churches and

theologians today may wish that all churches had bishops in historic suc-
cession, biblical scholarship has helped us to see that the threefold structure
of bishops, presbyters and deacons on which that model is based is not
universal to all or even most churches in the New Testament. Ecclesiologies and ministry structures vary greatly, from the hierarchy described in
the Pastoral Epistles (1 and 2 Tim, Titus), to the beloved community of
friendship that characterizes the Johannine community, to the prophetic
model of leadership characterizing the churches of the Apocalypse.

I am grateful that the LWF affirmed the diversity of the New Testament on the matter of ministry structure in the 2007 Lund Statement on
"Episcopal Ministry Within the Apostolicity of the Church." Surveying
the biblical tradition, the Lund document acknowledged that:

> The New Testament does not describe a single pattern of ministry, which can serve
> as a blueprint for later structures in the church. Rather, there is in the New Testa-
> ment a variety of forms reflecting developments at different places and times.[6]

I hope that similar acknowledgment of biblical diversities can be lifted up by
the LWF in statements on other matters as well, including moral issues.

Some of the diversity is found within a single biblical text. Some of the most
fascinating diversity is not simply between different biblical documents, but
also between different voices represented within a single document. This is
especially the case in the Old Testament—the way in Genesis, for example,
we can identify and retrieve different theologies of the Yahwist as contrasted
to the Priestly writer, as seen in their different creation accounts. We need
both creation accounts, with their different theologies and contexts, especially
for ecology. The richness is lost if we simply harmonize the layers.

In New Testament documents as well, we can identify different layers of theologies—the theology of the hypothetical "Q" community, for
example, that is now embedded in the Gospels of Matthew and Luke;
the theology of the women prophets in Corinth that can be heard behind
Paul's responses to it in 1 Corinthians; or the theology of the Philippian
community that might be reflected in the Christ Hymn of Philippians 2
that was perhaps taught to Paul by the Philippians themselves as part of
their mutual sharing.

---

[6] "Episcopal Ministry Within the Apostolicity of the Church: The Lund Statement by the Lutheran
World Federation," Lund, Sweden, 2007, at **www.lutheranworld.org/LWF_Documents/LWF_The_
Lund_Statement_2007.pdf**, accessed November 2009.

Eschatology is something I am working on in relation to environmental issues and the LWF climate change program. In order to move away from the escapist, earth denying eschatology of a text such as 2 Peter 3 we can embrace a more new creation oriented eschatology that is found in other texts.

My students are astonished to learn the huge variety of eschatologies in the New Testament, sometimes within the same document. Robert Kysar looks at the seemingly contradictory multiple eschatologies within the Gospel of John, noting that some verses depict salvation and eternal life as a future possibility, while other verses seem to suggest that eternal life is something we already have. In Kysar's view, the Fourth Evangelist received the futuristic eschatology from the tradition but felt it no longer adequate for the community. So the Fourth Evangelist lays alongside that tradition verses that seem to describe eternal life also as a quality of the believer's life in the present, as seen for example in Jesus' dialogue with Martha in John 11, or the statement in the high priestly prayer that "this is eternal life, that they may know you" (Jn 17:3).[7]

In the face of such diversity within biblical texts, is it the final author alone, and that author's theology, that has the authoritative canonical stamp—i.e., the Priestly writer who edited Genesis, or the author of the Pastoral Epistles (1 and 2 Tim, Titus) who may have been the collator of Paul's letter collection? Or, can we not also draw for our Christian life on some of the other, earlier theologies of the authors and communities preserved in submerged layers of these writings?

There is also diversity among interpreters, sometimes due to our different contexts, sometimes to different methodologies or simply to different scholarly judgments or convictions.

I work on the Apocalypse. Some of the best work on this text comes from postcolonial insights of people from marginalized communities—for example Pablo Richard, a Roman Catholic, who employs Latin American liberation insights; Brian Blount, an African American; Allan Boesak, a South African; Elisabeth Schüssler Fiorenza and Tina Pippin, two feminist scholars. Using the lens of empire, these interpreters see aspects of the text that previous interpretations have not seen, even while they may also differ among themselves about other aspects of interpretation.

---

[7] See, "Eternal Life is Now," in Robert Kysar, *John the Maverick Gospel* (Westminster John Knox, 1993), chapter 4.

The insights of critical feminist scholarship have also been important in opening up and retrieving the multiplicity of voices in the Bible. The letter of 1 Corinthians, for example, is often viewed as a case study in problematic disunity. But the church in Corinth can also be viewed as an example of a church learning to live with theological diversity on some issues, as part of its deeper unity in Christ. Elisabeth Schüssler Fiorenza has made the provocative suggestion that "it is Paul, and not the Corinthians, who understand their debates as party or school divisions."[8] Instead of adopting Paul's rhetoric of unity/disunity that can result in vilifying women and others in the Corinthian community, she hypothesizes that there was in Corinth a conversation or "broad theological movement of which Paul is a part." She suggests that we describe debates in the *ekklēsia* in Corinth not as division or disunity but rather "in terms of *parrēsia*—the free speech of citizens."[9]

Schüssler Fiorenza proposes the model of early Christianity as the "discipleship of equals," a democratic vision of *ekklēsia* that embraces diversity:

> The modification of the word "discipleship" with that of "equals" must not be understood as advocating sameness under the guise of universality. Rather it seeks to underscore equality in diversity as the central ethos of discipleship.[10]

Even when biblical scholars come from very similar contexts and use similar methodologies, they can come to different interpretations—for example, on the issue of homosexuality. I lift up for example the excellent paper coauthored by two of my North American New Testament colleagues, Arland Hultgren and Walter Taylor, who together analyzed five biblical passages often cited on homosexuality.[11] Careful exegesis characterizes the entirety of their study, including translation questions particularly related to 1 Corinthians 6:9–10 and Romans 1. Yet, they disagree about what church policy we should take. Exegetically the two interpreters share almost complete common ground, and each finds much

---

[8] Elisabeth Schüssler Fiorenza, "Rhetorical Situation and Historical Reconstruction in 1 Corinthians," in *New Testament Studies* 33 (1987), p. 395.

[9] Elisabeth Schüssler Fiorenza, "Paul and the Politics of Interpretation" in Richard A. Horsley (ed.), *Paul and Politics: Ekklesia, Israel, Imperium, Interpretation* (Harrisburg: Trinity Press International, 2000), pp. 51, 54.

[10] Elisabeth Schüssler Fiorenza, *Sharing Her Word: Feminist Biblical Interpretation in Context* (Boston: Beacon Press, 1998), p. 113.

[11] Arland J. Hultgren and Walter F. Taylor Jr., "Background Essay on Biblical Texts for 'Journey Together Faithfully, Part Two: The Church and Homosexuality,'" 2003, at **www.elca.org/What-We-Believe/ Social-Issues/Social-Statements/JTF-Human-Sexuality/Faithful-Journey-Resources/Historical- Documents.aspx**, accessed November 2009.

to commend in the other's position. Yet, disagreement is still possible, partly regarding the question of whether and how texts about same-sex practice in first-century Roman culture can even be applied to discussions of homosexuality and homosexual orientation today, since differences between ancient homosexual practice and contemporary understandings of homosexuality are so great.

Hultgren and Taylor write,

> The difference between interpreters should not be understood as a conflict between those who seek to be "true to Scripture" and those who seek to "twist the Bible" to their own liking. The disagreements are genuine. Nor is one approach intrinsically more "conservative" and the other more "liberal."

In instances such as this, when responsible biblical scholars disagree, perhaps the crucial question is whether and on what issues diversity must be church dividing. (And I believe both Hultgren and Taylor would agree that disagreements on homosexuality are not church dividing.)

The ELCA adopted a social statement on sexuality as well as ministry policy recommendations. The documents are intriguing in that they lay out four different positions on homosexuality and ministry, and argue that all four positions can be held by responsible biblically faithful Christians. There simply is no consensus right now, the proposed statement says. Although people from both extremes have attacked the document, I hope it will hold as a faithful, centrist, responsible model of honoring biblical diversity. The document's proposal for respecting the bound conscience of one another in the midst of our disagreement builds on the apostle Paul's approach to ethics in the Corinthian correspondence.

The great treasure of biblical diversity today

The question for us is this, How can we honor diversity as part of our unity in communion? How can we cherish transformative communion in the midst of our differences? How can we tell the biblical story, the story of God's mission, in such a way as truly to honor faithful diversity today?

My colleague David Rhoads wrote a wonderful, accessible, non-technical treatise on New Testament diversity aimed for congregational use.[12] His

---

[12] David Rhoads, *The Challenge of Diversity: The Witness of Paul and the Gospels* (Minneapolis: Fortress Press, 1996).

hope is that "experiencing the diversity in the New Testament will help to revitalize the church." He picks up on the insight put forward already in the 1934 by Walter Bauer, namely that the multiplicity of theologies and practices in the New Testament reflects a diversity that was there from the very beginning of Christianity.[13] Diversity was not the result of a fall from some earlier pristine unity. "God has provided for such diversity in the New Testament," Rhoads argues, "and we need it for our life together." He writes:

> Diversity in the Bible is a rich celebration of the complexities of the human condition and of the manifestations of God in our midst. The multiplicity of belief and practice in the New Testament promotes openness and leads us to welcome others who are different and to learn from them. The diversity in the canon undercuts the human tendency to claim absolute truth for any one Christian belief system. It stands against intolerance and urges us to depend on each other for a full witness to the truth of God. It is a call to respect and celebrate diversity in the church and in the world as an expression of God's love of diversity in creation.[14]

Rhoads uses the analogy of biodiversity to argue that canonical diversity may be important for our very mission and survival.

Recognizing God's grace in the other: Faithful diversity is not communion dividing

Recognizing diversity does not mean that "anything goes," as some have charged. How Paul dealt with food issues in 1 Corinthians 8–10 and Romans 14–15 by both permitting and limiting difference, out of regard for the weaker brother and sister, can be instructive for us on sexuality and other potentially divisive issues today. As David Horrell persuasively argues, Paul's concern was "not to resolve the substantive ethical issue under dispute, but rather, through inculcating a stance of other-regard in a context of communal solidarity, to construct a moral framework within

---

[13] See Walter Bauer, *Orthodoxy and Heresy in Earliest Christianity* (Philadelphia: Fortress, 1971; German original, Tübingen: J.C.B. Mohr, 1934)

[14] Rhoads, op. cit. (note 12), p. 11.

which a degree of diversity and difference can remain." [15] The ethical model that Paul carefully constructs in Romans and 1 Corinthians holds together both solidarity and difference. We can use such a framework in Lutheran contexts today.

In seeking stories of faithful diversity and how it might work for our churches and our communion today, I go back to the handshake of *koinonia* in Galatians 2. This narrative tells the story of what was perhaps the most contentious church meeting in history. Even the two biblical versions of the meeting are not in agreement. [16] Paul is furious with the Jerusalem leaders, and they are certainly furious with him. Neither side gives in. Yet their deep differences do not become church dividing because they are able to recognize the grace of God in the other person. "When . . . [they] recognized the grace was given to me," Paul writes (and we hope he also recognized the grace given to James and Cephas and John), "they gave to Barnabas and me the right hand of fellowship [*koinonia*]" (Gal 2:9). That handshake must have been an amazing moment. Paul and the Jerusalem leaders saw God's grace in the eyes of the other person, across their differences. The only concession that Paul says he made was not doctrinal or moral, but rather a commitment to "that we remember the poor, which was actually what I was eager to do" (Gal 2:10).

That kind of "aha" of experience of seeing God's grace in the other person, across the circle, can happen as we study the Bible today, as we seek to discern God's will. The goal is not to obliterate diversity, whether the diversity within the Bible or the diversity between interpreters. The goal is not even agreement, although agreement is wonderful. Rather, the goal is *koinonia*, communion in Christ. Across the table, across the circle, across the world, across our disagreements and differences, as we study the Bible in all its diversity, with our diversity of methods and perspectives and insights, we can look into the eyes of the other person and see the grace of God. That is true communion, true *koinonia* in Jesus Christ.

---

[15] David G. Horrell, *Solidarity and Difference: A Contemporary Reading of Paul's Ethics* (London: T&T Clark, 2005), p. 281.

[16] Acts 15 suggests that Paul made dietary concessions, agreeing to abstain from meat that had been strangled. Paul himself insists that he never made such a concession.

Marginal Readings: Implications for a Lutheran Hermeneutic and Communion

Monica Jyotsna Melanchthon

I come from a country of 1.2 billion people. In spite of the recent growth of the Indian economy, India has the second highest rate of poverty—after Nepal—among all Asian countries. Millions live in conditions that are less than human; they are vulnerable, discriminated against, marginalized, victimized and violated on account of their social and genetic makeup.

One's position at the bottom of caste, class and gender hierarchies is in itself the primary cause of vulnerability and marginality, as this position is associated with having the least rights, highest obligations and lowest status.[1] Thus, endemic gender- and caste discrimination and violence are the result of severely unequal social, economic and political power dynamics. Devoid of land, education and skills, obliged to perform certain occupations considered polluting, Dalit women, men and children depend on the dominant social groups for their livelihood. This dependence leads to violence, most commonly perpetrated by dominant caste males.

Doing theology in the midst of the stresses and strains of those who are ignored, rejected and sidelined requires going against the grain of traditional theological reflection that has been controlled and dominated by the privileged and so-called "upper caste." These issues of diversity, marginalization, authority and biblical interpretation present many challenges for Lutheran theological reflection in India. What is the significance of the margins for theological reflection? What is the Bible's significance for those marginalized by caste? How do the marginalized approach Scripture? How are sacred texts or traditions to be drawn on by and for those at the margins? What might a Lutheran hermeneutic be for those wanting to interpret and read Scripture from the perspective of those stigmatized by caste or at the margins of society or the church?

---

[1] Annie Namala, "Affirming the Image of God in Dalit Women: A Task for the Indian Church," in *In God's Image: Journal of Asian Women's Resource Centre for Culture and Theology*, vol. 26, no. 3 (September 2007), p. 10.

Margins and their significance for theological reflection

One significant insight of twentieth-century Christian theology is the notion of a "preferential option for the poor," i.e., that people who are marginalized have a claim to special consideration. Arising out of various theologies of liberation, this option for the economically disadvantaged and for those at the fringes of society has provided major new impulses for biblical studies, systematic theology, church history, ecclesial practice and the academic study of religion. Opting for the margins continues to be an important focus at a time when the gap between rich and poor is growing at an alarming rate in many parts of the world, and when other gaps, based on differences in gender, caste, sexual orientation or race, prevail.

Being marginalized is not simply a struggle between oppressor and oppressed, with the latter remaining submissive and passive. In their spatially conceived representation of exclusionary gestures, "margins have always been ambiguous signs which have served to frame the center in terms of indictment as well as approbation."[2] Theologians, sociologists and others have often categorized marginality as ecological, economic, socio-political or a combination of these. While it has been common to privilege one of these categories in order to explain how societies work, they are rarely mutually exclusive. In addition, since marginality is relative, virtually any group might be made marginal depending on people's past and present situations. Sometimes marginality can be imposed (in economic, political or cultural terms), and sometimes even actively chosen. Defining "margin" is a complex matter, requiring contextual sensitivity if it is to be useful for theologians.

Besides the uncertainty regarding how to define it, opting for the margins has also been challenged by postmodern shifts in intellectual, social, political and economic realities that replace preferential options with other emphases such as pluralism, otherness and difference. Opting for the margins is then reduced to the special interests of certain minority groups, or even rejected as antiquated and irrelevant today.

Entering further into the debate on marginality[3] can result in masking patterns of oppression and becoming deaf to voices from the margins. Instead, I acknowledge that the margins are simply those areas/places in society that are on the periphery, on the fringes, sometimes concealed.

---

[2] Sneja Gunew, *Framing Marginality: Multicultural Literary Studies* (Melbourne: University Press, 1994), p. 27.

[3] Cf. the collection of articles, in R.S. Sugirtharajah (ed.), *Still at the Margins: Biblical Scholarship Fifteen Years after Voices from the Margin* (New York: T&T Clark, 2008).

These places are neither deserted nor quiet, but crowded and noisy with people drawn from among a long list of individuals and communities who are deprived of privileges, whether on grounds of race, caste, tribe, gender, economy, politics, sexual orientation, mental health, physical disability, HIV/AIDS, etc. Those who live at the margins—or simply exist—cannot be reduced to or dismissed as "untouchables," "prostitutes," "criminals," "sinners," "downtrodden," "the oppressed," "minorities," "homosexuals," or even the "poor." They are not categories or statistics but women and men, flesh and blood, created, redeemed and loved.

In his recent book, *Margins: Site of Asian Theologies,* Felix Wilfred identifies three specific reasons why we need to pay attention to the margins.[4] Margins are the space of God's visitation—God is discernable and present in the margins. The biblical story reveals a God who journeys to the margins and who is at the periphery. Therefore, we are required to journey from the centers of power to the fringes of society to experience God in new ways and in new forms because God is present in the disturbing and unsettling questions raised by experiences at the margins. "She speaks when we are silent and allow ourselves to be challenged and taught by realities around us."[5] The resistance and hope expressed by communities at the margins, in the midst of demoralizing despondency, "slumdog" despair and powerlessness is a celebration of the power of God at the margins. God is at the margins and on the side of the poor; when we stand with those at the margins we are with God.

Margins are also places that enable those oppressed to affirm their self and identity—the language at the margins is of plurality and diversity because it is within difference that the poor and the marginalized have a space. They are places occupied by people who go unnoticed, misfits who seldom figure according to mainstream definitions and values. And yet, it is at the margins that they are affirmed and acknowledged. Difference is allowed to flourish here; they are empowered to come to a consciousness about who they are. Victims of domination resist assimilation by distinguishing themselves from others. By asserting their difference, they consciously perceive and acknowledge their collective selves. Difference is crucial for their subjecthood as principal agents of their own emancipation. In their assertion of difference, we also hear and discern God's language of plurality in practice.

Margins especially function as the sites of theologies. If margins are the space of God's visitation, it is here that theologies also need to begin.

---

[4] Felix Wilfred, *Margins: Site of Asian Theologies* (New Delhi: ISPCK, 2008), pp. xii–xx.

[5] Ibid., p. xii.

The complexity of the realities confronting communities at the margins is immeasurable. But, in spite of their "slumdog" existence, they bring to the fore reflections and interpretations that are subjective, based on knowledge derived from experience, which is more important than any quantitative generalization. They are pushing the church to overcome stagnation by disturbing the sterile complacency of the dominant social groups and traditions, and by challenging their set mores, fixed modes of looking at reality and established literary canons. These marginal readings and interpretations bring into focus neglected or suppressed aspects of experience, vision, language and reality and compel the academy and a communion of churches to observe itself critically and to refashion its mission and theology. The margins offer fresh, new and exciting resources for fashioning a theology that is unconventional, radical in spirit and orientation and made possible by religious and cultural borders that are fluid and porous.

We also need to pay attention to the margins because marginal voices widen theological horizons. This new set of voices broadens our theological horizons and allows us to reshape our theological guidelines. Marginal readings or the inclusion of hitherto suppressed voices enable a fresh theological direction and a "constructive reinterpretation in the task of theological reflection."[6] Marginal readings need to be heeded for their liberative potential since they free us from a narrow understanding of faith or self, conditioned by centers of tradition and power. They transform the understanding of the margins and those who inhabit these spaces and raise questions and issues that are either neglected or not often raised by the dominant. They free faith from being reduced to a matter of knowledge, truth and understanding and root these in concrete praxis.

Last, but not the least, the inclusion of marginal readings is a social, political and ecclesial task. Broadening the range of texts we attend to and issues we take seriously and encouraging the consideration of a range of marginalized voices in academic institutions and public debates, remain important social, political and ecclesial tasks. The stakes involved in such a diverse and multicultural project go beyond reducing parochialism and enlarging the understandings of the mainstream.[7] They go far beyond a simple "inclusion." Marginal readings need to be welcomed not only as critical interventions into mainstream Western culture's readings of biblical

---

[6] Joerg Rieger, *God and the Excluded: Visions and Blindspots in Contemporary Theology* (Minneapolis: Fortress, 2001), p. 99.

[7] Monica J. Melanchthon, "Unleashing the Power within: The Bible and Dalits," in Roland Boer and Fernando Segovia (eds), *The Future of the Biblical Past*, Semeia Studies Series (Atlanta: SBL, 2010), forthcoming.

texts, but also into many non-Western theological and biblical discourses, thus expanding their own vision. These readings are also cultural positions within the moral and political fabric of their social contexts; they are trying to expose ideologies and justifications for practices or institutions that are unjust and exclusionary, and that "dis-empower" and marginalize a great many who inhabit these contexts.

The centrality of the Bible for marginalized communities

The sacred scriptures of the Hindu Vedas were not accessible to those marginalized by caste because of their untouchable/Dalit status. Although the Bible was present in India already in the first century C.E., it was not available to these communities for several centuries because the early custodians of the Christian Scriptures in India limited its access. Scriptures, Christian or other, occupy an important place in marginalized communities, and have both the capacity to dis-empower, stigmatize, discriminate and bring death as well as to affirm, embrace and to bring life. Because they can bring death and life and because of their presence almost everywhere religion is discussed, sacred scriptures are particularly significant in the interface between religion and marginal experiences.

Interpretations of the Bible are polyvalent because of the difference in the social location, ideology, perspective and biases of the interpreter, the method employed and the conceptions of "meaning."[8] For those who represent institutional religion and sometimes also the academy, sacred materiality is a resource used to affirm and uphold orthodoxy. But the same sacred materiality, to those who are considered too polluted to touch or listen to Scripture, has offered the possibility of reaching out beyond the constraints of orthodoxy in order to address their realities. The Bible's relevance lies in its use and not in its mere possession.[9] Hence, when it became possible for the Dalits to have access to Scripture, the Bible became "plurivalent" in its use as a colonizing book, a meta-symbol of the colonialists, to inculcate Western manners, values and symbols, a medium

---

[8] Mark Allan Powell, "The Social/Cultural Context of Biblical Interpretation Today: Features, Assumptions, Effects and Challenges," in David C. Ratke (ed.), *Hearing the Word: Lutheran Hermeneutics—A Vision of Life under the Gospel* (Minneapolis, MN: Lutheran University Press, 2006), pp. 59ff.

[9] Walter Altmann, *Luther and Liberation: A Latin American Perspective*, transl. by Mary M. Solberg (Minneapolis: Fortress, 1992), p. 55; cf. also Terence Fretheim, "The Authority of the Bible and the Imaging of God," in William P. Brown (ed.), *Engaging Biblical Authority* (Louisville/London: Westminster/John Knox, 2007), p. 45.

through which education and literacy became available, and an icon in a culture with a history of iconizing material objects.[10] Whatever the initial aim, it was popular among the newly converted, because it was accessible to all who could read irrespective of race, caste or gender. It served as a means of emancipation for the colonized.

The Bible holds a central place in theologizing at the margins, because it is seen as a source of power and comfort and provides continuity with Christian identity and tradition.[11] The Bible is also significant because of the commonality that exists between their experience and the struggles and those of marginalized communities of the Bible. This is probably the first and most important consideration—the points of convergence between the biblical world and the world of the marginalized today.[12] The biblical dictum of a preferential option for the poor and the marginalized struggle for justice, equality and freedom is one such point of convergence.

This affinity between the marginalized of the Bible and the subjugated today contributes to the appeal that the Bible holds for them. The potential of biblical texts for negotiating and renegotiating liberation in the light of their subjugated experience makes possible the discovery of God within their social and cultural milieus and their liberation from oppressive forces. The Bible equips one to expose sin and call people to repentance. It is a source of life, and more specifically for the life of the community.

Features of marginal readings

There are several features that bind marginal readings of the Bible. When approached with a Dalit consciousness[13] and by socially engaged Dalit scholars/activists, the sacred texts do not have predetermined meanings

---

[10] Sathianathan Clarke, "Viewing the Bible through the Eyes and Ears of Subalterns in India," in *Biblical Interpretation*, 10, 3 (2002), pp. 245–66.

[11] Dhyanchand Carr, "Dalit Theology is Biblical and it Makes the Gospel Relevant," in A. P. Nirmal (ed.), *A Reader in Dalit Theology* (Chennai: Gurukul, nd), pp. 71–84.

[12] K. Jesuratnam, "Towards a Dalit Liberative Hermeneutic: Re-reading the Psalms of Lament," in *Bangalore Theological Forum*, vol. 34, no. 1 (June 2002), pp. 2–3.

[13] "a mind-set influenced not only by the Dalit experience of suffering and rejection but also of overcoming the same [...]. The term *dalit* [...] affirms their determination to annihilate slavery, both internal and external, and their visions for an egalitarian, casteless society. Deenabandhu Manchala, "Reading together with the Dalits: An Exploration for Common Hermeneutical Directions Amidst Plurality of Interpretations," Unpublished (nd), p. 4.

or a dominant trajectory—their meaning in the context of marginalization must be contended. As Carlos Mesters puts it:

> The people's main interest is not to interpret the Bible, but to interpret life with the help of the Bible. They try to be faithful, not primarily to the meaning the text has in itself (the historical and literal meaning), but to the meaning they discover in the text for their lives.[14]

Dalits have learned hard lessons under two gurus—poverty and caste—while Dalit women have a third guru, namely gender discrimination. The first has taught them sacrifice, patience and forbearance. The second and third have taught them resilience and struggle. Their reading, interpreting and theologizing starts, as in all other liberation theologies, from their experiences and their engagement. It starts with their context and their experience at the bottom of Indian society. The point of departure is their experience of struggle for survival and liberation.

Context and experience, tested and revised in conversation with others is the starting point for these interpretations. The appeal to experience as a source of knowledge in the hands of those who feel oppressed and discriminated against is useful in opposing authoritarian powers. The strength of this appeal to experience lies in the fact that it is shared by others. Experience is never pure or unmediated; it is always affected by the communities and circumstances in which we live. Appealing to experience means acknowledging the fact that experiences are often ambiguous, certainly limited and often contradictory.

Hence, a Dalit reading of John 4 will emphasize the manner in which Dalits are hindered from drawing water from the wells or drinking from the pots of the dominant castes. The story of Cain and Abel is read with an emphasis on Abel as the dominant land-owning class who victimized Cain as a result of his profession as a shepherd, traditionally understood as a polluting occupation. The Babylonian captivity is interpreted as caste captivity, Job is seen as the prototype of Dalits, and the prophets are seen as the champions of the poor and the cause of justice.[15] In his book, *Towards Dalit Hermeneutics*, James Massey

---

[14] Carlos Mesters, *Defenseless Flower: A New Reading of the Bible*, transl. by Francis McDonagh (Maryknoll, NY: Orbis, 1989), p. 9.

[15] V. Devasahayam, *Outside the Camp: Bible Studies in Dalit Perspective* (Chennai: Gurukul, 1992); *Doing Dalit Theology in Biblical Key* (Chennai: Gurukul/ISPCK, 1997); See also the article by A. Maria Arul Raja, "New Exorcism and Dalit Assertion: A Reinterpretation of Mark 5:1–20," pp. 346ff.; John Jeyaharan, "A Dalit Reading of Lord's Prayer," in V. Devasahayam (ed.), *Frontiers of Dalit Theology* (Chennai/New Delhi: Gurukul/ISPCK, 1997), pp. 357ff.

draws many parallels, both etymological and experiential, between Dalits and the Hebrew *dal* or *dallim* in the Hebrew Bible.[16] The story of the woman with the flow of blood, and her stigmatization and discrimination, resonate with the Dalit experience of stigmatization and discrimination. Jesus is the "Word made flesh who lived among us"—emphasizing "lived among us"—identified with us, suffered with us and liberated us from the enslavement of caste.[17] Paying serious attention to the context is one way of exhibiting responsibility to the faith community on behalf of whom the text is being interpreted.

From this insight arises the widely evoked "hermeneutic of suspicion." At its foundation lies the assumption that in every claim to knowledge someone's vested interests are operating, generally those of the dominant and powerful in society. If this is the case, then we must be suspicious of all knowledge claims, we must come to see how they reflect and serve the interests of the powerful while victimizing the marginalized.

The Bible is received as a text, a result of human effort that arises from a particular context. In other words, the Bible becomes the Word when read in community and in light of the community's experience and consciousness— shaped by the affirmation of people's roots, collective struggle, experiences of suffering and of liberation, and the vision of liberation and restoration. The ultimate goal is to instill in the community the impetus to strive for political and social liberation and to provide the community with possible blueprints for acting toward liberation, a new identity and fullness of life. This process, propelling the text into life in order to influence change, is textual activism. The Bible—and Christianity as a whole—"contain something of truth not because of its origins, but because it liberates people now from specific forms of oppression."[18] Therefore, reading and interpreting the text play a major part in the social, cultural and political mobilization of marginalized communities and for the maintaining and preserving life.

The effectiveness and relevance of a reading is measured by the extent to which a reading touches the lives of the individual and the community. There is therefore a special sensitivity to the practical implications of the reading. New interpretations are futile unless they motivate and provoke the community into action. Hence, marginal readings, born out of a context of

---

[16] James Massey, *Towards Dalit Hermeneutics* (New Delhi: ISPCK, 1994).

[17] V. Devasahayam, *Outside the Camp. Bible Studies in Dalit Perspective* (Chennai: Gurukul Lutheran Theological College and Research Institute, 1992); V. Devasahayam, *Doing Dalit Theology in Biblical Key* (Chennai: Gurukul/ISPCK, 1997).

[18] Susan Welch, *Communities of Resistance and Solidarity: A Feminist Theology of Liberation* (Maryknoll, NY: Orbis, 1985), p. 53.

oppression and injustice and a spiritual experience with God, are readings that seek to be of service to the community. They start from a meeting with God, a meeting that takes place within a situation of challenge, one that awakens Christians to a contemplative commitment and to develop a spirituality of protest. They have also been termed "combative readings" since they seek to equip the community with the power to rebel, resist and liberate and provide a biblical basis for doing so.

The shift from their particular experience to the Bible, from the Bible to action, and then back again to the Bible is emphasized, requiring a process of mutual critique and validation between experience and text. Only then can one envision liberation, the renewal of the church and the transformation of society. Marginal biblical hermeneutics are closely bound up with their direct involvement in the process of production and hard physical labor.[19] Dalits contribute with their physical labor to the maintenance of the entire society's life and hence are committed to its preservation. Life needs to be protected. They thus are suspicious of all traditions and ideologies that threaten life by legitimizing subjugation and oppression.

The fact that Dalits lack the basics necessary for leading a dignified life makes Dalit readers very sensitive to the present moment.[20] They challenge the way in which dominant theological and social determinism seeks to keep people in positions of subjugation. They reject scriptural and social traditions and employ creatively performed rituals[21]—song, dance and acting[22]—to reread and revise oppressive traditions in order to address their predicament.

For the marginalized, studying the Bible is a matter of faith. Biblical research is not merely an intellectual exercise but ultimately a way to respond to God. This provides both the motivation and goal in all aspects of biblical research. But this faith is more than intellect. It is character-

---

[19] Felix Wilfred, "Towards a Subaltern Hermeneutics: Beyond the Contemporary Polarities in the Interpretation of Religious Traditions," in *Jeevadhara* 26/151 (1996), p. 57.

[20] Felix Wilfred, *The Sling of Utopia: Struggles for a Different Society* (New Delhi: ISPCK, 2000), p. 150.

[21] Simon Charsely citing Max Gluckman, *Rituals of Rebellion in South-East Africa* (Manchester: Manchester University Press, 1954), identifies these performances as "rituals of rebellion," in Simon Charsely, "Interpreting Untouchability: The Performance of Caste in Andhra Pradesh, South India," in *Asian Folklore Studies*, 63 (2004), p. 287, fn. 11.

[22] Through his study of the Madiga community (traditionally cobblers) in Andhra Pradesh, Charsely shows how they undermine the claimed superiority of the dominant Brahman. For example, "The ability to move and skin dead cattle is given a forcefully positive evaluation. The eating of beef is not represented as a mistake," in "Interpreting Untouchability," ibid., p. 285.

ized and defined by its "earthliness,"[23] indicating urgency, immediacy and directness, bound up with life's material and physical realities and needs. An anonymous poet writes about God who comes to her every day in the form of two hundred grams of gruel; it is this gruel God who sustains her and gives her life and the energy to survive.[24]

Marginal readings use oral resources, rituals, symbols and enactments and other rituals of rebellion to understand biblical texts. They welcome imaginative, creative and non-formal methodologies for reading and interpreting the Bible. Since marginal communities are collective by nature, and places where learning is engendered through collective and communal exercises, the resulting interpretation is rich.

They are ecclesial because these communities are rooted in the church even in those instances where the institutional church has not been supportive of their cause.

> They accept and proclaim their belonging to these churches, experiencing this belonging as a reference and sometimes as a challenge. But they share a common feeling that the church of Christ is God's instrument for the liberation of the human spirit and for demonstrating the first fruits of God's reign. They are rooted in the church and their resolve to read from within the church in accord with the longings and aspirations of the people of God is something they share in common.[25]

Despite their strong criticism of ecclesiastical institutions, they are actively involved in the life of the church and working for its transformation. One can say that the theologians of struggle have not given up on the church. Sometimes, in spite of the church, the people will rise.

There has been an irruption of these voices from the margins, one that cuts across gender, race, caste, class and religion. The challenges they pose are radical and may be construed as threatening to the church. In ongoing theological work, we often do not take seriously the concerns or the articulations of our partners from different contexts. If we can exist without them year after year then there is no compelling reason why they should be taken seriously at all. But the church cannot pretend any longer to hide behind the

---

[23] Wilfred, op. cit. (note 19), p. 58.

[24] Anonymous, "From Jaini Bi—With Love," in Alison O'Grady (ed.), *Voices of Women: An Asian Anthology* (Singapore: Asian Christian Women's Conference, 1978), p. 11.

[25] Maria Clara Luccheti Bingemer, "Preface – Third World Theologies: Conversion to Others," in K. C. Abraham, *Third World Theologies: Commonalities and Divergences* (Maryknoll: NY: Orbis, 1993), pp. vii–xiv.

facade of neutrality. These readings challenge the community to discern a new way of being church. The hope lies in the fact that the creative and liberating side of the church has been expanding, and so has the consciousness that the church does not exist for itself but for the life of the world.

Harnessing texts for the transformation of the marginalized

The following charge has been made:

> Liberation theologies of various sorts have found great favor in Lutheran World Federation circles in recent years, and that remains evident in this volume's papers. The tacit assumption of numerous essays [. . .] could be stated as, "Our politics is better than your politics, and the sooner our kind takes over the better." Needless to say, fitting such a notion into theological containers most of us would recognize as Lutheran takes some powerful magic.[26]

> Our theological discussion [. . .] has been divided into a conservative insistence on the dogmatic tradition, and a liberal repudiation of dogmatic content in exchange for an ethic of shared humanity [. . .]. Every article of the Confession of Faith has explosive and aggressive significance for the status quo of the old world, and an article that leaves our relationship [. . .] to society as it was, is not worthy to be an article of the Christian Faith.[27]

Throughout India, people struggle for food, security and land to overcome violence and to recover human dignity. It is both a challenge and an imperative to read and interpret Scripture and tradition and to understand the propositions of our faith in a social and political sense that will not only transform the individual but also renew and restructure society and the church on principles of justice and freedom.

> Confessions of faith which do not have as their consequence far-reaching social changes in this world, are matters of private recreation, and therefore have long been tolerated as irrelevant and harmless. We shall only be able to make clear

---

[26] Frederick Niedner in his review of Niels Henrik Gregersen, Bo Holm and Ted Peters (eds), *The Gift of Grace: The Future of Lutheran Theology* (Minneapolis: Augsburg Fortress, 2004), at **www.crossings.org/ thursday/2006/thur031606.shtml**, accessed November 2009.

[27] Helmut Gollwitzer, *The Rich Christians and Poor Lazarus,* transl. by David Cairns (New York: Macmillan, 1970), p. 3.

to our contemporaries the relevance of every article of our Confession of Faith, if we make clear its political and social revolutionary significance for society.[28]

But does it really require "magic" to harness Lutheran ideals and doctrine for the sake of the marginalized? Or for purposes of "liberty and freedom?" Are social and political engagements in variance with Lutheranism? Why does a liberational reading of Scripture or interpretation of doctrine and tradition worry some? Does not the gospel seek to liberate society and its individuals from oppression, be it political, social or religious? When did "justice" or "freedom" become bad words?

That Luther's social conscience undergirded much of his teaching and preaching is beyond doubt. Luther may not have foreseen or expected a social and religious revolution, but his preaching and writing generated one among the people of his time, since they gave or perhaps appeared to give religious sanction to separatist political initiatives. His call to Christians to read and interpret the Scripture themselves gave a religious boost to people's yearning for emancipation. By putting men and women in charge of their own destinies, he made an incalculable cultural impact. When

his declaration that a man[29] must above all things follow his own conscience even if that means resisting his temporal and spiritual overlords—spread throughout Europe, it signaled to the majority of the people who were, or fancied themselves to be, in some or other way oppressed, that they could take on the system and win.[30]

Such was the transforming power of Luther's teaching. In many ways, this stresses the fact that words, whether written or spoken, trigger surprising and unexpected responses from the hearers.

It has been said that the church's best secret before Luther was the Bible. This secret, when exposed by Luther, generated volatile and unexpected results. The Reformation brought about a "breakthrough in biblical interpretation"[31] and questioned many of the inherited commonplaces. For Luther, the Bible was not just a repository of doctrines, but a "living communication that was

---

[28] Ibid., p. 2.

[29] While it is LWF editorial policy to use inclusive language, this has been left uncorrected in quoted material, here and throughout the publication.

[30] Derek Wilson, *Out of the Storm: The Life and Legacy of Martin Luther* (London: Hutchinson, 2007), p. 344.

[31] Darrell Jodock, *The Church's Bible: Its Contemporary Authority* (Minneapolis: Fortress, 1989), p. 22.

not properly Word until it was effectively communicated and internalized by human beings."[32] Luther therefore gave the community the open Bible and permitted them so to speak—by applying reason to the plain text—to challenge centuries of official church teaching. Luther encouraged people to use their God-given intellect to question everything. Question they did, bringing into play not only their intellect but also knowledge derived from experience. Luther himself "exploited his own experience in order to understand scripture and more importantly, to understand his own life."[33] This enduring legacy brought recognition for the ordinary readers' right and capability to interpret the Scriptures.

Implications for Lutheran biblical hermeneutics

What are the ingredients of a Lutheran hermeneutic of biblical interpretation? How might marginal readings enrich the articulation of a Lutheran hermeneutic? Is there a space for principles such as liberation, justice, love and life within this hermeneutic?

The following criteria have been identified as employed in a Lutheran reading of Scripture:

- The context of the text
- Experience/context of the interpreter[34]—"the social location of the interpreter and the religious community to which he or she belongs"[35]
- Loyalty to the ideals of the gospel, in other words a strong Christological base[36]—"what is important and central and true about Scripture is whatever shows forth Christ"[37]

---

[32] Ibid.

[33] David C. Ratke, "Introduction," in David C. Ratke (ed.) *Hearing the Word: Lutheran Hermeneutics* (Minneapolis, MN: Lutheran University Press, 2006), p. 9.

[34] Scott Hendrix, "The Interpretation of the Bible According to Luther and the Confessions or Did Luther Have a (Lutheran) Hermeneutic," in Ratke, ibid., pp. 13ff.

[35] Richard Perry, "What sort of Claim does the Bible have today?" in Ratke, ibid., p. 75.

[36] Márta Cserháti, "Experience and Expertise in Understanding the Bible: Responsive and Responsible Readings," in Reinhard Boettcher (ed.), *Witnessing to God's Faithfulness: Issues of Biblical Authority,* LWF Studies 2006 (Geneva: The Lutheran World Federation, 2006), pp. 177ff.

[37] Cf. Helmut T. Lehrmann (ed.) *Luther's Works,* vol. 35 (Philadelphia: Muhlenberg Press, 1960), p. 236; Diane Jacobson, "Reading Strategies in the Light of Biblical Diversity," in Boettcher, ibid., p. 55.

- Gospel and law that point to Christ—"demands for justice and con-demnation of sin can and do show forth Christ" [38]
- Gospel (content) and Scripture (document)
- Meaning (semantics) and impact (pragmatics) of a text[39]
- Conversation and dialogue
- Personal transformation and self-improvement[40]
- Canon within the canon[41]—criteria or core values/principles such as "God's unconditional love;" "Jesus Christ as center;" "justification by grace through faith;"[42] "salvation (also understood as life in its fullness)"
- Reading in community.[43]

Scott Hendrix concludes his analysis of Luther's treatment of Scripture by saying,

> I would therefore, not say, that Luther had a single hermeneutical method or principle, but a hermeneutical vision. By that I mean: Luther had a vision of what life under the gospel could and should be. The Christians of his day were not using scripture from a distance but trying to live within its world and find-ing their way as early Christians had to do. For Luther the Reformation was a missionary enterprise that faced unprecedented situations. To meet them, he and his colleagues drew on all their resources, chief among them the gospel message and scriptures, to mold as best they could an evangelical community.[44]

What might marginal readings bring to this list and hermeneutical vision? What might this evangelical community look like and what was its basis? I believe all these keys or criteria to be open to interpretation. Socially engaged Dalit readers revere the Bible for its potential to liberate those who have suffered centuries of exploitative oppression and perverse cruelties. There is a genuine

---

[38] Jacobson, ibid., p. 56.

[39] James W. Voelz, "Toward a Distinctive Lutheran Hermeneutic," in Ratke, op. cit. (note 33), pp. 98ff.

[40] Jane Strohl, "The Social/Cultural Context of Biblical Interpretation Today," in Ratke, ibid., p. 69.

[41] Márta Cserháti, "Finding the Keys: Unity and Diversity in the Bible," in Boettcher, op. cit. (note 36), pp. 65ff.

[42] Ibid., pp. 68ff.

[43] Diane Jacobson, "Tools for Biblical Interpretation: Imagination and Critical Reflection," in Boettcher, op. cit. (note 36), p. 126.

[44] Scott Hendrix, "The Interpretation of the Bible According to Luther and the Confessions or Did Luther Have a (Lutheran) Hermeneutic?" in Ratke, op. cit. (note 33), p. 31.

longing for freedom of the community from social, religious and cultural bondage. A liberative reading of Scripture is understood to be consistent with the character, requirements and obligations of God. This emancipatory liberation is the authoritative lens through which the Bible is read. Hence, while marginal people would accept the principles/criteria listed above, it also requires that these principles are employed for the purposes of life and liberation. Although the detail of the hermeneutic might differ from one community to another, there is an overall inclusive and compassionate "shape" to the hermeneutic employed by marginal readers. Guided by compassion and justice rather than fidelity to religious orthodoxy, a marginal hermeneutic wrestles with biblical texts in diverse ways in order to grasp their redemptive detail and potential.

Marginal readings are not simply oppositional or counter readings; they also attempt to undo the power of dominant readings that represent themselves as universal. Above all, they emphasize the need for the proclamation of liberty to those enslaved by systems of oppression. They critique singular understandings and assertions that minimize their God-given authenticity and the actualization of this gift.[45]

Implications for life in communion

> The very cohesion of the LWF could be at stake unless ways are found constructively to come to terms with conflicting approaches to the Bible. The stakes are high and the situation complex. On the one hand, to hold the Bible as the Word of God in high esteem has always been one of the hallmarks of the Lutheran tradition. It has been appreciated as the sole norm for the church's life, preaching and teaching [. . .]. On the other hand, in the actual life of the church, questions regarding the authority of the Bible have been raised in various ways.[46]

The issue of the authority of the Bible is a sensitive matter and can be divisive. While I do not want to enter into the debates surrounding the authority of Scripture, I would like to acknowledge that most people within the communion, knowingly or unknowingly, live and make decisions that are informed by the Bible. The Bible brings focus and clarity to all aspects of their lives. In the minds of many, the world of the Bible and the world

---

[45] Katie G. Cannon, "The Biblical Mainstay of Liberation," in Brown, op. cit. (note 9), p. 23.

[46] Reinhard Boettcher, "Introduction," in Boettcher, op. cit. (note 36), p. 9.

of the church occupy identical spaces in their imagination.[47] A relationship is developed over time and hence sentiments run high when there is a discussion on the authority of the Bible. The Bible is authoritative in various and diverse ways and this diversity becomes apparent in the varied interpretations and readings in the Lutheran communion. But if we are to take seriously the lived experiences of others, this means we must hear the voice of "the other," and other ways of reading.

The Bible is God's gift to the church, for which we are grateful. Recently, at a consultation on "Dalits and Mission," the leader asked us to reflect on what the Bible was for us and then he asked us to tell him what we wished the Bible were. The responses were revealing. One wished that it had a few blank pages; another wished the Bible did not end with a "full stop"; and still another wished that there were less violence in the Bible. "The Bible does not always say what you thought it did—or wish it did. The only way to move forward through and past that offense is by more study, more probing and questioning."[48] What Ellen Davis says is significant:

> Receiving the Scriptures as God's gift means opening our minds to be changed by them; it does not mean relinquishing the right to disagree with some of what we encounter there—even the necessity of disagreeing on some significant points of faith and practice—since the biblical writers disagree among themselves, even within each Testament. Indeed, the very fact of internal disagreement is crucial for our understanding of scriptural authority and how the Bible itself fosters a critical consciousness; even those established by authoritative texts, may be challenged and debated within the community of faith. Every biblical writer who departs from the tradition does so by highlighting other neglected elements of the tradition; every innovation is established on an older foundation [. . .] if we disagree on a given point, then it must be in obedience to what we, in community with other Christians, discern to be the larger or more fundamental message of the Scriptures. In other words, disagreement represents a critical judgment, based on keen awareness of the complexity of Scripture and reached in the context of the church's ongoing worship, prayer, and study.[49]

Therefore, it seems to me that as members of the Lutheran communion we need to come to such a judgment slowly and perhaps reluctantly, to realize that we

---

[47] Serene Jones, "Inhabiting Scripture, Dreaming Bible," in Brown, op. cit. (note 9), p. 75.

[48] Ellen F. Davis, "The Soil that is Scripture," in Brown, ibid., p. 37.

[49] Davis, ibid., p. 38.

may not be able to accept everyone's view. This would be a sign of maturity.[50] But we need to continue to study the Bible and examine the implications of our interpretations critically to see whether they can be brought into full conversation with Scripture and the Christian tradition. We need to practice the virtues of humility,[51] charity and patience[52] in our approach and readings of the Bible. We must also show charity toward those who read the text differently. In doing so, some of our dissents and disagreements can be reversed. Such interpretative humility and charity may foster God's work of reconciliation within the communion and enrich life within communion.

Theology and biblical interpretation, therefore, must be a conversation between the text and the interpreter and between readers and not a proclamation designed to silence critical debate. If theology is to accomplish the goal of transformation/conversion/salvation/life, it requires the hearing of heretofore unheard voices. Sharon Welch refers to this process as the "insurrection of subjugated knowledges."[53] These are voices which have existed, says Chopp, "[. . .] on the underside, on the margins, in death itself,"[54] and this authentic hearing of the other is "transformative communication,"[55] because when we truly attend to the lives of those who have been dispossessed we must examine our own participation in the structures of oppression. This hearing necessitates changes in practice because we can no longer proceed under the assumption that our own experience is the sum of reality. In fact, as Daniel Maguire has argued, the view from the margins is likely to be a far more clear-sighted view.[56]

Perhaps more constructively, it is in this engaged dialogue between different perspectives that human understanding of God, and of Christian discipleship in the modern word, is most likely to be enlarged. A truly critical theology will always be a dialectical theology, not fixed on one track solutions, but ready to listen and to learn new truths from unexpected

[50] Ibid.

[51] Humility is here understood as being able to admit that none of our interpretations is definitive.

[52] Davis, op. cit. (note 48), pp. 36ff.

[53] Sharon D. Welch, *Communities of Resistance and Solidarity* (Maryknoll, N.Y.: Orbis Books, 1985), pp. 44–46.

[54] Rebecca S. Chopp, *The Praxis of Suffering: An Interpretation of Liberation and Political Theologies* (Maryknoll, New York: Orbis Books, 1986), p. 121.

[55] Sharon D. Welch, *A Feminist Ethic of Risk* (Minneapolis: Fortress Press, 1990), pp. 129–36.

[56] Daniel C. Maguire, "The Feminization of God and Ethics," in *Christianity and Crisis* (March 15, 1982), pp. 59–67, here, p. 62.

directions including interpretations of the biblical text offered from the margins.[57] If a cross fertilization of ideas is encouraged one can emerge more clearly aware of one's own identity and determined to live and develop one's theological mission as a contemplative commitment, in which methodology, choice of subject matter and systematic examination of the experience and struggles of the oppressed will combine to produce a real experience of God and proper attention to the God of others. As theologians, we are called to see the revelation of God shining in the faces of others, those who are different from us, and to make our theology an effective and gratuitous instrument of conversion and liberation.

---

[57] Cserháti, op. cit. (note 36), pp. 177ff.

"Whoever Hears You Hears Me": Hearing the Voice of Christ as We Listen to One Another Interpret the Bible

Dean Zweck

Introduction

According to the Lutheran understanding of Scripture, Christ is at the center as the Word made flesh. It is not only the person of Christ that is central, but all that Christ has done for us and for our salvation: his life, death and resurrection. Because of Christ and through the working of the Holy Spirit, God makes us his own in baptism, forgives us our sins, restores and heals us. We are born anew to a living hope through the resurrection of Christ. In and through Christ, God is making all things new—a promise and hope that include the whole creation.

This transformative gospel lies at the heart of the biblical narrative. Both in the world of the Bible and in the world of today we see people living out their faith in transformed lives (Rom 12:2). Being in the world, yet not of it, Christians can be open to perspectives and practices from their cultural contexts that become transformative in light of the gospel. In this process, which is undergirded by the faithful hearing of God's Word, there is affirmation and adaptation, but also refutation. Being attentive to other realities, perspectives and practices is to recognize that in these also there are wisdom, knowledge and goodness from God, from which we can learn and which we can appropriate. Other perspectives and practices can open our eyes and enrich our lives to see and experience the gospel working in ways that we were not formerly aware of.

Furthermore, as we listen to one another interpret the message of the Bible in a global communion, we can be deeply enriched in faith and life by appreciating and appropriating the gospel illumined perspectives and faith expressions of our sisters and brothers living in their very different situations.

In this article, examples illustrating this approach are given from the Bible, from the time of the Lutheran Reformation and from the writer's faith and life experiences of living and working in other cultural contexts.

Paul: From Damascus to Athens

Paul speaks of his own conversion and transformation in various places, primarily in Galatians 1:13–17 and 1 Corinthians 15:8–10.[1] He speaks of himself as one who had violently persecuted the church of God, but who, because of the revelation of God's Son to him, now proclaims Christ among the Gentiles. "But by the grace of God I am what I am," he writes, "and his grace toward me has not been in vain" (1 Cor 15:10).

As God's chosen apostle to the Gentiles, Paul intentionally became "all things to all people, that [he] might by all means save some" (1 Cor 9:22). With that intention, Paul travelled far and wide and eventually found himself in Athens, where he contended for Jesus as Israel's Messiah in the synagogue and proclaimed "the good news about Jesus and the resurrection" in the market place (Acts 17:17). There, Luke tells us, Paul entered into dialogue with Epicurean and Stoic philosophers, some of whom politely asked him about the "new teaching" he was presenting, and then took him away from the din of the *agora* to the serene space on top of the Hill of Ares, the traditional place for Athenian philosophers to meet for debate. Here, on the Areopagus, in a momentous speech, Luke presents Paul not so much as a Jewish itinerant preacher, but as a Christian philosopher.

In an eloquent oration (Acts 17:22–31), the Christian speaker first makes contact with his hearers by showing appreciation for their religiosity, and then focuses in particular on one object of their devotion: the unadorned altar with its inscription, "to an unknown god." From this starting point Paul announces his theme: "What therefore you worship as unknown, this I proclaim to you" (Acts 17:23). In rhetorically correct style, the speaker now moves into the main body of the speech (the *probatio*), and, in the manner of Stoic treatises on theology, sets forth carefully reasoned arguments for the existence of one true God and God's gracious endowment of the world for the benefit of humanity.

I have argued elsewhere that the real dialogue in the Areopagus speech is between Paul and the Stoics.[2] The dialogue proceeds from the assumption that the natural theology of the Stoics had developed a notion of God compatible enough with Christian proclamation to be used as a significant point of contact. Stoic treatises on theology conventionally divided the discussion into three parts, which we find also in the Areopagus speech: God, the world

---

[1] See also 1 Tim 1:12–16.

[2] Dean Zweck, "The Exordium of the Areopagus Speech," in *NTS* 35 (1989), pp. 94–103; also "The Areopagus Speech of Acts 17," in *Lutheran Theological Journal* 21 (Dec. 1987), pp. 111–22.

and religion.[3] The speaker on the Areopagus links up with well-established Hellenistic proofs for the existence and nature of the Deity: God's creative activity, God's providential governance of the cosmos and God's care of humanity. The points of contact that are made are not haphazard, but follow a pattern typical of Stoic exposition on the subject of religion.[4]

This linking of the biblical message to Hellenistic ways of thought cannot be demonstrated exhaustively here, but let three examples suffice. The unknown god is first identified as "the God who made the world and everything in it" (Acts 17:24). The Stoic philosopher Epictetus (AD 55–135) uses virtually the same words: "God has made all things in the cosmos."[5] The speech argues that God should be recognized because God gives to all people life and breath and everything (Acts 17:24), and cares for them by establishing "the times of their existence and the boundaries of the places where they would live" (Acts 17:26). This links with elaborate Stoic arguments for the existence of God based on the evidence of God's gracious provision. Dio Chrysostom (ca. AD 40–120) mentions the seasons as one such proof: humans love and admire the divinity "also because they observed seasons and saw that it is for our preservation that they come with perfect regularity."[6] In describing humanity's relationship to God (Acts 17:27–28), the speech quotes directly from the literature of Hellenism: God is "not far" from each one of us,[7] in God "we live and move and have our being,"[8] "for we are indeed his offspring."[9]

The speech not only makes points of contact, but also establishes points of refutation. Since there is only one God, the Creator and Sustainer of the cosmos, it is folly to build all manner of shrines and images, as if these could contain or represent God (Acts 17:4; 29). Enlightened philosophers already know this.[10] To the extent that they have correctly perceived the nature of

---

[3] Cicero, *De Natura Deorum*, 2.3; Acts 17:24–29.

[4] As exhibited in book 2 of Cicero's *De Natura Deorum*. Classical references sourced from the *Loeb Classical Library* series.

[5] Epictetus 4.7.6 (*ho theos panta pepoiēken ta en tō kosmō*).

[6] Dio Chrys. *Or.* 12.32.

[7] *ou makrān* very probably reproduces a topos in Greek popular philosophy. Dio Chrysostom (*Or.* 12.28) says that the people of long ago "were not dispersed far away [*ou makrān*] nor outside of the divinity by themselves."

[8] Possibly a quote from Epimenides of Crete. Epimenides of Crete was a semi-mythical, sixth-century BC Greek seer and philosopher/poet.

[9] The exact words are found in a hymn to Zeus by the Stoic poet Aratus, *Phaenomena* 5.

[10] E.g., Strabo 16.2.35: "What man, then, if he has any sense, could be bold enough to fabricate an image of God resembling any creature among us? Nay, people should leave off all image-carving, and [...] should worship God without an image." Strabo (63/64 BC–ca. AD 24) was a Greek historian, geographer and philosopher.

God and acknowledged him appropriately, they fit Peter's description in the Cornelius episode: "I truly understand that God shows no partiality, but in every nation anyone who fears him and does what is right is acceptable to him." (Acts 10:34–35). And yet, the message of repentance toward God is for all without exception, because all must appear before the one whom God has appointed to judge the world in righteousness. At the same time, there is wonderful hope: God has given "assurance" (Greek: *pistis*) to all by raising this man from the dead (Acts 17:30–31).

With consummate skill, Luke shows that the apostle, whose intention was to be all things to all people, was as good as his word. In the speech, we find a Christian rhetor who has entered the thought world of his hearers, and made it his own to such an extent that he is able to able to enhance the Jewish/biblical understanding of one true and living God, Creator of all things, by employing worthy notions of divinity in Hellenistic philosophy, the Stoic tradition in particular and attuning them to key ideas found in the Hebrew Bible. The Areopagus speech represents a beginning point in the long journey of the ongoing dialogue between Christian faith and philosophy.[11]

Augsburg, 1530: A culmination of transformative perspectives and practices

Lutherans are of many stripes and many kinds, but what holds them together in their diversity is a common confession. Lutheran churches are churches of the Augsburg Confession.

The sixteenth-century Reformation began in no small part because the church of that time was teaching certain non-transformative perspectives, and, as a consequence, was advocating numerous non-transformative practices. Because late medieval Christendom was in many ways a closed system in which other perspectives and practices were relentlessly stifled and even stamped out by force (cf. the Inquisition), the way forward was to go backwards, that is, to go back to the sources (*ad fontes*). In the light of those sources—the New Testament in particular—early Lutheran Reformers critiqued the teaching and life of the church of their time, and, finding them wanting, went on boldly to proclaim a rediscovered evangelical perspective, on the basis of which they forged a corresponding set of transformative practices.

---

[11] Hans Conzelmann describes the speech as "the most momentous document from the beginnings of that extraordinary confrontation between Christianity and philosophy," in "The Address of Paul on the Areopagus," in Leander E. Keck and J. Louis Martyn (eds), *Studies in Luke–Acts* (Nashville: Abingdon, 1966), p. 217.

For Luther, transformation came from his study of the Scriptures, the task assigned to him by his wise superior, Staupitz. The more Luther studied and lectured in the Scriptures, the more he discovered a new perspective. We cannot trace that journey in detail, but the full evangelical breakthrough came when Luther finally understood what the righteousness of God really is. Looking back on his life from near its end, Luther wrote about his transformative breakthrough. He describes how it was a single word in Romans 1:17 that still stood in his way: "In it [the gospel] the righteousness of God is revealed." He wrote:

> At last, by the mercy of God, meditating day and night, I gave heed to the context of the words, namely, "In it the righteousness of God is revealed, as it is written, 'He who through faith is righteous shall live.'" There I began to understand that the righteousness of God is that by which the righteous live by a gift of God, namely by faith. And this is the meaning: the righteousness of God is revealed by the gospel, namely, the passive righteousness with which merciful God justifies us by faith, as it is written, "He who through faith is righteous shall live." Here I felt that I was altogether born again and had entered paradise itself through open gates. Here a totally other face of the entire Scripture showed itself to me.[12]

What we have here is the gaining of a transformative perspective. Here, Luther discovered the gospel as "the power of God for salvation" (Rom 1:16). Here, Luther gained a perspective that was to change him from a questioning monk, bold enough to post the Ninety-five Theses about indulgences, to a driven reformer, ready and willing to put in place the transformative practices that go hand in glove with a transformative gospel.

Luther's evangelical perspective and early Lutheran thinking about its implications for churchly practice culminated in the eloquent confession made at Augsburg, 25 June 1530. Much has been written about the Augsburg Confession, but here I would like to make just a few points. At the heart of this confession is a particular way of speaking the gospel that is absolutely clear, and prevents any kind of Pelagian muddying of the waters. This is, of course, the article on justification:

> Likewise, they teach that human beings cannot be justified by God by their own powers, merits, or works. But they are justified as a gift on account of Christ through faith when they believe that they are received into grace and that their

---

[12] Martin Luther, "Preface to the Complete Edition of Luther's Latin Writings, 1545," in Helmut Lehmann (ed.), *Luther's Works*, vol. 34 (Philadelphia: Muhlenberg Press, 1960), p. 337.

sins are forgiven on account of Christ, who by his death made satisfaction for our sins. God reckons this faith as righteousness (Romans 3 [:21–28] and 4 [:5]).[13]

In Article IV of the Augsburg Confession justification functions as the overarching transformative perspective that informs both the structure of the confession and the way each article is worded and presented. Let us put this simply.

- Article I: begins with the Triune God, Creator of all things
- Article II: the biggest problem in God's good creation is original sin and its consequences
- Article III: the sending of the Son of God to be the Savior from sin
- Article IV: how the saving work of Christ is appropriated—justification by faith
- Article V: how God provides the ministry of the gospel and the sacraments so that we may obtain such faith
- Articles VI–VIII: how justification results in the new obedience of the justified and their community in the church
- Articles IX–X: how the grace that justifies comes to us in the sacraments.[14]

There is a logical progression here leading up to and proceeding from the central article on justification.

The evangelical faith confessed at Augsburg not only expressed itself in an integrated and coherent theological perspective, but also in enunciating the transformative practices that issue forth from that perspective. As the Confession moves along, the practices increasingly receive more attention. For the gospel to run its course, there needs to be good order in the church and persons who are properly called (Article XIV), there needs to be a sorting out of which traditions help the gospel and which ones need to go (Article XV), Christians need to know about their relationship to the civil government (Article XVI), and so forth. The last part of the Confession (Articles XXII–XXVIII) deals with "Articles in Which an Account Is Given of the Abuses That Have Been Corrected."[15] In light of the gospel and of the rediscovered evangelical perspective, some things need to change or be discontinued in the life of the church.

---

[13] "The Augsburg Confession—Latin Text—Article IV: Justification," in Robert Kolb and Timothy Wengert (eds), *The Book of Concord: The Confessions of the Evangelical Lutheran Church* (Minneapolis: Fortress Press, 2000), pp. 39–41.

[14] Cf. the analysis in Günther Gassmann and Scott Hendrix, *Fortress Introduction to the Lutheran Confessions* (Minneapolis: Fortress, 1999), p. 79.

[15] Kolb and Wengert, op. cit. (note 13), pp. 61–103, here p. 61.

> Nevertheless, the ancient rites are, for the most part, diligently observed among us. For the accusation is false that all ceremonies and ancient ordinances are abolished in our churches. Truth is, there has been a public outcry that certain abuses have become fused to the common rites. Because such abuses could not be approved with a good conscience, they have been corrected to some extent.[16]

Implied here is that this is a work in progress. Transformation is taking place in the evangelical church's practice, in view of the fact that certain practices had crept into the life of the church that obscured the gospel.

At the time of the Reformation, a transformative, evangelical perspective resulted in transformative practices that promoted the gospel in the life of the church. We need to appreciate how renewing and life giving this was for the church of that time and to ponder what it means for us today, for the church is always in need of reformation (*ecclesia semper reformanda est*). We can do this by asking how the gospel might best be communicated to the people of our time in their differing cultural contexts. What is the big God question of our time? Maybe it is not so much, How can I find a gracious God? as, How can I find God at all? What is God's good news for our time, and how might we best express it? What in our cultures helps us say it? What is God saying to us through other perspectives? How do we interpret these perspectives in light of the gospel? As Christians, what can we learn from one another's perspectives and practices that have emerged and developed as we have faithfully and for a long time heard and interpreted the Scriptures in our various cultural contexts?

Anutu in New Guinea[17]

As a Christian, a pastor and a teacher of theology, I feel that my faith and life have been enriched by the perspectives and practices of the Papua New Guinean Christians among whom I lived for many years. One memory that has not faded is of meeting a very old man in a village in Papua New Guinea, not long after I had arrived in the country. They said he was one hundred years old, and he himself told me that as a small boy, perched on his father's shoulders, he had seen "Senior" Flierl (the pioneer missionary from Neuendettelsau). During our

---

[16] Ibid., p. 59.

[17] *Anutu* is a traditional indigenous name for God that is commonly used in the northeastern part of Papua New Guinea. In the Kotte language, God was also called "Mâreng-fung"–origin of the earth.

long conversation, I asked him what the coming of the gospel had meant for his people. He thought for a while and said, "It meant that we could sleep."

I was not expecting that answer, and for this reason I still remember it, and all the more because in subsequent years I discovered how typical and how true that answer was. Typical, because Niuginians have an uncanny way of using a simple picture to convey a profound truth. And how true, because the coming of the gospel made deep, untroubled, refreshing sleep a reality. Such was the fear of enemies, whether physical or spiritual, that they often used a specially carved wooden support or stool that would keep the head propped up, so that one would not sleep too deeply and could have one's ears open for the warning sounds of approaching hostility.

Especially in the early days, the gospel was experienced as a most welcome and transformative message that delivered people from paralyzing fear and bestowed upon them a peace they had never known: peace with God through Jesus Christ, who is our peace (Eph 2:14); peace from the endless cycle of trying to placate demanding spirits; peace with former enemies through the breaking of spears at baptism; and peace with neighboring people with whom one's group had been feuding so long that even languages parted ways. The transformative power of the gospel meant deep peace and deep sleep. The old man's answer was "spot on."

The theology of this transformative gospel is reflected in the hymnody of the Evangelical Lutheran Church in Papua New Guinea. There is a strong recurring emphasis on being rescued from darkness and now walking in the light; of being trapped in consuming guilt and anger, and God coming to bring peace; of being delivered from a dark prison and now rejoicing in God. Here are some examples.

A song by Wahaoc from Wareo in the Finschhafen area:[18]

> He led us, that Messiah,
> from the hand of Satan
> he led us, led us.
>
> Our Lord drew us up,
> us, out of the mire.
> For him let us live, let us live, as his heritage, let us live.

---

[18] Author's own translation from Kotte. No. 253, in the *Lutheran Gae Buk*, revised edition (Madang, PNG: Kristen Pres, 1960).

O friend, let us praise our heavenly Lord,
O yes, friend, let us praise
our heavenly Lord, O yes, let us extol him.

A song by Nawasio Gedisa translated from Jabem into Tok Pisin.[19]

O Jesus came and stayed,
he is with us.
Let us truly give thanks to him,
now and forever.
> *Alleluia, -leluia,*
> *praise the name of God*
> *Alleluia, -leluia, alleluia.*

Many years ago
Flierl arrived at Simbang.
Brought the Good News to us,
joy and peace.

Our ancestors were in darkness
here on the earth.
The light of God has arisen now
and it gathers us.

Let all us Christians
praise the name of Christ.
He is the Child of God.
O, all of you come!

Holy Spirit, you come now,
come into our hearts.
Guide our church
to do your work.

---

[19] Author's own translation from Tok Pisin. No. 331, in *Rejoice and Sing*, Papua New Guinea edition (Adelaide: Lutheran Publishing House, 1978).

A song by Desiang, from Wemo, Finschhafen:[20]

> You owner of peace, ooe,
> Lord, you owner of peace, ooe,
> make peace, ooe,
> Lord, make peace, won't you.
>
> Guilty, guilty, ooe,
> Guilty, a heap of guilt, ooe,
> make peace, ooe,
> Lord, make peace, won't you.
>
> Unravel the knot of anger,
> that animosity against friend,
> its onset, ooe,
> Lord, chase it away!

These examples from the hymnody aptly illustrate my main idea: at the heart of the biblical narrative lies the transformative gospel, and that as people are transformed by this central message they can adapt perspectives and practices from their cultural contexts that become transformative in the light of that gospel. Furthermore, as we listen to one another interpret the message of the Bible in a global communion, we can be deeply enriched by appropriating the gospel illumined perspectives and expressions of faith of our sisters and brothers in their very different contexts.

A couple of snapshots from the land "down under"

Australia has been called "the South land of the Holy Spirit,"[21] but it has also been called "the most godless place under heaven."[22] There is a sense in which that is true, because Australia is a very secular and materialistic

---

[20] No. 431, in op. cit. (note 18).

[21] Muriel Porter, *Land of the Spirit?: The Australian Religious Experience* (Geneva: World Council of Churches, 1990), p. ix.

[22] Ian Breward, *Australia: "The Most Godless Place Under Heaven"?* (Adelaide: Lutheran Publishing House, 1988), title page.

culture and not many people go to church regularly. And yet, God is in this land, and always has been.

Like the Athenians of Acts 17, the Aboriginal people, in their diversity of beliefs, also acknowledged the Creator. Aboriginal Christians, looking back at the time of their ancestors, can relate to the first words in the letter to the Hebrews: "Long ago God spoke to our ancestors in many and various ways by the prophets." Reflecting on this text a group of Aboriginal Christians said this:

> We believe that this text applies equally well to the ancestors of our Aboriginal people as it does to the ancestors of the people of Israel. The Creator Spirit spoke to us in many ways, especially through the land which links us to the Creator Spirit.

As one in our workshop group said:

> Aboriginal culture is spiritual. I am spiritual. Inside of me is spirit and land, both given to me by the Creator Spirit. There is a piece of land in me, and it keeps drawing me back like a magnet to the land from which I came. Because the land, too, is spiritual.

> This land owns me. The only piece of land I can claim a spiritual connection with—a connection between me and the land—is the piece of land under the tree where I was born, the place where my mother buried my afterbirth and umbilical cord. The spiritual link with that piece of land goes back to the ancestors in the Dreaming. This is both a personal and sacred connection—between me and the land, me and my ancestors.[23]

I read those words and the book in which they are written eleven years ago, and that gave me some insight into the way Aboriginal people relate to the land and the pain they must feel in being dispossessed of it, as happened under the *terra nullius* policy that has only recently been overturned.[24]

Reading about it in a book is one thing, but actually hearing an Aboriginal person saying it is another. About two years ago, I went to the Red Centre, as it is called, to teach at a course for Aboriginal pastors,

---

[23] The Rainbow Spirit Elders, *Rainbow Spirit Theology: Towards and Australian Aboriginal Theology* (Blackburn, Victoria: HarperCollins, 1997), p. 4.

[24] This was the policy that regarded the land as vacant on the pretext that Aboriginal peoples were nomadic and therefore did not own the land.

evangelists and church workers. Our "campus" was a clearing out in the bush, and we sat in warm sunshine on the red earth under the deep blue canopy of the sky. It was cold at night, and we slept in swags (a kind of sleeping bag) alongside body-length fires. My companion was the old Pastor Davey Ingkamala. Before retiring at night, we sat by the fire and he told me many stories. He told me how some years previously he had gone through the traditional initiation that he had missed out on as a young person. He said that an important part of initiation was learning the ancestral stories about the Dreaming, and how if you do not have these stories you are in effect landless and not fully recognized as a male in the tribe. Since many of the characters in the stories were originally regarded as divinities, it was interesting to hear how he related both to the stories and the characters in them. For him, involvement in the stories means no compromise of his Christian faith, because in his hearing of them now everything is undergirded by faith in one true and living God, the Creator. And yet, as he said, the stories are important, because without them he cannot belong properly, either to the land or to his own people.

Years earlier, Davey Ingkamala told the story of his conversion and subsequent life as an evangelist and pastor which has been published.[25] What is striking is his strong faith that the One he knows as Creator of all is a God of very great love, who does not give up on sinners.

> I still remember the words that God spoke to me earlier on [this was in a vision of blinding light], "First the heat will burn you." I can see that God's Word is true and strong. He does not speak for no reason, nor without effect. His word has power. Whatever he says, happens. So today I thank and praise God with all my heart that he has called me to do this work, to be a true and honest worker for him. God has shown me, a sinner, his very great love. I keep on thinking about the fact that God really is a God of love. That his love is without limit, and that in the Lord Jesus Christ our Saviour, it embraces the whole earth.[26]

My second Australian "snapshot" is just that. It is a photo of a war memorial in Papua New Guinea that consists simply of a tall block of black stone, with just one word on it: "mateship." The memorial is situated at one end of the

---

[25] "Pastor Davey Ingkamala's Story," transl. from Arrarnta by John Pfitzner, in Paul G. E. Albrecht, *From Mission to Church 1877–2002: Finke River Mission* (Adelaide: Finke River Mission, 2002), pp. 222–5.

[26] Ibid, p. 225.

long and torturous Kokoda Track, along which thousands of young Australian soldiers made their way during one of the battles of World War II.

Mateship is the name given to the strong egalitarian bond between Australians, especially in times of hardship. It was the bond between the harshly treated convicts who came on the first fleet of ships in 1788. It was the bond between settlers trying to come to terms with the extreme isolation and hardship that came with trying to carve out a new existence in the harshness of the Australian bush. It was the special bond between Aussie soldiers and those who walked with them during the world wars and other conflicts. No longer simply a male, "blokey" thing, but a bond between and inclusive of all Australians, mateship is the virtue that comes to the fore when tragedy strikes—as it did so powerfully during and after the apocalyptic bushfires that ravaged Victoria in early 2009.

It is almost self-evident that the notion of mateship has possibilities for Christian theology and life in the Australian context. I cannot unpack that here, but just a couple of starters. One starter would be in connection with the theology of the cross. "No one has greater love than this, to lay down one's life for one's friends" (Jn 15:13). And further on in the same passage: "I do not call you servants any longer […] but I have called you friends" (Jn 15:15). Both of those notions are at the heart of mateship. Mateship, whether in time of war or in fighting terrible fires, means being willing to risk your life, and even lay down your life, for your mates. There is no hierarchy in mateship because we are all mates together. Mateship is like the body of Christ as Paul describes it in 1 Corinthians 12:12–26, in which there are many members, and where foot or eye has no right to lord it over others, but where "the members may have the same care for one another. If one member suffers, all suffer together with it; if one member is honored, all rejoice together with it" (1 Cor 25b–26).

Conclusion

The March 2009 conference at Augsburg challenged a diverse gathering of theologians from around the world to think deeply about diversity, and in particular, how they can "learn from cultural, gender, social, economic, political and interreligious realities different from their own and be transformed by them."[27] The recognition of our Lutheran diversity is salutary,

---

[27] Background paper for the March 2009 Augsburg conference.

and the challenge to learn from diverse realities in our various contexts is timely. At the same time, however, we need to hold on to our unity. "Yes, diversity is wonderful," said some of the African voices in the biblical seminar group at the conference (if I may give the gist of what they said), "but what holds us together? What constitutes our unity?" St Paul's image of diverse members in one body is helpful here:

> For just as the body is one and has many members, and the many members of the body being many are one body, so also Christ. For in the one Spirit we all were baptized into one body—whether Jews or Greeks or slaves or free [. . .]. And you are the body of Christ and members individually (1 Cor 12:12–13, 27, literal translation).

Our unity consists, and exists, paradoxically in our diversity, but only because that diversity is held together in Christ, whose body we are. Our diversity is a wonderful gift, and so is the unity in Christ that holds us together. Revitalization and renewal happen best in the church when the Word truly becomes flesh—when Christ is truly present in the many members, when Christ is authentically heard and interpreted by diverse voices in diverse contexts, as I have tried to show here. Christians can be open to perspectives and practices from their cultural contexts that are good and helpful in their own right, and become transformative in the light of the gospel because they help Christians to appropriate and live out the gospel more deeply in their life situations.

As we have seen with Paul in Athens, with Lutheran confessors in the sixteenth century, and with the gospel at work in our own time, there is in our conversation with other realities both affirmation and appropriation, but sometimes also refutation. This calls for wisdom, for discerning what God wants to give us not only in God's Word, but also in God's world, because, as it says in James, "Every good endowment and every perfect gift is from above, coming down from the Father of lights" (Jas 1:17, RSV). In light of the gospel, our theology and practice and our faith and life can be deeply enriched and made more relevant as we hear one another interpret the Bible in our many and various contexts.

A Critical Look at the Ethiopian "Wax and Gold" Tradition

Girma Mohammed

What is the wax and gold tradition?

The wax and gold tradition is distinctive to Ethiopia, especially as embodied in and promoted by the Ethiopian Orthodox Church.[1] This tradition can be defined as a "poetic form which is built on two semantic layers": the figurative meaning of the words is called wax while the hidden and "actual" significance is known as gold.[2] Messay Kebede elaborates, "The prototype being the superposition within a single verb of the apparent meaning in the hidden significance, ambiguity, or a double entendre pervades the whole style."[3]

As powerfully manifested in the Ethiopian literary tradition, this tradition provides a dualistic framework for understanding reality, with a continuous tension (rather than coherence) between the material and spiritual. In keeping with this framework, Christians ought to side with the spiritual rather than the material realm, which, according to this conception, has a close affinity to that which is evil. Therefore, political and ecclesiastical authorities are ascribed spiritual power. As a result, spiritual and pious

---

[1] The recent census indicates that of the total population, sixty-two percent are Christians (18.4 percent of whom are Protestant); thirty-two percent are Muslim and six percent practice traditional religions. Despite comprising various religious commitments, the Ethiopian Orthodox Church is the single most powerful church in Ethiopian history. Besides having a stake in the political power, many believe the Ethiopian Orthodox Church to be the custodian of Ethiopian civilization as well as the originator of the Ethiopian worldview and philosophy, for example, as materialized in the notion of *Etiopiawinet* (Ethiopianness). There is no religious group (including Islam in Ethiopia) which is not influenced and/or affected by the wax and gold worldview and philosophy. Certainly, many Protestant believers still claim that Ethiopia is a nation of covenant, and the influence of the wax and gold philosophy is clearly evident in their interpretive methods, sermons and ways of life.

[2] Donald N. Levine, *Wax and Gold: Tradition and Innovation in Ethiopian Culture* (Chicago: University of Chicago Press, 1965), p. 5.

[3] Kebede Messay, *Survival and Modernization: Ethiopia's Enigmatic Present: A Philosophical Discourse* (Asmara: The Red Sea Press, 1999), p. 180.

people and authorities are considered untouchable. According to this system, there is no separation between the theological and the political.

Yet, the dualism in the wax and gold tradition seems to have served unintended purposes—the ambiguity surrounding it has at times provided space to criticize people who otherwise were beyond critique. Consider an example: Aleka Gebre-Hana, a famous Ethiopian priest and *bale-qene* (poet), was invited by a friend for dinner. While waiting for food to be served, he was disgusted to see a rat jumping out of the *mesob* (traditional breadbasket) where his friends had put the *enjera* (the Ethiopian equivalent of pancake), which is usually served with diverse sorts of stews and sauces known as *wett*. However, the hosting family did not realize that Alaka G. Hana had seen the unexpected (and understandably unpleasant) guest of the dinner party–*ayt* (rat). As a priest, Alalaka G. Hana, who had a reputation of unleashing scathing criticism even on authorities (using the wax and gold poetic system), had to say a blessing after the dinner. Employing a wax and gold approach, he said:

> Belanew tetanew ke enjeraw ke wetu
> Egziabeher yestelegne ke mesobu aytu

The *hebere-qal* (double-layered word) in this poem is *aytu*. It could be rendered as, I have enjoyed your dinner and I pray that you may not lack food on your table. However, the gold (deeper meaning) of the *hebre-qal* has a completely different rendering, which is very distant from a blessing, as the word *aytu* can also mean "that rat." The deeper meaning, the gold, therefore is: I have eaten your food but do not think that I have not seen that rat jumping out of the *mesob*. Hence, in the disguise of a blessing, Alaka G. Hana criticized his friend for having served him such unhygienic food.

Literatures are controlled by indirections when "suffused with parables and protracted symbolisms." As the result, conversations are "full of evasive remarks."[4] Instead of what is being talked about, people would be looking for hidden meanings and motives behind the words uttered. Aesthetically, Levine has described the wax and gold tradition as a "genius of the Amhara"—an ethnic group, which is responsible for inventing and spreading this particular way of communication. Levine goes even further: the wax and gold tradition is not only a way of communication, it is indeed a way of life.[5]

---

[4] Donald N. Levine, *Flight from Ambiguity: Essays in Social and Cultural Theory* (Illinois: University of Chicago Press, 1985), p. 25.

[5] Ibid., p. 28.

What is the historical background of such a poetic and literary tradition? In Ethiopia, formal education was started by the Ethiopian Orthodox Church and included reading, liturgy, poetry and interpretation. These were closely linked to tradition and dogma and maintained or reproduced rather than creatively engaging the existing theological and/or philosophical conceptions. *Ye-qene bet* (school of poetry) was different in offering students the opportunity to express their individuality, while, at least on the surface, respecting tradition and dogma.

Historically, the Alexandrian church gave birth to the Ethiopian Orthodox Church. The Alexandrian church was known for espousing Greek philosophy, especially Platonism. Therefore, besides elements from traditional religious practices (to which the Ethiopian Orthodox Church is often known to be open), the Platonic concept of dualism can well be identified as one of the sources of the wax and gold tradition. As a result, in this tradition, the material aspect of reality is often used as a window to reach a "higher" reality—the sacred. Moreover, in the Ethiopian Orthodox Church the spiritual and hidden meaning has priority over the literal meaning.

Sociopolitical implications

While Levine and Messay concur that the *semena worq* (wax and gold) phenomenon is a highly distinctive contribution to Ethiopian culture, they disagree on the social and philosophical significance of this tradition. I will not go into the complexity of their disagreements in this article.[6] However, both of them fail to question the adequacy of the dualistic philosophical impetus behind the tradition itself.

The wax and gold tradition has its merits. For instance, it is aware of religion's influence on public affairs and has used religion rather effectively in shaping the the nation's cultural identity. It has kept a profoundly diverse nation together by forging a religiously tinged national meta-narrative. Argu-

---

[6] Levine outlines at least four social purposes of wax and gold phenomenon. First, according to Levine, it provides the medium for an exhaustive supply of humor. Second, wax and gold could serve as a means to insult one's fellow in a socially acceptable manner. Third, it can be one of the techniques of defending the sphere of privacy against excessive intrusion. Fourth, it could serve as a media to criticize authority. Messay, who portrays that the wax and gold tradition as a "poetic style that is deemed to be the crowning achievement of erudition in the traditional society," criticizes Levin's work for failing to acknowledge the place the wax and gold tradition is supposed to occupy. Messay reasons, first, that Levine's argument emphasizes the pivotal place of authority and individualism rather than the poetic nature itself. Second, his list of the functions of the wax and gold tradition hardly fulfills people's way of life, which he thinks is evident in this particular poetic tradition.

ably, Ethiopia's extraordinary resistance to foreign occupation and eventual victory in the battle of Adwa (over Italian forces in the twentieth century) was a living testament to the Ethiopian "grand story." Moreover, except for political and social uprisings triggered by political élites and leaders, Ethiopian ethnic groups are well known for their peaceful coexistence.[7] This tradition has also helped the nation to maintain its distinctive identity and civilization. This includes, but is not limited to, culture, writings, *fidel* (alphabet) and numbering. As Ayele Bekerie argues,[8] the Ethiopic (Ge'ez) writing system is a gateway to the Ethiopian organization of thought patterns. Ayele stresses that "it may also enable us to probe the scope of human liberty that permits the creation of ways and means to improve and enhance 'beingness' and togetherness." Hence, these writings are "rich sources of human intellectual activities, such as history, philosophy, social order, psychology and aesthetics."[9] This tradition has made Ethiopia somewhat unconventional or unique among African nations. Moreover, it is difficult to understand "Ethiopianness" without understanding the wax and gold philosophy.

However, the adverse legacy of the wax and gold paradigm is glaring. Notwithstanding the aesthetic significance of ambiguity and its space for individual creativity, the wax and gold tradition is archaic and unchanging. This apparent paradox has been explored by scholars such as Nimrod Raphaeli and Teodros Kiros. Raphaeli speaks about a philosophical category that is "resistant to change," while Teodros talks about a philosophy which is adaptable. How can these contradictory senses be present in the same wax and gold tradition? According to the wax and gold tradition, Ethiopia has a preordained national meta-narrative. Questioning this is not allowed because it is considered to be sacrosanct and therefore, fixed. At the same time, wax and gold philosophers seem to have been aware that times do change as do cultural norms and perceptions. Yet, any notion of change is often met by suspicion and resistance in this paradigm, precisely because it might create a kind of situation where time-honored traditions become subjects of modern scrutiny.

Ambiguity therefore is used to tame the incoming (foreign) ideas and value systems to legitimize the popular "grand story," rather than scrutinizing it. This is precisely because beliefs, literatures and ideologies are adapted,

---

[7] This however is far from claiming Ethiopian has never experienced ethnic marginalization. However, amid some exhibited ethnic marginalization and exclusion, they seem to avoid a major inter-ethnic clash. This is partially because ethnic groups have a tradition of dealing with inter-ethnic conflicts in a cultural and religious manner that helped to avoid sliding into major conflict against one another.

[8] Ayele Bekerie, *Ethiopic, An African Writing System. Its History and Principles* (Asmara: Red Sea Press, 1997).

[9] Ibid., p. 3.

modified, added to and subtracted from to fit the status quo. Interestingly, the wax and gold paradigm does not leave new ideas unaccounted for, but either domesticates or bans them. Domestication intends to tailor the incoming ideas to fit the already existing conceptions. Therefore, changing the basic wax and gold paradigm is resisted and avoided. Those who might insist on or demand change face excommunication, or even extinction.[10]

The effect of uncritically accepting the wax and gold philosophy on society and politics is not hard to detect. This can be illuminated through Levine's comparison between the Ethiopian wax and gold conception and American culture. The American way of life, Levine remarks, "affords little room for the cultivation of ambiguity" because "[t]he dominant American temper calls for clear and direct communication." Few American philosophers would question Kaplan's contention that "[a]mbiguity is the common cold of the pathology of language."[11]

The Ethiopian wax and gold mentality, in contrast, is "indirect and secretive."[12] Language, as Chaim Rosen observes, is a "primary means of both self-defense and also of offense."[13] Rosen continues,

> One must live a long time in midst of Ethiopians, speaking with them [. . .], in order to begin to appreciate how much calculation is invested in each phrase. That he who desires to do harm may always be polite, that he who wishes to deliver an insult may include it in a finely wrought compliment, is a part of general understanding of human nature.[14]

This also has notable social and political implications. Transparency and trust are vital in a society where people depend on interpersonal and interethnic interaction. This is important not only in terms of economic justice (such as fair distribution of land), but it is also an essential aspect of the exchange of ideas, culture and beliefs. However, the wax and gold mentality does not appear to help this, but rather to contribute to a deep distrust in society. In other words, despite having a glorious national meta-

---

[10] The story of the so-called *Stefanosawiyan* (= Stephenites), who tried to reform the Ethiopian Orthodox Church and ended up being eliminated by both persecution and martyrdom, is a good example.

[11] Levine, op. cit. (note 4), p. 28.

[12] Ibid., p. 25.

[13] Tania Schwarz, *Ethiopian Jewish Immigrants in Israel: The Homeland Postponed* (London: Routledge, 2001), p. 133.

[14] Ibid.

narrative that is traced back to the Solomonic line in ancient Israel, this has led to smaller narratives being pushed to the periphery. The place of power and the notion of mystery play a crucial role in the wax and gold interpretive philosophy.

Contentious meaning

Interpretive philosophies have origins and agendas. The wax and gold hermeneutic is a product of an ideology that was prevalent in Ethiopia for more than a millennium and half. As an ideological tool, it had agendas: legitimizing the divine origin of the authorities; portraying the church (i.e., the Ethiopian Orthodox Church) as an inseparable partner in power sharing with the nation; unifying the nation under one king and one church; restricting power to certain ethnicities (in the name of the Solomonic dynasty); and creating a strictly hierarchical society. Therefore, the wax and gold hermeneutic had (and still has) its own "bible" with its own peculiar meaning.

Interestingly, the notion of covenant[15] is used as a means for adjudicating in the interpretive process. Then the term (covenant) becomes a political and ecclesiastical catchword. The use of the notion of covenant was intended to connect Ethiopia to the covenant of ancient Israel, and as a result, Ethiopian Christianity to ancient Judaism. Adrian Hastings' observation seems to be valid when he characterizes covenantal trajectory as something that

> [. . .] provides at one and the same time the justification for religious identity of Ethiopia as Israel, with all its Judaic practices, for the supreme authority of its kings as heirs of Solomon, and for the sacredness of wooden *tabot* (the Ark of the covenant), central to the Ethiopian liturgy, whose original was in Axum sacramental replicas in every church throughout the country.[16]

Nonetheless, instead of being a social and religious platform for unity and coherence, the covenant became a breeding ground for domestic disunity and international isolation. Besides, Ethiopia, as a nation that effectively

---

[15] Covenant has a special affinity to the Ethiopian society for several reasons. First, the nation is believed to have direct (blood) relationship with Israel of which the narrative of the Queen of Sheba (in the Old Testament) is the basis. Second, the nation is perceived still to be hosting the Ark of the Covenant and Christianity, side by side. Third, a dramatic eschatological blessing is a part of constant prayers even in the Protestant Churches in Ethiopia. This expectation is based on the promise of Psalms 68—the promise that "Ethiopia will stretch her hands unto God."

[16] Adrian Hastings, *The Church in Africa, 1450–1950* (Oxford: Clarendon Press, 1994), p. 21.

resisted foreign occupation, should have led Africa to democratization. Instead, being heavily reliant on a "self-created bible," it isolated the nation from the global movement of democratization and modernization.

Ironically, the wax and gold tradition has also served, albeit unintentionally, as a source of help for ordinary Ethiopians. First, people have remained enchanted with the spiritual realm. As a result, even when things seem to be unbearable, it has provided people with a sense of hope and optimism and helps ordinary people break away from the present ideological mantra, in favor of what is considered to be more spiritual. Moreover, it has created an ethnic and religious tolerance for living in a profoundly pluralistic society. Second, in a context where the worth of the individual amounts to little more than their ethnic identity, it creates a space for individuality in interpreting the Bible and in other areas of human endeavor. Third, the same tradition has been used especially to deconstruct the ideology behind the people who are at the helm of power. In fact, it was the only means people could turn to in order to register their discontent with the political and ecclesiastical authorities, even though this had to occur in veiled ways. The ambiguity provides them with a space to sing about justice and preach about equality in situations where directly demanding justice can be hazardous. Even then, the "hermeneutical space" in a culture formed by the wax and gold hermeneutic is profoundly based on a deep sense of negation, contempt and suspicion towards the material aspects of reality and its powers (both political and ecclesiastical). This has adverse effects on society.

To return to question with which we began, there are two parties using the wax and gold hermeneutical tool for different reasons: one is to demand unconditional national and ecclesiastical unity, the other, to realize freedom. The same means of adjudication—that is the covenant—is used by both parties: one to create an hierarchical society and the other to promote equality. Whose meaning is legitimate? My contention is, none and both. There are some grains of truth in both persuasions, but neither one is convincingly complete. For instance, while the former appeals to unity (both ecclesiastic and national) it leaves no room for individual, religious and ethnic freedom. Patriotism, ideology, dogma and tradition, in the name of the covenant, have trumped the value of individuals and individuality. The latter rightfully demands individuality, equality and freedom. However, the demands are not motivated by love, but marred by a painful past, suspicion and contempt toward those who are considered "other." An hermeneutic based on negation can be an effective tool to deconstruct the "powers." However, it lacks a positive basis, tool and rhythm for reconstruction.

Biblical hermeneutics, I contend, should seriously account for human experiences such as repression, diversity, injustices, inequality, etc. Formulating an hermeneutic, which claims to be unconditioned by human experiences, as a way of repressing others in the name of dogma, unity and even scientific neutrality, is objectionable. However, elevating human experiences as the ultimate horizon in hermeneutics is equally objectionable.

Rather, biblical hermeneutics should take the biblical worldview as the ultimate horizon. This horizon takes a theology of creation—what God intends for our relationship with God, others and the wider world—as the launching pad for hermeneutics. That assumes that there is one loving God of one organic human race, whose love transcends race, gender and social status. Under One Father, we celebrate our differences, but not fragmentation, we cherish unity, but not patronization. Whereas this might sound too idealistic, such a biblical hermeneutics and worldview recognize the Fall and its sweeping consequences, as well as the promise of redemption. Redemption, with its far-reaching spiritual and social consequence, is the unshakable foundation for love and justice. This helps to filter the counter-productive elements in human experiences. Further, it works to enhance forgiveness, rather than bearing grudges and seeking revenge. It promotes equality and freedom, in place of suppression and patronization.

Concluding remarks

There may be too much interest today in listening to differences, divergences and deviations, which can keep us divided by nationality, race, skin color, ethnicity, language, culture, gender, etc. This does not take much effort but, at times, just seems to follow assimilated cultural and religious impulses. Totalitarian unity is no better. It may take nothing more than sheer force, violence and inflexible determination to reach one goal at the expense of everything and everybody.

Biblical interpretation is a science, requiring human imagination and hard work. It is an art—it must sift through delicate lines to keep the body of Christ united, without destroying the beauty in diversity. As it develops, it accounts for changing political, economic and cultural situations. Then, and only then, can we overcome ideologies which reduce the richness of biblical teachings to single, social and political principles and in the process, overcome hatred, contempt and social fragmentation.

Mutual Fecundation:[1] The Creative Interplay of Texts and New Contexts

Duane A. Priebe

God reveals God; we can speak of God only on the basis of revelation. This revelation is embedded in traditions and texts through which God continues to illuminate our world and to address us with transforming power. Scripture, as God's Word, in some sense belongs to the reality of God and to the structure of the world. It encompasses the origin, meaning and destiny of all things. With variations, this is true of the Torah, the Vedas and the Qur'an.[2]

According to Christians, the Word through whom God created all things became incarnate in Jesus Christ (Jn 1:1–14). Through Christ and in Christ God draws all creation into its ultimate destiny. God's Word in Scripture has its center in Jesus Christ through whom everything receives its proper meaning. Conversely, Jesus Christ came within the context of Israel's Scriptures, and it is through the whole of Scripture that Jesus Christ encounters us as who he is. Luther speaks of the Bible as the cradle of Christ.

This is a version of the hermeneutical circle of the whole and the parts. Jesus Christ is the whole in whom the Bible and all its parts come to their truth, while we can understand Christ only in the context of the whole of Scripture. Further, everything exists through and for Jesus Christ and is reconciled to God through his death (Col 1:15–20). What God has done in Christ can be understood only in the context of the entire history of the world and its cultures. Conversely, he is the whole through whom our world, cultures and histories come into their truth.[3]

It is through wrestling with the words of Scripture that Jesus Christ encounters us as the Word of God's love for the world. Hans-Georg Ga-

---

[1] I have borrowed this phrase from Raimon Panikkar, although we may use it differently.

[2] This would have to be said differently for Buddhism, which sets aside the question of God.

[3] This does not mean that Christianity is the whole, or the culmination of history. Christians participate with all human beings in the question of the truth of our world before God. For Christians, that question centers in Jesus Christ, explores what it means to see our world in his light and interprets him in the context of our world.

damer argues that the truth of a work of art or literature is present and accessible only in that work, not anywhere else. A picture, for example, "presents something which, without it, would not present itself in this way."[4] The picture is "essentially tied to the original," which could also present itself in other ways. But if the original "presents itself in this way, this is no longer any incidental event but belongs to its own being. Every such presentation is an ontological event and occupies the same ontological level as what is represented." By being re-presented, the original "experiences, as it were, an increase in being."[5] "Word and image [. . .] allow what they present to be for the first time truly what it is."[6]

This is also true of Scripture. Israel's history is the history of God's engagement with the world as that history is "re-presented" in the Bible. Similarly, we have access to Jesus Christ as the event of God's saving love for the world only in the four "re-presentations" of Jesus Christ in the Gospels in conversation with the rest of the New Testament and with Israel's Scriptures. The Bible belongs essentially to Israel's history as the history of God's revelation and to the event of Jesus Christ. It is the enduring product of that revelatory history through which God continues to address people.

According to the Reformation Scripture principle, the Bible is its own interpreter. It speaks directly to us, although its power to do so is informed by the cultural and religious traditions that link us to the text and enrich its potential to speak to us. Its meaning is not controlled by an external key, whether dogma or the methods of the scholarly academy. This power of a text to transcend historical distance is not peculiar to Scripture.[7] Gadamer suggests that classical literature "preserves itself precisely because it is significant in itself and interprets itself," transcending historical distance. It is classical because the duration of its "power to speak directly is fundamentally unlimited."[8]

Jonathan Z. Smith argues that a closed canon is a limited set of words which, through the creative process of interpretation, extend their domain

[4] Hans-Georg Gadamer, *Truth and Method*, transl. and revised by Joel Weinsheimer and Donald G. Marshall (New York: Crossroad, 1989; London & New York: Continuum, 2004), p. 46 [53]. Where they differ, page numbers in the 1989 edition will be in square brackets.

[5] Ibid., p. 135 [140].

[6] Ibid., p. 137 [143].

[7] According to Gadamer, what is classical "does not first require the overcoming of historical distance, for in its own constant mediation it overcomes this distance by itself. ... [W]e belong to that world" of the work, and the work also "belongs to our world." Ibid., p. 290.

[8] Ibid., p. 290.

"over everything that is known or everything that exists without altering the canon."[9] The truth of Scripture lies in its power to take up the whole complex of human life, culture and history into a creative conversation with God. In that conversation, our understanding both of what God has done in Jesus Christ and of our world are transformed.

Gadamer describes this ongoing process of understanding as a "merging of horizons"[10] in which "the meaning of a text goes beyond its author," and its discovery "is never finished."[11]

The Bible offers many examples of the interpretive interplay between an event or statement and new contexts, generating new meaning. We will look at two examples from the New Testament related to Jesus' death and one from Israel's Scriptures related to the interplay between Canaanite and Israel's religious traditions.

Two New Testament examples

Mark 14:1–11: The woman who anoints Jesus. The story of the woman's action is transformed and redeemed when Jesus sets it in the context of his death, and it interprets his death.

Mark frequently uses a literary technique of sandwiching one or more narratives within another, making them mutually interpretive. This story entails two such sandwiches. First, the woman's action anticipates the story of the women who cannot perform the customary anointing after Jesus' death (Mk 16:1), framing the narrative of his death.

Second, the woman's story is framed by the plot to arrest and kill Jesus. The chief priests and scribes plot to do so, but not during the feast (Mk 14:1–2). Then Judas makes it possible (Mk 14:10–11). The narrative sequence suggests that Jesus' defense of the woman leads to his betrayal and death.[12]

---

[9] Jonathan Z. Smith, "Sacred Persistence: Toward a Redescription of Canon," in Jonathan Z. Smith, *Imagining Religion: From Babylon to Jonestown* (Chicago and London: University of Chicago Press, 1982), p. 48.

[10] Gadamer, op. cit. (note 4), pp. 299–306 [302–7].

[11] Ibid., pp. 296, 298.

[12] This is a different question from Judas's actual motivation. As one moves from Mark 14:1–11 to Matthew 26:1–16 to John 12:1–8, the initially indirect association of Judas with those who object becomes more explicit, while the reason for objecting moves from concern for the poor to personal greed, and the connection with the betrayal moves into the background.

The story says nothing about the woman or what she might have intended. She might have been wealthy or poor. She might have been carried away by the moment, later to regret it. We do not know.

By interpreting her action in light of the needs of the poor, some condemned it as a foolish waste at best or as impious. Passover was a time to give particular attention to the needs of the poor; Jesus himself had told the rich man to sell all he had and give it to the poor. The anonymous "some" includes the reader and invites us to consider whether we would react differently—if we did not know the end of the story.

Through setting it in the context of his death and burial, Jesus also creates meaning for what the woman did. In so doing, he transforms and redeems it. He makes it a beautiful thing: she prepares his body for burial. In addition, he makes it an integral part of the gospel preached throughout the world. Her story now belongs to Jesus' identity and to the meaning of his death for the world. The narrative structure in which the story of Jesus' death is framed by the issue of anointing his body for burial indicates the importance of this story for interpreting his death.

The narrative sequence suggests that Judas betrayed Jesus in response to what the woman did and to Jesus' defense of her. This made possible what previously seemed impossible (vv. 1–2), that is, Jesus' secret arrest. Mark's narrative even allows a charitable interpretation of Judas's motivation: that he was deeply troubled by what the woman did and Jesus' defense of her, because he was committed to the cause of the poor, which Jesus himself had supported.[13]

The interplay between the woman's action and Jesus' betrayal, death and burial offers one interpretation of Jesus' death: Jesus died because he defended the woman and sinners[14] against their accusers—and, perhaps, in order to defend them. On the other hand, by being set in the context of his death, her action is transformed and redeemed. The story of the woman and the story of Jesus' death on the cross mutually interpret each other. Neither has the same meaning apart from the other.

John 11:48–53: Caiaphas's prophecy. Caiaphas's hostile statement is transformed into prophecy in light of Jesus' death, and it interprets Jesus' death.

In John 11:25–26, Jesus claims that he is the resurrection and life. Death has no power over those who believe in him, as evinced by the raising of Lazarus.

---

[13] See Mark 10:17–22. According to the Sermon on the Mount, a person cannot serve two masters (Mt 6:24).

[14] This parallels the series of conflict stories in Mark 2:1–3:6, in which Jesus' claims to authority to forgive sins and to be lord over the Sabbath leads to a consultation about how to destroy Jesus.

While earlier there was opposition to Jesus, at this point Jesus begins to be seen as dangerous (Jn 11:45–53). The threat of death, whether physical or otherwise, is one basic way rulers, individuals, and groups try to control others. If Jesus is the source of life beyond the power of death, the threat of death has lost its power.

The chief priests and Pharisees worry that if everyone believes in Jesus, the Romans will assert their control by destroying the temple and the nation. Caiaphas says, "[. . .] it is better for you to have one man die for the people than to have the whole nation destroyed" (Jn 11:50). Jesus' death would undermine his claim to be the source of life beyond the power of death. So they plot how to kill him (Jn 11:53).

What Caiaphas intended is clear: get rid of Jesus before the Romans decide to get rid of us. It was a hostile statement. He did not intend to prophesy. But in light of Jesus' death as the event of God's saving love, John interprets it as a prophecy that "[. . .] Jesus was about to die for the nation, and not for the nation only, but to gather into one the dispersed children of God" (Jn 11:51–52). This new meaning requires no change to Caiaphas's words.

Set in the context of Jesus' death, this story and Caiaphas's hostile words are transformed into a prophecy of salvation through Jesus' death. Caiaphas's prophecy interprets Jesus' death, and the narrative links it to his claim to be the resurrection and the life. Jesus' death transforms and redeems Caiaphas's words. The two belong together. Through this mutual interpretation, each receives a meaning it would not have apart from the other.

Set in the context of Jesus Christ's death, both the woman's action in anointing Jesus and Caiaphas's statement gain new meaning in a way that transforms and redeems them. In turn, each in its own way contributes to the meaning of Jesus' death. Thus, each comes into its own truth.

Is this not what it means for sins to be forgiven and for sinners to be justified? The biologist René Dubos once suggested forgiveness of sins is a power that transforms sin and error into new creative possibilities for the future—it is not merely a matter of setting them aside or forgetting them. In this sense, forgiveness of sins is the dynamic of the evolutionary process.

These stories illuminate the relation of Israel's Scriptures to Jesus Christ. Mediated through the literary and interpretive traditions of first-century Judaism, Israel's Scriptures provide the language within which God's action in the incarnation, death and resurrection of Jesus Christ can be understood. At the same time, what happens in Jesus Christ transforms how Israel's Scriptures are read and understood.

If Jesus Christ is the event of God's love for the world, including all nations with their varied cultures, these stories also provide a paradigm for what happens when the message of the gospel is spoken into the varied matrix of people's lives, languages and cultures.[15]

One Old Testament example

Hosea 1–3: While Hosea rejects worship of Ba'al, he also incorporates certain traditions about Ba'al into his vision of the identity and activity of Israel's God.

Hosea announced God's judgment on the northern kingdom of Israel for their idolatrous worship of the Canaanite deity Ba'al. Ba'al was involved in two conflicts over who would rule. First, Ba'al's victory over Yamm (Sea)[16] produced the order necessary for agriculture. Second, the conflict between Ba'al and Anat (Ba'al's sister and wife) and Mot (Death) circled around fertility, the issue of life versus death. All were first generation descendants of El, the Creator of the creatures.

Many Canaanites, who always worshipped Ba'al, were politically assimilated into Israel. For many Israelites, the fertility rituals associated with the worship of Ba'al seemed to meet practical needs. The rain falling to earth to nourish plants was associated with sexual relations between Ba'al and Anat, and young women ensured their fertility by a brief period of prostitution at temples of Ba'al.

While Hosea opposes the worship of Ba'al, he also integrates elements of the Canaanite traditions into the way he speaks of Israel's God. The sexual relationship between Ba'al and Anat is transformed into the non-sexual relationship between YHWH and Israel as God's unfaithful wife. In her idolatry, she pursues other lovers and ascribes to them what YHWH alone gives (Hos 2:5, 8). YHWH becomes both the source of fertility and agricultural prosperity and the source of drought (Hos 2:8, 9, 12). Ultimate salvation, in which God says, "You are my people," and they answer, "You are my God," is portrayed as the relationship between a husband and wife. In that relationship, the gifts God's people receive

---

[15] Lamin Sanneh demonstrates how this process in translation contributes to the pluralism and cultural diversity of Christianity. See especially Lamin Sanneh, *Translating the Message: The Missionary Impact of Culture* (Maryknoll, NY: Orbis, 1989); Lamin Sanneh, *Whose Religion Is Christianity? The Gospel Beyond the West* (Grand Rapids, MI: Wm. B. Eerdmans, 2003). Translating the Bible into new languages brings elements of that culture into the biblical message, and the gospel both assimilates and transforms that culture.

[16] The Ugaritic (the language of the Canaanite texts found at Ugarit north of Palestine) word *yam* was used as the name of the Canaanite god of river and sea.

from God are imaged in terms of the gifts of fertility that were ascribed to Ba'al (Hos 3:16–23; 14:4–8).

In Israel's traditions, Israel's God is frequently identified with El, the Creator of the creatures. God's rule is also coupled with imagery of victory over the sea and ordering the world (Ps 93). This theme portrays God's victory over destructive powers, like enemy nations (Isa 17:12–14), sin (Ps 32:1–7) and personal distress (Ps 69), as well as God's activity establishing world order (Ps 74:12–17). Jesus gives life to the dead and stills the wind and sea (Mk 4:35–41), and in the new creation the Sea (Yamm) is no more (Rev 21:1). In Israel's Scriptures, the battle with Mot plays no role. By the time of Christ, however, it plays some role in Israel's traditions, and in the New Testament, Death (Mot) is the last enemy to be defeated (1 Cor 15:24–28).

This is one among many examples of how elements of other religious traditions were assimilated and transformed by Israel. That which was received was shaped in new ways by the new context. The One who is the Creator and orders the agricultural world, giving fertility and prosperity, is the God who called Abraham and led Israel out of Egypt. But what is assimilated also transforms Israel's understanding of God and God's activity.

The persuasive power of Israel's religious traditions was deeply linked with their capacity to assimilate ideas and themes from their religiously plural environment, transforming them and being transformed, without losing their own identity. This identity centered in the Creator of all things, who called Abraham, led Israel out of Egypt and promised to bless the nations through them. This potential to move toward a more universal horizon, assimilating, transforming and being transformed in engagement with other religious traditions and cultures without losing its identity, is fundamental to the truth of the message of Christ.

Two modern cross-cultural examples

Two examples illustrate possibilities for new insight that may arise as texts are heard and contemplated in new contexts, whether or not they illuminate the passages' original meaning.

Genesis 1 and Hindu tradition: The creation story in Genesis 1:1–2:3 continues to fascinate people from a wide variety of backgrounds. The first word, *bereshith*, can be translated in three different ways: "in the beginning God created," suggesting creation out of nothing; "when God began to create," suggesting it is a matter of ordering a primordial "chaos"; or "by means of the beginning God created," which Judaism took to mean "by means of wisdom," based on Proverbs 8:22. Judaism read it in all three ways.

Current scholarship leans toward the second translation in view of Near Eastern mythology, linking the establishment and ordering of the world with conflict and victory over the Sea (e.g., Ps 89:5–12). Genesis 1 clearly reflects the influence of the Babylonian creation myth, *Enuma elish*, especially in dividing the waters on the second day and ordering the sun, moon and stars on the fourth. The word *tehom*, deep, may also suggest the name of the Babylonian goddess Tiamat. Marduk, a descendant of Apsu and Tiamat, who were the primordial divine waters, defeated Tiamat, cut her watery body in half and in the space between ordered the sun, moon and stars, symbolizing the gods. Such an interpretation would also resonate with the Canaanite stories of the battle between Ba'al and Yamm.

But there are some problems with this. The Canaanite "Creator of the creatures" with whom Israel's God is identified is El, not Ba'al. Second, as gods who came to be in time, neither Marduk nor Ba'al was the ultimate divine reality. Third, in the Canaanite or Babylonian context, the "chaos" of Genesis 1:2 would be seen as alternate deities, not as Plato's disorganized matter. That would be hard to imagine at a time when the author of Isaiah 40–56 was speaking of the incomprehensible transcendence and power of God, to whom nothing can be compared.

In fact, the Babylonian *Enuma elish* does not construe the primordial state as chaos. Initially the watery bodies of the primordial deities, Apsu and Tiamat (fresh water and salt water), are mingled and comingled as a single, undifferentiated whole. This is a state of perfect symmetry and peaceful harmony, not chaos. When they give birth to the gods, this symmetry is broken. The children are troublesome and noisy, and their ways and deeds are disgusting and offensive to their parents. The conflict is between the harmony of the ideal past and the disharmony and broken symmetry of the present and threatening future. Although it has to do with the realm of the gods, this movement is roughly analogous to the evolutionary cosmology of contemporary science. The physicist Heinz Pagels spoke of the initial state of the universe as one of "perfect symmetry."[17] The universe and life within it then developed through an unpredictable process of symmetry breaking.

The basic structure of Genesis 1:1–2:3, moving from 1:1–2 to God creating everything by speaking, has no real parallel in ancient Near Eastern texts.

---

[17] Heinz Pagels, *Perfect Symmetry: The Search for the Beginning of Time* (New York: Bantam Books, 1991).

The closest analogy is found in Hindu texts. Barbara A. Holdrege agues that the cosmos is formed in "a two-stage process in which an unmanifest state of undifferentiated unity gives rise to a manifest state through a series of discrete speech-acts."[18] Initially, the word that transcends all speech and belongs to the essence of the "Absolute" is imaged as an infinite dark sea with the cosmic egg, the source of life and of all creation, floating on its surface. This word, Om, contains all knowledge and speech and is the unmanifested Veda. After some time, this unexpressed word becomes differentiated into sounds and syllables in speech, through which the creation is produced. These words constitute the Vedas.

This pattern roughly corresponds to the broad pattern of Genesis 1:1–2:3. This suggests reading Genesis 1:1–2:3 as a narrative in which creation takes place: through the one word that belongs to the essence of God becoming differentiated into words through divine speech. In later Judaism, this word becomes identified with the Torah; in the New Testament, with Jesus Christ. The creation story would then read as a movement from the initial symmetry of Genesis 1:2, to the increasing diversity of creation through the power of God's speech to break symmetry and to create new realities, which God sees as good.

Reading Mark 6:30–44 in Papua New Guinea: Melanesian mythical traditions speak of the death and burial of a hero as the origin of the crops central to people's lives. This story can take many forms. One version is the story of two brothers. Every night, after the younger brother falls asleep, the older goes out into the forest and returns in the morning. Curious, one night the younger brother follows him. He sees his older brother in a clearing, rooting in the ground like a pig. Realizing that he has been seen, the older brother orders the younger to murder him brutally. He is then to bury the older brother in the field, build a fence around the place and return later. When the younger brother returns, he finds the enclosure filled with pigs.

In different versions of the story, the benefit may be sweet potatoes or other necessities instead of pigs. The brutal death is always voluntary, and it produces what is necessary for the community's life.

---

[18] Barbara A. Holdrege, *Veda and Torah: Transcending the Textuality of Scripture* (Albany NY: SUNY, 1996), p. 49. See the discussion of "Veda and Creation," pp. 29–129. Also Barbara Holdrege, "Veda and Torah: The Word Embodied in Scripture," in Hananya Goodman (ed.), *Between Jerusalem and Benares: Comparative Studies in Judaism and Hinduism* (Albany, NY: SUNY, 1994), pp. 119–36. She builds in part F.B.J. Kuiper's reconstruction of the Vedic cosmogonic myth, in F.B.J. Kuiper, "Cosmogony and Conception: A Query," in *History of Religions* 10 (1970), pp. 91–138.

In this context, I was invited to preach on the story of the feeding of the 5,000 in Mark 6:30–44. Three times the narrative says that they are in the desert. Yet, Jesus commands them to sit in the green grass and feeds them (Mk 6:39). While originally the text reflects the promise that in the time of salvation the desert shall become fruitful (Isa 35), in the New Guinean context it naturally evokes a new meaning. Jesus Christ, who voluntarily died a brutal death on the cross, becomes the source of life and of everything necessary for life. So, wherever this crucified Jesus is, even in the desert, even retroactively, there is green grass and more than enough food for all.

These two examples illustrate how reading biblical texts in the context of other cultures and religious traditions can create new meaning for those passages. The biblical texts, in turn, transform those traditions by drawing them into the story of the Creator of the universe, who sends God's Son into the world to suffer and die to give life to a world that is turned toward death in so many ways.

Two non-Christian examples

If the Bible is the Word of the One who created the universe, it belongs to the world, not only to Christians. Often non-Christians read the Bible and contemplate the story of Jesus Christ as the event of God's salvation in powerful ways. Sometimes they understand the point more clearly than Christians.

Keshub Chunder Sen: Keshub Chunder Sen (1838–1884) was a powerful, deeply religious, influential figure in nineteenth-century India. Fascinated by Jesus Christ, Sen made him central to his devotional life, and devoted his energy to proclaiming Christ. Sen assimilated Jesus into the framework of his Hindu bhakti tradition, and his interest in Christ modified his Hinduism. As a result, he made important contributions to the language and categories for an indigenous Indian Christian theology.

In a powerful lecture, "That Marvelous Mystery—The Trinity" (1882),[19] Sen tells the story of creation in a way that merges biblical and Hindu narratives. Drawing on the imagery of Rig Veda X, 129, he identifies "Jehovah"

---

[19] David C. Scott (ed.), *Keshub Chunder Sen: A Selection*, Library of Indian Christian Theology, Companion Series No. 1 (Bangalore: Christian Literature Society, 1979), pp. 219–47.

with the "Supreme Brahma of the Veda and the Vedanta," whose might is "yet unmanifested," sleeping in eternal silence and impenetrable darkness. No one can comprehend and thought cannot approach this mysterious, infinite One.[20]

Then, in the silence and darkness, a voice cries out and creation springs forth. The universe, with all its beauty and variety, was created through that one almighty Word. "What was creation but the wisdom of God going out of its secret chambers and taking visible shape, His potential energy asserting itself in unending activities?"[21] Creation is a "continued process [. . .] a continued evolution of creative force [. . .]. The silent Divinity began to speak, and His speech, His word, a continued breathing of force is creation."[22]

The ultimate purpose of creation is universal redemption through Jesus Christ, in whom the primary creative force of God's Word, manifested in "endless varieties" in the evolutionary process, at last takes form. "God sent His only begotten Son in order to make all His children, one and all, sons and heirs of God." In Jesus Christ, "the last manifestation of Divinity is Divine humanity." In the Spirit's power, all people are made sons and daughters of God, "partakers of Divine life."[23]

An abiding contribution is Sen's association of the Trinity with the Hindu philosophical idea that Brahman, the Absolute, is Satchidānanda: *Sat*, existence; *Cit*, consciousness or Word; and *Ānanda*, bliss. This engenders Sen's Trinitarian description of the history of creation and redemption.

> The apex is the very God Jehovah, the Supreme Brahma of the Vedas. Alone, in His own eternal glory, He dwells. From Him comes down the Son in a direct line, an emanation from Divinity. Thus, God descends and touches one end of the base of humanity. Then, running all along the base, God permeates the world, and then by the power of the Holy Spirit drags up regenerated humanity to Himself. Divinity coming down to humanity is the Son; Divinity carrying up humanity to heaven is the Holy Spirit. This is the whole philosophy of redemption.[24]

---

[20] Ibid., p. 224.

[21] Ibid., p. 225.

[22] Ibid., pp. 225–6.

[23] Ibid., pp. 226–7.

[24] Ibid., p. 226.

The Man Who Never Died:[25] Dr Gopal Singh (1917–1990) was a Sikh scholar, poet and critic. He was the first to translate the *Sri Guru Granth Sahib*, the Sikh Scripture, into English. His long poem, *The Man Who Never Died,* is a meditation on the life of Jesus and his teaching.

Singh sets the theme on the opening page:

> This is the story of the Man
> Who never died:
> and who proclaimed
> that he who's born
> must be re-born;
> and he who's dead
> must rise from the state of death.
> For it is not in the nature of man to die,
> but to live from no-time to no-time.[26]

Jesus' birth among the animals in the stable established "the identity of man with all life and with no-life." His birth went unnoticed in a land where God's people lived, worshipped, and suffered. No one noticed or knew who he was, except "a single wonderstruck star" and "three stray Wisemen of the East [. . .]. Even though the whole universe reverberated/with the song of the Angels of Light."[27]

The poem is filled with wonderful paradoxes. God permeates everything and God's grace surrounds us, even though we do not know it. In contrast to human beings, "who go to the man who has, /God goes to the man who hasn't" and is always "at thy beck and call, the more/when you need Him most and own Him least."[28] People demand Jesus' death, because otherwise "'He'll destroy all the ancient values of man. /And the kings shall lose their glory [. . .] /The poor shall lose their misery and the harlots their ill repute."[29] "Destiny destroys us in two ways: /By refusing our wants/or by fulfilling them! /But, he who wills as God Wills/escapes both!"[30]

---

[25] Gopal Singh, *The Man Who Never Died* (Honesdale, PA: The Himalayan International Institute of Yoga Science and Philosophy of the USA, 1990).

[26] Ibid., p. 1.

[27] Ibid., p. 10.

[28] Ibid., p. 36.

[29] Ibid., p. 61.

[30] Ibid., p. 67.

Some people seek Jesus' death to avoid his claim. Others see his death as tragic, failing to see that God comes only through pain and that "[s]alvation is possible only in a tragic world."[31] When people thought he was finished, he rose from the dead and said to believers,

> Nothing dies in the realm of God [...]
> Only the past dies or the present,
> but the future lives forever.
> And, I'm the future of man.
> To me, being and non-being were always one.
> I always was and never was![32]

These authors speak powerfully about God's saving action in Jesus Christ from another context, which can seem strange and at times make us uncomfortable. We Christians are often tempted to defend Christ from different religious and cultural interpretations that we see as problematic. But Christ does not need our defense.

In fact, non-Christians often see the meaning of Jesus Christ more clearly than Christians. The last time I was in Bangalore, India, I was privileged to attend the premiere of a traditional Indian dance drama, "Prince of Peace," that told the story of Jesus. In a time of conflict between religious communities, it portrayed Jesus as one who, through his life, death and resurrection, had the power to reconcile people across all boundaries and divisions: men and women, righteous and sinners, Jews and Gentiles, and so on throughout the world. It was written by a Muslim, funded by a Hindu and produced by another Hindu.

Conclusion

For religious traditions that include a canon of scripture, those who live in an open-ended, shared conversation with those texts are living in an open-ended, shared conversation with the voice at the foundation of the universe.[33] The power of Scripture to speak in new, life-giving ways in new contexts speaks to its truth.

---

[31] Ibid., p. 65.

[32] Ibid., p. 69.

[33] See Wilfred Cantwell Smith, *What is Scripture? A Comparative Approach* (Minneapolis: Fortress Press, 1994), p. 242.

As people read the Bible and contemplate the Christian message in various cultural, linguistic, and religious contexts, the text speaks God's Word into those contexts in different ways. Gadamer speaks of a merging of horizons.[34] A horizon is what a person sees from a particular standpoint. We all live in historical and cultural horizons that both shape and limit what we can see and understand. In one important sense, the Bible is less culturally controlled than any of our theological frameworks. The texts were originally written within the horizons of cultural, linguistic and religious contexts different from any we might bring to it.

As we wrestle with biblical texts, letting them question our assumptions and presuppositions and hearing their claim to truth, the strange horizon of the world of the text and the horizon of our world engage each other in a transformative way that creates a new, merged horizon. Through conversation between these interpretations, everyone comes to a deeper and richer understanding of what God has done in Jesus Christ. This process will not be completed until we see all creation summed up into Jesus Christ, from whom and for whom all things exist, and in whom all things hold together (Col 1:15–20).

---

[34] Gadamer, *op. cit.* (note 4), pp. 305–6.

Rethinking Lutheran Engagement with Religious Plurality

J. Paul Rajashekar

"Theology is an unending wisdom, because it can never be learned completely."[1] This statement of Luther's expresses a remarkable understanding of theology as experience and as wisdom that is never complete. Luther notes that the human being hears and learns, but also loses such understanding, time and again, from the ears and from the heart, thus distorting what has been learned, which is learned all over again within the context of one's struggles (*Anfechtung*). Luther's persistent doubts and struggles to understand the meaning of God's promises made him a theologian. Hence, according to Luther, theology has no finality other than how it is lived out and experienced in the context of God's promises for the world.

Luther's extensive writings are a testimony to his ongoing struggles to relate faith to ever-new situations and contexts. Instead of honing in on one text or refining a single tome or treatise, Luther wrote new treatises or tracts as the context demanded, willing to rethink his views in relation to theological issues and practices. He frequently distinguished his theological claims from those of his medieval scholastic forebearers, willing to reshape elements of the theology he had inherited and reformulate them into his context. Luther, of course, lived in a religiously homogenized context, where everyone was a Christian, nominally at least, save the few marginalized Jews. The tradition Luther gave birth to inevitably bears the marks of its context and time.

One does not need to belabor the point that the Lutheran theological tradition emerged in the culturally and religiously circumscribed context of medieval Europe. Acknowledging this implies that Luther and his medieval contemporaries had only very limited exposure to the world of religious plurality. Their understanding was limited to biblical Judaism (understood primarily as a religion of the law) and to the writings of "pagan" religious philosophers. The rise of Islam, especially the military threat from the

---

[1] *WA* 40, III: 63–17f., cited in Oswald Bayer, *Martin Luther's Theology. A Contemporary Interpretation*, transl. by Thomas H. Trapp (Grand Rapids: William B. Eerdmans, 2008), p. 31.

Ottoman Empire, presented a new religio-political reality and crisis during the period of the Reformation. Unlike their Catholic contemporaries, the Protestant Reformers had little interest in or acquaintance with the religions of Asia and the newly discovered world, nor did they possess the necessary literary resources that would help them to understand other religions or engage theologically with issues of religious plurality. When faced with new situations, they looked to the Scriptures and the teachings of the apostles and early church fathers for clues as to how to respond to the problem of non-Christian religions. Furthermore, Luther and the medieval Protestant Reformers lacked direct contact with people of other faiths or the lived experience of religious pluralism in their society. Their responses to religious plurality therefore were primarily in the form of polemics, if not, proselytism.

Justification and "godlessness"

As heirs of the Lutheran tradition, we live at a different time and in a different religious context and our awareness of religious plurality differs significantly from that of earlier periods in Christian history. During the course of the last century, the Christian awareness and exposure to people of other faiths have undergone a sea change. After World War II, the widely held belief in the West that the forces of secularism and secularization will eventually undermine the influence of religion in society has proved to be wide of the mark. Despite a decline in church membership in the West, our world has experienced a tremendous religious resurgence in the latter half of the twentieth century. Nonetheless, it has taken a long while for Lutherans to recognize this reality. The culturally and religiously circumscribed theological assumptions of European Lutherans have held sway over Lutheran thinking and thus inhibited Lutheran engagement with religious diversity and plurality.

At the 1963 Lutheran World Federation (LWF) Assembly in Helsinki, the discussion on a draft document on "justification" began with an analysis of the human situation. The draft document characterized the human situation by using the typically Barthian phrase "godlessness." Given the theological climate of the post-World War II era, the pervasive awareness of secularism and secularization and the emergence of Marxism as a powerful ideology in Eastern Europe, the phrase "godlessness" made much sense to Europeans. Interestingly, a lone voice from India, that of

Dr. P. David, objected to that phrase, stating that he came from a context where "godlessness" was not so self-evident. On the contrary, he thought that "gods" were everywhere![2]

The drafters of the document, however, took no notice of this comment. In the final version of the document, approved by the then Commission on Theology following the Assembly, the phrase "godlessness" was retained as a universal description of the human situation.[3]

I cite this to illustrate that the reality of religious plurality, a phenomenon self-evident in much of the non-Western world, was not obvious to those Lutherans living in Germany and Scandinavia, nor to those in North America, who had not yet experienced the impact of the 1965 Asian Immigration Act that brought Asian immigrants and their religious faiths to the shores of North America. The experiences and theological assumptions of Western Lutherans took precedence over the views of Lutherans hailing from non-Western cultures. As a result, Lutheran reflections on the reality of religious pluralism did not progress much and had to wait until the 1980s.

Lutheran encounters with religious pluralism

With the establishment in 1984 of an office for "The Church and People of Other Faiths" in the LWF, the Lutheran awareness of the challenge of religious plurality was still processed through European religious histories and experiences. The discussions in the Commission on Studies focused on the issue of articulating a *theologia religionum*. What this phrase meant was subject to debate within the Commission. While for some it referred to a rigorous Christian apologetics that accorded Christianity a preeminent place among the world's religions, for others it was an attempt to provide a rationale for continued missionary engagement. There were also those who saw it as an attempt to develop a theology for interreligious dialogue. In the 1980s, certain quarters regarded the word "dialogue" with deep suspicion, since it suggested a notion of "parity" among religions, and the work of this office was constantly under pressure to articulate a Christian apologetics in the context of Christian mission.

---

[2] See the Lutheran World Federation, *Proceedings of the Fourth Assembly of The Lutheran World Federation, Helsinki, July 30–August 11, 1963* (Berlin: Lutherisches Verlagshaus, 1965), pp. 248–54.

[3] Ibid., pp. 352–7; see Appendix III for the final version approved by the Commission on Theology, pp. 476–82.

Today, all that has changed. What a difference a couple of decades can make in the lives of the church and the world! From the mid-1980s onwards, there has been a rigorous academic discussion on issues of religious plurality.[4] The subsequent studies undertaken by the LWF Office for the Church and People of Other Faiths focused on dealing with the challenges of religious pluralism.[5] In the intervening years, contexts that were once predominantly mono-religious had gradually become multireligious. Religions, once primarily confined to their geographical origins, have become "deterritorialized," and are now literally "global" or "world" religions. To be sure, the profoundness of religious diversity and its impact on society vary from context to context but the polemics and proselytism of the past eras have been challenged and subject to rigorous scrutiny in all contexts. The experience of people of other faiths has taught us that other people are not postulates of our doctrines, that is, we cannot define others according to our theological logic. Rather, they are neighbors whose faith and witness challenge us to articulate what we believe and profess, not over against them but in relation to them.

These developments have led to a greater awareness of the significance of interreligious dialogue and to an acknowledgement of the values, beliefs and contributions of other religious traditions. Although certain "theologies of hostility" toward other faiths may still exist in some contexts and cultures, Christians today generally accept that the reality of religious diversity is here to stay and is unlikely to disappear; if anything, it will become more

---

[4] The early discussions in the Western academy focused on the typologies of "exclusivism," "inclusivism" and "pluralism" as a way of describing and analyzing theological responses to religious pluralism. Exclusivism has been associated with the position that salvation can be found only through the person and work of Jesus Christ and that saving grace is not mediated through other religions. Inclusivism refers to the position that salvation extends beyond the boundaries of the church and that other religions play some positive role in God's plan for humanity. Pluralism refers to the position that all religions are culturally conditioned, yet valid or authentic responses to the divine or ultimate Reality. For a representative sample of more recent discussions or constructive proposals based on Trinitarian, liberationist, dialogical, comparative and postcolonial perspectives consult, Gavin D'Costa, *The Meaning of Religions and the Trinity* (Maryknoll: Orbis, 2000); Francis X. Clooney, *Theology After Vedanta: An Experiment in Comparative Theology* (Albany: State University of New York Press, 1993); M. Dhavamony, *Christian Theology of Religions: A Systematic Reflection on the Christian Understanding of World Religions* (Bern: Peter Lang, 1998); John Hick, *A Christian Theology of Religions: The Rainbow of Faiths* (Louisville: Westminster John Knox, 1995); S. Mark Heim, *The Depth of the Riches: A Trinitarian Theology of Religious Ends* (Grand Rapids: Eerdmans, 2001); Paul F. Knitter, *Introducing Theologies of Religions* (Maryknoll: Orbis, 2002); Jacques Dupuis, S. J., *Toward a Christian Theology of Religious Pluralism* (Maryknoll: Orbis, 2006). For an evangelical or Pentecostal perspective, see Harold Netland, *Encountering Religious Pluralism: The Challenge of Christian Faith and Mission* (Downers Grove: Intervarsity, 2001); Amos Young, *The Spirit Poured out on all Flesh: Pentecostalism and the Possibility of Global Theology* (Grand Rapids: Baker Academic, 2005).

[5] See Hance A. O. Mwakabana (ed.), *Theological Perspectives on Other Faiths: Toward a Christian Theology of Religions*, LWF Documentation No. 41 (Geneva: The Lutheran World Federation, 1997).

pronounced. What to make of this reality theologically or how to engage with it are fundamental questions.

The challenge before us today goes beyond the task of constructing a theology of religions or a theology of religious plurality. Our focus has shifted toward an articulation of a Christian theology that is informed and chastened by a dialogical engagement with people of other faiths. In other words, the issue before us needs to be addressed within the broader framework of Christian theology today. Traditionally, the frontiers of theology have always been set within its own perimeters. In the past, theological articulations have relied solely on the canons of one's own community, sacred texts, traditions, culture, heritage and hermeneutic. It was hardly conceivable that they could also lie within the sphere of other faiths—be they Hindu, Muslim or Buddhist. In today's context, such a self-sufficient posture of theology has become increasingly untenable. Theology is now challenged to broaden its scope and task by interrogating religious diversity in our midst and critically examining all self-legitimating claims and practices of faiths in our midst—including our own—in order to foster a bona fide relationship among people of various religious faiths.

This task goes beyond constructing a theological hypothesis that would grudgingly accord a place for other religious traditions within our doctrinal schema. Rather, we are challenged to articulate how our acknowledgement of religious diversity redefines our self-understanding. In other words, a critical reexamination and reconceptualization of our inherited theological categories is essential in order for us to shift from an exclusivist to an inclusive understanding of other religious faiths. Christian theological articulations must go beyond the traditional self-referential to a cross-referential posture and engagement.[6] This, I believe, is the task of theology today.

It is in the context of a dialogical engagement that Christians gain a better grasp of the faith, values and commitments of people of other faiths, and thus are better equipped to articulate their self-identity and calling in the midst of and in relation to others. Without a dialogical experience, all our theological proposals may turn out to be mere academic hypotheses or theoretical abstractions, divorced from the reality of lived experience. The task before us is to articulate a Christian theology that is dialogically grounded and publicly accountable in relation to the claims and counterclaims put forward by others. Do Lutheran theological categories of

---

[6] My use of the terns, "self-referential" and "cross-referential" comes from Kenneth Cragg, *Christ and the Faiths* (Philadelphia: Westminster Press, 1987).

understanding allow for such an engagement with the world of plurality? How may we rethink or reformulate our inherited categories in the service of the theological task before us today? I shall attempt to respond to these questions by offering an hermeneutical perspective that may open up new possibilities for engagement with people of other faiths.

Lutheran exclusivism

Lutheran theologians, desiring to do theology in the matrix of religious pluralism, are invariably up against categories of exclusivism in the Lutheran tradition. While the Lutheran tradition did not explicitly subscribe to the patristic dictum, *extra ecclesiam nulla salus* (outside the church there is no salvation), in Lutheran self-understanding it undoubtedly meant *extra Christum nulla salus* (outside Christ there is no salvation). The Lutheran tendency toward exclusivism, therefore, is derived from a doctrinal interpretation of biblical texts. The absoluteness of the Christian claim is thus articulated in terms of the "Lutheran *solas*:" s*olus Deus, solus Christus, sola gratia, sola scriptura, solo verbo, sola fide* and so on. The doctrinal language of "God alone," "Christ alone," "grace alone," "Scripture alone," "Word alone" and "faith alone" are all intertwined, and reinforce claims of Lutheran exclusivism.[7]

By their very nature, the Lutheran *solas* make exclusive Christian claims. But they do so in the form of a circular argument. In a multi-faith society, a generic affirmation of faith in "God alone" may not meet with great resistance (except of course by atheists). However, the Lutheran hermeneutic is not content with a theocentric view of reality that easily accommodates other religious beliefs in terms of grace and truth. The Lutheran view of "God alone" is imposed by a decisive limitation in the claim, "Christ alone." Lutherans claim that we cannot know God apart from the revealed Christ. But, this "Christ alone" claim does not represent a "cosmic Christ" or a "universal *logos*." Rather, it points to the historical Jesus Christ. The Lutheran way of interpreting Christ is invariably tied to faith in Christ, which in turn comes by the hearing of the Word (*ex auditu*). The Word alone is not any word, not even the words of Scripture, but a word of promise that

---

[7] A fuller discussion on Lutheran attempts to understand other faiths is found in J. Paul Rajashekar (ed.), *Religious Pluralism and Lutheran Theology*, LWF Report 23/24 (Geneva: The Lutheran World Federation, 1988). Essays by Paul Varo Martinson, Theodore M. Ludwig and Carl Braaten in this volume focus on the issues of the dialectic of the law and gospel in relation to a Lutheran theology of religions.

points to grace alone. The grace alone refers back to what God has done in and through Christ alone.

The circularity of the argument and the series of qualifications a Lutheran hermeneutic imposes on understanding the faith lead to the impression that Lutheran tradition is intent on keeping the gospel as exclusive as possible, where Christian engagement with religious plurality is possible only according to our terms. The *solas* appear to draw a rigid boundary between believers and outsiders. Put differently, it seems that the Lutheran understanding precludes a positive dialogue with persons of other faiths, unless others subscribe to the doctrinal claims of Lutherans.

The Lutheran dialectic

Thoughtful Lutherans may question an exclusivist reading of the Lutheran *solas* because Lutheran theological assumptions and biblical hermeneutics do not support a fundamentalist stance. The *solas*, so Lutherans claim, are only one side of the dialectic of engagement in the world. The intent of the *solas*, despite their exclusive claims, is not to erect a mighty fortress around Lutherans. Lutheran theologians have therefore sought to temper the exclusive claims of the *solas* by pointing to the dialectic of the law and gospel, along with the corresponding distinctions between the God's "left hand" and God's "right hand," and the realm of creation and the realm of redemption. Many have argued that the dialectic of law and gospel, and the other corresponding distinctions, are not intended to make a rigid separation between Christians and others in the world.

God is indeed the Creator of the world and therefore all people have some knowledge of God and God's law, and if God's law is the foundation of all human laws, then Christians and others are subject to them. Thus, in the realm of creation, all humans live in mutual interaction with one another without distinction. Since God relates with all people through the modality of the law, which is grounded in human reason and natural law, Christians must engage in dialogue with others and appreciate their social and moral contributions. Therefore, Lutheran theologians have affirmed all positive, spiritual, moral and societal values that uphold justice, peace and the integrity of God's creation and have encouraged cooperation with such endeavors.

The Lutheran dialectic of law and gospel stops short of affirming any salvific values in the realm of creation. Although all people, regardless of their faith convictions, are subject to God's law and its restraining and sustaining function in the world, only Christians have the knowledge of God's redemptive work in Christ Jesus. All people have an element of natural theology or knowledge of God in their faith stories, but not all of them have a sure and certain knowledge of Christ. Those who do not explicitly profess the name of Christ lack the experience of a gracious God and are therefore engaged in works of self-salvation. The Lutheran "yes" to the world of religious plurality in God's creation, it turns out, is a decisive "no" to the religious values and claims of others. Because others lack a proper knowledge of Christ through faith, their faith and beliefs lack salvific validity. Whatever knowledge others possess—especially people of other faiths—is ambiguous, insufficient and incomplete. Because others lack a proper knowledge of Christ and salvation, they lack the gospel.

The Lutheran dialectic of the "yes" and "no" to the world of religious plurality may provide a basis for Lutheran engagement in evangelizing the world. It allows us to encounter others positively as God's children, to live and work together in ordering our world. It encourages Lutherans to share the good news of Jesus Christ with those who have not heard the gospel and to invite them to participate in God's kingdom, inaugurated by Jesus Christ. But, the Lutheran dialectic of law and gospel can also instill a negative bias against others because they lack the gospel and may lead our efforts in proselytizing them. Despite the positive values that we may find in others, they are ultimately deficient in their understanding of God and salvation. Therefore, Lutheran engagement becomes a word of judgment against others. But then, what is the point of a dialogical engagement with others if ultimately all their religious values are deficient or insufficient? Christian dialogue with others in this case becomes a disguised form of monologue.

Toward a Lutheran theology of engagement

The traditional Lutheran *solas* have made the Christian engagement with others problematic because of their claim to exclusivism and exclusion. Moreover, the Lutheran dialectic of law and gospel is not without difficulties in our attempt to articulate a relevant Christian theology that is not condescending toward the beliefs of others. It is important to remember that in Lutheran theology, law and gospel are categories that help us to understand God's dealings with the world. They are primarily analytical tools and not categories of judgment. They represent two modes of God's relation to the world. They are to be distinguished, but not separated. The dialectic, therefore, insists on holding together simultaneously two divergent modes of God's activity in the world.

The dialectic of the *simul*, what we understand as "simultaneously," is a fundamental presupposition of almost all Lutheran doctrinal affirmations. Lutheran theology understands God's revelation as simultaneously hidden and revealed; God's activity occurs simultaneously through the work of the left hand and right hand; Christ is simultaneously human and divine; God's saving activity occurs simultaneously through law and gospel; the Christian is simultaneously saint and sinner; the sacrament of bread and wine is simultaneously the body and blood; the kingdom of God is simultaneously present here and now and not yet. This emphasis on the *simuls* in Lutheran theology opens up possibilities for a positive engagement with all people in our world. A proper understanding of the *simuls,* in fact, pushes us away from an exclusive stance in matters of faith and invites us into an inclusive engagement with people.[8]

While the *solas* hold us back by their exclusive claims, the *simuls* thrust us into an open posture toward the world. They are thus juxtaposed in a dialectical relationship. The *solas*, "Christ alone," "faith alone," "grace alone," provide the necessary anchor for our participation in the world and our encounters with people of other faiths, or no faith. Without such an anchor, our conversations with people become ambiguous and lack any particular religious commitment. But, if the *solas* alone were to prevail, our conversations would become restricted. In order to be effective anchors of faith, the *solas* need the *simuls.*

On the other hand, by affirming God's inclusive love for the world, the Lutheran *simuls* free us to affirm the reality of God's grace and truth in the world, wherever they may be found. The *simuls* recognize that God is at work through the instrumentality of both law and gospel. This occurs whenever the Christian community hears the Word and receives the sacraments. However, this same God is also at work among other peoples in and through the dialectic of law and gospel. It is part of the biblical

---

[8] The insight was organically suggested by Theodore Ludwig, "Some Lutheran Reflections on Religious Pluralism," in Rajashekar, op. cit (note 7). It was further developed by Paul Varo Martinson in an unpublished paper, "Salvation and Religions: From *Sola* to *Simul*." The author of this essay is indebted to both these scholars and other Lutheran scholars who were part of an international study group between 1985–1992. I have explored these ideas in another essay under the title, "Navigating Difficult Questions," in Richard H. Bliese & Craig Van Gelder (eds), *The Evangelizing Church: A Lutheran Contribution* (Minneapolis: Augsburg Fortress, 2005), pp. 92–112.

testimony that God is active in creation in love, and insofar as Christ is the medium of creation, God's love also finds expression among people of other faiths. The Lutheran *simuls*, therefore, encourage us confidently to explore the mysterious ways in which God is present among other people and we may even meet Christ among them.

If the *simuls* alone were the criteria without the *solas*, Christians would have no reference point for their engagement with others. We would have no way of distinguishing the authentic and the spurious, or the divine and the demonic. The *simuls* are grounded in the *solas*. The *solas* and the *simuls* therefore need each other and must be held together. A tension exists within these two categories of understanding, simultaneously pushing us in two different directions. Nonetheless, in holding on to this tension, we are provided with a foundation for articulating a Christian theology that takes account of the faith and practices of people of other faiths in our self-understanding.

Some concluding thoughts

The intent of the preceding analysis is to emphasize interreligious dialogue as the necessary prerequisite for doing theology in religiously pluralistic contexts. I have used the Lutheran doctrinal categories of *solas* and *simuls* as analytical tools for understanding and grounding our interreligious engagement. Understood as categories of analysis, hermeneutical tools and not as theological truths, they open up possibilities of encounter without prejudice toward others or their faith. My analysis serves the purpose of freeing Lutherans for a *bona fide* engagement with people of other faiths. What I have proposed provides a mode of doing theology in a pluralistic world. My analysis does not in any way offer a systematic theology of religions but rather invites Christians to focus their energies in a different direction. That is dialogue. The focus of dialogue, among other things, is to engage in mutual theological discoveries that strengthen our faith in relation to other faiths.

Why a dialogical starting point is essential for theology is not hard to justify. It is the nature of pluralism that invariably challenges each and every faith to articulate its claims to legitimacy and religious self-sufficiency. Pluralism, implicitly or explicitly, raises the question by what authority faiths make such and such a claim. In the face of such questioning, all claims to authority, whether grounded in Scripture, tradition community or history, are subject to intense scrutiny. In a globalized world, where religious ideas traverse every which way, influencing and shaping religious commitments and worldviews, claims to religious absolutism, superiority and exclusivism have become highly questionable. This is not to deny or undermine the exclusive content and contours of religious faiths in their historical specificity, but the fact is, the exclusive claims originated in a religiously circumscribed context makes them problematic in pluralistic contexts. Hence, the demand to rethink Lutheran theology today.

Furthermore, exclusivist claims for the superiority of one's beliefs are not merely internal claims heard within the confines of one's religious community but are also heard by those outside of it. When those claims are translated into overt or covert forms of persuasion or proselytism, they become problematic in the context of religious and social pluralism. This pressing issue warrants further theological reflection in pluralistic societies. Claims of exclusivism, accompanied by overt proselytism, are often perceived by others as an assault on their beliefs or ways of life. Whatever internal scriptural, doctrinal or inner warrant there may be within a religious community, outwardly religious communities in open societies tend to be a bit circumspect, if not, embarrassed, about proselytizing activities.

The idea of proselytism often brings about some theological discomfort among Christians and therefore there is a tendency to soften or hide under benign or non-threatening rubrics such as "sharing the faith," "reaching out in love," or "witnessing." Christians in minority situations may view the issue differently. However carefully Christians may nuance the meaning of mission, evangelism, witness and evangelization in their theological self-understanding, these categories are often conflated with proselytism in public discourse. In the minds of the public, proselytism seems to have an unethical or improper ring to it. In religiously plural and culturally diverse contexts, the ethics of proselytism invariably comes into collision with the assumptions of pluralism. Thus, the church's missiology, too, is in need of critical rethinking. Proselytism, religious absolutism and fundamentalism are some of the issues that are a source of conflict in many societies. Theological articulations of the Christian faith cannot ignore these issues affecting communal life. It is precisely for this reason that all theological articulation needs to be grounded in a dialogical engagement with the world.

I conclude this article with a final observation. The dialogical approach I am advocating here is a complex one. All theology is a product of dialogue, although the dialogue partners or interlocutors have varied from context to context and from age to age. Theology has always been in dialogue with philosophies, worldviews, ideologies and science. Sometimes, the dialogue has been internal or intra-Christian, and, at other times, external or extra-Christian. Interreligious dialogue often involves texts, traditions, philosophies, myths and folklore, and, more importantly, the people who embody their faith in diverse ways. Our understanding of the other in a dialogical process is often fraught with problems. The beliefs and testimonies of others, despite our best efforts to comprehend them, often remain alien and strange in our hearing. In a true sense they are "alien witnesses" who demand our attention and even a response. The witness of other faiths challenges us to articulate our faith as intelligibly as possible in relation to others. Hence, theology can no longer be done in isolation without a dialogical engagement with others. Put differently, the challenge before us in a religiously plural situation is not so much constructing a theology of religions, but rather rethinking Christian theology in its totality in light of the depth and riches that one discovers in a sustained dialogical praxis. Constructing a relevant Christian theology today warrants that we place all our theological assumptions in a position of vulnerability. The dialectic of the *solas* and the *simuls* calls us to be vulnerable before others in order to be loyal to Christ!

Luther's Perspectives on the Communio Sanctorum in Dialogue with Traditional Japanese Spirituality

Motoo Ishii

Ancestral rites seem to pose an obstacle for Christian mission in Japan since, even in this secularized age, they continue to influence ordinary people. These rites are closely linked to Japanese Buddhism, and it is not possible to share the gospel without connecting with Japanese spirituality as found in Japanese ancestral rites. The question confronting the churches is how the Christian faith can respond to this spirituality in terms of Christian spirituality and thus take root on Japanese soil. In accordance with *lex orandi, lex credendi*, theology must be embodied and closely related to practices.

In the following, I shall explore two traditional Japanese spiritualities and how the concept of *communio sanctorum*, as elaborated by Martin Luther, might address them. At the same time, I will examine how Japanese spirituality could challenge traditional Western Christian thinking. Some may critique this as possibly compromising the Christian faith, while others will see it as a real dialogue between the Christian faith (in a Lutheran vein) and the spiritual needs in a different religious setting.

Behind the practice of ancestral rites lie two traditional types of spiritualities that are nurtured in Japanese culture: community oriented spirituality and nature oriented spirituality.

Community oriented spirituality

Shuichi Kato writes about five features of Japanese views of death and life:

> First, a family, a blood-community, and a "mura" (local village) community have the living and the dead as its members. Death is just to move from the first status to the second as a member of the same community. In this sense, it is better than ostracism. [...] Second, it is essential to die in a good manner

in a community. The good manner is to die without disgracing benefits of the
community and to die according to a way that the community established.[1]

This describes a community oriented Japanese spirituality, which does not
make a sharp division between the living and the dead, but overcomes the
crisis of death.

According to traditional Japanese thought, the souls of the dead become
kami (god) or *hotoke* (Buddha), that is, they are saved through ancestral
rites. In turn, the spirit of the dead blesses the living. Here we can see the
interdependent relationship between the living and the souls of the dead,
who together constitute Japanese community, with the family and village
(*mura*) at its core. They are living as members of the same community. This
community oriented spirituality brings harmony and benefits to the community that may be more important than individual happiness.

Nature oriented spirituality

In nature oriented spirituality, the Japanese want gradually to return to
nature after their death and be united with the cycle and flow of life and
death in nature. Through the ancestral rites, the souls of the dead return
to nature and unite with the collective ancestral spirit. Traditionally, the
Japanese think of mountains as the dwelling places of souls and spirits. In
addition, the ancestral spirit could become the spirit of the mountain, or god
of the community. Nature nurtures the whole community of which ancestors
are members, even after their death. Such nature oriented spirituality also
expresses itself in an animistic worldview. Recently, Japanese scholars such
as Takeshi Umemura have insisted that in light of the ecological crisis, such
an animistic view can teach Japanese society and the Western world to take
care of nature and the whole of life. In *A Single Drop of Water in a Mighty
River*, the Japanese writer, Hiroyuki Itsuki, expresses this as follows:

> I want to rethink that we are just small beings. It is true, however, that there
> is a life of heaven and earth even in a single dewdrop on a leaf though it is just
> small. If the expression "life" is exaggerated, I can paraphrase it into "a breath
> of the universe." [. . .] "A human being is just a single drop of water in a mighty
> river." He/she is just a small drop of water but it is a drop which makes a huge

---

[1] Shuichi Kato, M. Risch, R.J. Lifton, *Japanese View of Death and Life,* II (Tokyo: Iwanami, 1977), p. 209.

flow of water and a part of rhythm which moves towards the eternal time, I just feel so gazing the water.[2]

In nature oriented spirituality, people humble themselves and seek a way to live in and with nature, and to entrust themselves to it. In its cosmological worldview, it does not contradict but complements a community oriented spirituality

Implications of Luther's communio sanctorum for Japanese spirituality

The Christian concept of *communio sanctorum*, the communion (or community) of the saints, as found in the Third Article of the Apostles' Creed, expresses how people are saved through the work of the Holy Spirit. Since the Reformation, many Protestants have understood this in juxtaposition to the Roman Catholic Church. Luther regarded the church as the assembly of believers, and, according to Article XII of the Augsburg Confession, the concept of *communio sanctorum* is understood as the community of saints. This suggests a way of interacting with Japanese spirituality.

Community of saints including the living and the dead

In the Middle Ages, a saint was understood as one who died after having lived a faithful and holy life that merits salvation. For Luther, however, being a saint does not imply being such a special person; a saint is simply a believer. All believers are sinful but, at the same time, righteous, because of Christ. Holiness came to be understood as that which comes from God and is given to all believers by faith alone, not because of a believer's works. Because of God's love through Christ, all believers are saints.

Luther's position was that there are only two kinds of saints, those living and those dead.[3] Before God, both are living in eternal life that is ours through Christ. In the Eucharist, we have a foretaste of the banquet of heaven with all the saints. Such Christian community, with the living and the dead, could be a response to Japanese community oriented spirituality.

---

[2] Hiroyuki Itsuki, *A Single Drop of Water in a Mighty River* (Tokyo: Gentosha, 1998), pp. 21, 25.

[3] Lennart Pinomaa, *Faith Victorious: An Introduction to Luther's Theology*, transl. by Walter J. Kukkonen (Lima, Ohio: Academic Renewal Press, 1963), p. 114.

In pastoral terms, it is important for Christians to believe that what the gospel promises will be realized through the community of saints, which is especially consoling in the face of death. As Luther put it,

> [I]n the hour of his death no Christian should doubt that he is not alone. He can be certain, as the sacraments point out, that a great many eyes are upon him: first, the eyes of God and of Christ himself, for the Christian believes his words and clings to his sacraments; then also, the eyes of the dear angels, of the saints, and of all Christians. [4]

It is in the *communio sanctorum*, in which Christ exists at the center, that the eternal life which Christ promises and gives is realized. Hence, the dying person can be at rest, liberated from loneliness, taken into the community of saints. This is a concrete response to a community oriented spirituality. Many Japanese Christians appreciate Holy Communion as a symbol and actual event through which, by Christ's grace, they can meet a beloved one who has passed away.

Communio sanctorum shows forth comprehensive salvation

In Japanese nature oriented spirituality, there is a close relationship and continuity between human beings and nature; salvation is sought through union with nature. Such spirituality is important today because of the ecological crisis. One critique of Western Christianity is that it bears responsibility for this crisis insofar as it refers to human beings as rulers over the rest of creation, and that it is too anthropocentric.

In Christian theology, however, it is not the human being but God who is at the center and ruler of all creation. Also, human beings are taken from the dust of the earth and destined to return to dust. Biblical spirituality recognizes the continuity between human beings and nature and the smallness of human beings. Moreover, human sin is the cause of the destruction of God's creation. Human begins become aware of their responsibility when made conscious of sin. In order to solve the problem of sin, we must be saved first and renewed as agents to work in and for God's world.

The concept of *communio sanctorum* points to the location where salvation is realized through the Holy Spirit. In Protestantism, the *communio sanctorum* is known as the assembly of believers. Luther also uses it in terms

---

[4] Martin Luther, "A Sermon on Preparing to Die, 1519," in Helmut T. Lehman (ed.), *Luther's Works*, vol. 42 (Philadelphia: Fortress Press, 1969), p. 112.

of participation or sharing in holy things,[5] but in a different sense than the Roman Catholic Church. In medieval tradition, these holy things were the sacraments and merits of saints, but for Luther the holy things are the blessings each believer is given.[6] In the *communio sanctorum*, all believers share their possessions.[7] Therefore, the concept of *communio sanctorum* does not necessarily mean the community of believers, but also the sharing of all things that believers are given by God in this world. According to Luther's Large Catechism, all is given by God the Creator. Everything we need to live is named there, including the human body, nature, the sun and the stars in heaven.[8] If those who are saved by Christ share all things in the *communio sanctorum*, then all creatures share and partake in salvation. Therefore, the concept of the *communio sanctorum* implies salvation not only for human beings, but also for the rest of the creation.

At the center of this image of salvation, is the end of human sin as accomplished by Christ, and proclaimed through the *communio sanctorum*. In this sense, the Christian message of salvation correlates with Japanese nature oriented spirituality. Christian spirituality looks forward to the salvation of the whole world, including nature and the relationship between human beings and nature in the *communio sanctorum*. It is a comprehensive concept of salvation because at its center is God's comprehensive work for salvation.

Luther does not fully develop this image of salvation in the *communio sanctorum*, which includes the world of nature. However, in Lutheran theology it is possible to show and remember how Christians concretely participate in ecological concerns, through the bread and wine of Holy Communion:

> The "how" of Christ's presence remains as inexplicable in the sacrament as elsewhere. It is a presence that remains "hidden" even though visible media are used in the sacrament. The earthly element is [. . .] a fit vehicle of the divine presence and it, too, the common stuff of our daily life, participates in the new creation which has already begun.[9]

---

[5] Pinomaa, op. cit. (note 3), p. 119.

[6] Robert Kolb and Timothy J. Wengert, *The Book of Concord: The Confessions of the Evangelical Lutheran Church* (Philadelphia: Fortress Press, 2000), p. 438.

[7] Paul Althaus, *The Theology of Martin Luther*, transl. by Robert C. Schultz (Philadelphia: Fortress Press, 1966), pp. 294–7.

[8] Kolb and Wengert, op. cit. (note 6), p. 41.

[9] Evangelical Lutheran Church in America, *Renewing Worship 2: Principles for Worship* (Minneapolis: Augsburg Fortress, 2002), p. 123.

What is important here is the participation of earthly things in the new creation, as in how bread and wine are also the body and blood of Christ. Through the Lord's Supper we receive not only the remission of sin, but also a glimpse of the new creation in Christ, with cosmological and eschatological dimensions of salvation.

How Japanese spirituality challenges Christians

Will non-believers be saved?

Will ancestors be saved who did not have a chance to hear the gospel or to become a Christian before they died? Questions such as, Can my grandmother be saved even though before she died she did not have a chance to go to church? are being asked. This is the biggest issue facing the Christian mission in Japan.

As explained above, in community oriented spirituality, there is a mutual and interdependent relationship between the living and the dead. Therefore, the living can do something for the salvation of the dead by means of ancestral rites. In Christianity, is there anything to be done for their salvation? Is the concept of *communio sanctorum* exclusive? If so, its efficacy in relation to Japanese spirituality would be quite limited.

In this regard, Berentsen clearly distinguishes between *communio sanctorum* and *communio familiae*. He refers to Fasholé-Luke, an African Protestant theologian, who also compares African ancestor worship with the communion of the saints and concludes, "that even non-Christians can be embraced within the communion of Saints, in spite of his emphasis on the significance of the sacraments in the understanding of *communio sanctorum*."[10] Against Fasholé-Luke's ambiguous position, Berentsen says, "the New Testament does not allow a theology of mission to exploit the idea of the communion of saints in the direction of an obscuring integration with *communio familiae* in order to solve the problem of the pre-Christian dead."[11]

Then what could be an appropriate answer to the Japanese community oriented spirituality? Simply saying, "entrust them to the will of God," does not seem enough. Of course, this is true but the answer does not go far enough in helping those who have to face this question.

---

[10] Jan-Martin Berentsen, *Grave and Gospel* (Leiden: E. J. Brill, 1985), p. 213.

[11] Ibid., p. 214.

Allowing the dead "really to die"

Through ancestral rites, the bereaved help the dead go to heaven. This means that the bereaved enable the deceased really to die through a series of rituals that continue for thirty-three years. The soul of the dead unites with the collective ancestral spirit through these rites. In Japanese spirituality, a person "lives and dies" as they are remembered repeatedly in these ancestral rites.

Kunio Yanagida wrote a kind of diary while he experienced his beloved son dying after an attempted suicide. He reports that he had nursed his brain-dead son. He talked to him because, as a journalist, he had learned a lot about brain death: "there is a big difference between death in general (the third person's death) and the beloved person's death (the second person's death)." Then, after a few days, Yanagida told his son, "it is enough that you have done well, now I allow you to go."

It could be said that "the second person's death" is a kind of process of accepting the death of the deceased as real and allowing the bereaved to grieve. This also shows the undivided nature of "the first person's death" and "the second person's death" in Japanese spirituality because until Yanagida accepted his son's death, the son had not really died yet in spite of being biologically dead.

Life is more than being biologically alive. Rather, life is shared among people who are interrelated. Japanese spirituality knows that the meaning of an individual life is found in the relationship with others, especially in relationships of love. The individual's life does not end with biological death but, rather, in "receiving the hearts of the dead." This challenges Western individualism.

Michiko Ishimure is a Japanese writer who has grappled with Minamata, a neurological syndrome caused by severe mercury poisoning. For the sake of those who suffer from this disease in the polluted city of Minamata, she wants to draw attention to what has occurred. She wants to be a kind of shaman, acting against how capitalism exploits and harms nature and all of life. She is trying to listen to the voice of the spirits and the souls of the dead and the living who have not been pacified. Otherwise, they will never be saved, which means that they cannot die completely, and the world in which we live will not be reliable.

It is the solidarity between the living and the dead in Japanese spirituality that seeks to make life peaceful, safe and plentiful in the coming age. Ishimure feels that it is our responsibility to live in this solidarity. According to such an understanding, it is not sufficient only to entrust the souls of the dead into God's hands without also saying what the bereaved received from the deceased.

The individual and communal nature of life in Christ

Each Christian is united with Christ through baptism. The assembly of believers then becomes the church as the body of Christ. This may seem to be the logical sequence but it does not express how faith occurs. If there is no church and no one proclaiming the gospel or listening to it, then there is no Christian. In the community of believers, in which the witness of Christ is shared, there a Christian is born. An individual believer can exist only in the community of saints (*communio sanctorum)* in which Christ is present at the center, active in both individual Christians and the community as whole.

In Christian spirituality, an individual is never forsaken by the community of saints, while in Japanese community oriented spirituality, an individual is required to live and die for the community. In nature oriented spirituality, an individual will eventually disappear into the flow of the river.

It could be said that the Japanese know that their own self is small and thus humble. Christians know through faith that their own self is sinful and perishable before God, but also that God loves them in spite of their sin, and saves them. Christ works for the salvation of those who should be damned. An individual believer is united with Christ and saved through the *communio sanctorum.*

Concerning the salvation of non-Christian ancestors, I propose that we think of their souls within the context of the church as the body of Christ. It is not that they are in the communion of saints, or involved in the community. This would imply that the dead could be evangelized, which we cannot support. But we also cannot say that they are outside of salvation. We can say that we commit them to the hands of God. Then we could think of them in the context of the church, which is the body of Christ who was crucified, died and resurrected for our salvation. When we commit them to the hands of God, we commit them to Christ who loves those who are not worthy to be loved. Therefore, we can think of dead ancestors in the context of the same communion in which we are living.

Practically, it is important to think of non-Christian ancestors in the context of the church as the *communio sanctorum*, because this implies that the church will care for them. Instead of Buddhist ancestral rites, we hold services in which we give thanks and praise to God for our dead ancestors and share the love of God as found in the lives of those who have died. In such memorial services, we entrust them to God.

The communal nature of communio sanctorum

Luther talks about the communal nature of faith in unity with Christ and others:

> The immeasurable grace and mercy of God is given us in this sacrament to the end that we might put from us all misery and tribulation [Anfechtung] and lay it upon the community [of saints], and especially on Christ. Then we may with joy find strength and comfort, and say, "Though I am a sinner and have fallen, though this or that misfortune has befallen me, nevertheless I will go to the sacrament to receive a sign from God that I have on my side Christ's righteousness, life, and sufferings, with all holy angels and the blessed in heaven and all pious men on earth. If I die, I am not alone in death; if I suffer, they suffer with me. [I know that] all my misfortune is shared with Christ and the saints, because I have a sure sign of their love toward me." See, this is the benefit to be derived from this sacrament; this is the use we should make of it. Then the heart cannot but rejoice and be strengthened.[12]

My life is no longer just only my own, but rather shared with all saints because everything is shared with saints in the *communio sanctorum*.[13] This is not an undivided unity as in Japanese spirituality. It is, however, in contrast to modern individualism, in which it seems that each person has the right to decide for themselves, without others. But in the *communio sanctorum*, Christians feel for and take care of each other.

> You must feel with sorrow all the dishonor done to Christ in his holy Word, all the misery of Christendom, all the unjust suffering of the innocent, with which the world is everywhere filled to overflowing. You must fight, work, pray, and—if you cannot do more—have heartfelt sympathy. See, this is what it means to bear in your turn the misfortune and adversity of Christ and his saints. Here the saying of Paul is fulfilled, "Bear one another's burdens, and so fulfill the

---

[12] Martin Luther, "The Blessed Sacrament of the Holy and True Body of Christ, and the Brotherhoods, 1519," in Helmut T. Lehmann (ed.), *Luther's Works*, vol. 55 (Philadelphia: Fortress Press, 1960), p. 54.

[13] Althaus, op. cit. (note 7), pp. 297–303.

law of Christ" [Gal. 6:2]. See, as you uphold all of them, so they all in turn uphold you; and all things are in common, both good and evil. Then all things become easy, and the evil spirit cannot stand up against this fellowship.[14]

As believers we share with one another, so too is there sharing between the saints in heaven and the saints on earth. The bereaved receives what the deceased was thinking, feeling and committed to at death. If someone died in a war, the person would leave a strong desire for peace, so that the bereaved can take over the work for peace. Such relationships between the dead and the living must be assured in the Christian faith. Yet, because of our sinful nature, caution is also necessary, as described by Luther upon the death of his young daughter, Magdalene:

This love of which I speak is natural love, which, although in itself good and human, must be crucified with us so that the good, acceptable, and perfect will of God may be done. For God's Son, through whom and by whom all things were made, gave his very life although this was neither deserved nor required of him.[15]

Luther sees that even his love for his own daughter, which seems good in itself, must still be subservient to God's will, and thus "crucified." Christians must empty themselves and seek the salvation of others rather than benefits for themselves.

From this point of view, it can be said that through the *communio sanctorum* we can pray more positively for the salvation of non-Christian ancestors. In a community oriented spirituality, the Japanese people feel a close relationship with their beloved ones, for whom they have a natural love. In such a relationship, the deceased is not just dead, but living in the bereaved. If the bereaved person accepts being saved and united with Christ, the deceased living in this person is also saved. Both the bereaved and the dead are "crucified" in faith and purified by Christ love.

This is a tentative answer to Japanese spirituality. It must not be a dogmatic statement, but rather a practical and pastoral response: "Your non-Christian grandma, who is in your heart and mind, partakes in Christ's loving salvation through your faith."

---

[14] Luther, op. cit. (note 12), p. 54.

[15] Martin Luther, *Luther: Letters of Spiritual Counsel*, ed. and transl. by Theodore G. Tappert (Westminster: John Knox, 1955), p. 81.

What God has Created will not be Lost: Toward a More Inclusive Soteriology

Kristin Johnston Largen

Since rejecting Marcionite theology early in the church's life, Christians have consistently affirmed that the God of salvation is also the God of creation; the God of the New Testament is also the God of the Hebrew Scriptures. With this affirmation as its foundation, this chapter explores the relationship between creation and salvation and the ramifications of that relationship for Christian eschatological thinking, particularly as it pertains to non-Christians.[1] I proceed through a discussion of the following three affirmations: first, God is the Creator of all; second, God is in a loving relationship with all; and third, that relationship does not end at death.

God as Creator of all

The affirmation I begin with is the Christian belief that God is the Creator of all. Christians take this statement for granted and typically do not give it much thought—of course it is so, and how could it be otherwise? However, it is worth noting that while this supposition is fundamental for Christian thought, not all major world religions use this language, or construct the God/universe relationship in the same way. For example, Buddhism explicitly rejects the notion of the Buddha as creator; and Hinduism sets the whole concept of creation in the larger context of a cyclical understanding of time, where different manifestations of the divine are responsible for the different movements of creation, preservation and destruction within that cycle.

For Christians, however, the claim that God is Creator of heaven and earth is foundational, and there are two important theological assertions inherent in

---

[1] I recognize the problems inherent in using the language of "non-Christians" or "other religions." I use these terms for lack of a better functional option, and in light of the fact that the context for my teaching and research is primarily a Christian one, and that I am a Christian theologian, speaking from a Christian perspective. I do not mean to suggest, however, that all religions can/should be judged against the standard of Christianity.

this claim that should be noted and affirmed: the love God has for creation, and God's ongoing creative activity, which points to God's continued participation and presence within creation. In order to explicate these two assertions, I want to begin by looking at how Christians envision and describe this Creator God. To do that, I suggest one particular root metaphor that can be used to unpack the theological ramifications of naming God "Creator."

While Christians agree that God is the Creator, there is some debate as to what this creative activity looks like, and how best to envision God the Creator: what metaphor is richest and most suggestive? Even a cursory perusal of Scripture shows that we have a variety of models to choose from when thinking about God's creative activity. For example, Ian Barbour notes the following options: the image of God as "purposeful designer imposing order on chaos," which we find in the creation stories in Genesis; "God as a potter forming an object," found in both Jeremiah and Isaiah; God as "an architect laying out the foundations of a building," from Job 38; and, of course, we have multiple images of God as "Lord and King, ruling the universe to bring about intended purposes."[2] Certainly, all of these models are important, in that they preserve key theological affirmations about God, such as God's power to bring something out of nothing and God's absolute sovereignty over creation.

Nonetheless, all of these models fall short in one fundamental category—what God's creative activity says about the ongoing and sustained relationship of love God has with creation. In his book, *God in Creation*, Jürgen Moltmann describes this aspect of God's creative work.

> God the Creator of heaven and earth is present in each of [God's] creatures and in the fellowship of creation which they share [. . .]. Through the powers and potentialities of the Spirit, the Creator indwells the creatures God has made, animates them, holds them in life, and leads them into the future of God's kingdom.[3]

This understanding of God's generative activity leads Moltmann away from language of causality, which reinforces God's transcendence over the cosmos, in favor of creative language that invites Christians to view God's connection to the cosmos as "an intricate web of unilateral, reciprocal and

---

[2] Ian Barbour, *Religion in an Age of Science* (San Francisco, CA: Harper & Row, 1990), p. 176.

[3] Jürgen Moltmann, *God in Creation. A New Theology of Creation and the Spirit of God,* transl. by Margaret Kohl (Minneapolis: Fortress Press, 1993), p. 14.

many-sided relationships [. . .] which describe a cosmic community of living between God the Spirit and all [God's] created beings."[4]

Following Moltmann's insights here, I suggest as my root metaphor the image of God as a mother—particularly as a birthing mother.[5] The place I begin is Psalm 139, particularly verses 13–16:

> For it was you who formed my inward parts; you knit me together in my mother's womb. I praise you, for I am fearfully and wonderfully made. [. . .] My frame was not hidden from you, when I was being made in secret, intricately woven in the depths of the earth. Your eyes beheld my unformed substance. In your book were written all the days that were formed for me, when none of them as yet existed.

This image is echoed further in Isaiah 43:

> But now thus says the Lord, [the One] who created you, O Jacob [the One] who formed you, O Israel: Do not fear, for I have redeemed you; I have called you by name, you are mine. When you pass through the waters, I will be with you; and through the rivers, they shall not overwhelm you; when you walk through fire you shall not be burned, and the flame shall not consume you [. . .] [b]ecause you are precious in my sight, and honored, and I love you [. . .]. Do not fear, for I am with you.

In these lovely images, we see a God who takes an active role in the formation of each of God's children, a God who knows each of us intimately and cares about each of us passionately. And, perhaps even more importantly, the Bible witnesses to the fact that God's loving and creative activity does not end at a specific moment, but is ongoing and continues throughout our lifetimes, with the promise that God is always with us and watches over us with a mother's abiding love for her children.

Several important aspects of this metaphor are particularly appealing. First, this metaphor affirms an intimate connection between God and creation whereby creation is not external but internal to God—a very part of God's being and thus inseparable from God, the source of all existence. In her essay, "Heaven and Earth are Filled with Your Glory," Elizabeth

---

[4] Ibid.

[5] Both Barbour and Moltmann argue that motherly images of God are particularly appropriate for envisioning God's creative work for a variety of reasons. Barbour argues that the parental analogy, particularly that of God as mother, is "a particularly appropriate image of God's relation to the world." Barbour, op. cit. (note 2), p. 176. Moltmann argues that motherly categories best bring out that special creative work of God that consists in "letting-be," ibid., p. 88.

Johnson elaborates on this connection between God and the cosmos using the concept of God's glory, the *kabod YHWH*. She writes:

> [T]he glory of God is a luminous metaphor for the elusive nearness of the transcendent God glimpsed in and through the wondrous processes of nature, the history of freedom, and communities where justice and peace prevail. Using the term "glory of God" signifies that the incomprehensible holy mystery of God indwells the natural and human world as source, sustaining power, and goal of the universe, enlivening and loving it into liberating communion.[6]

In this way, she emphasizes that God is not best imaged and understood as over and above creation, apart from it and detached, but instead, "[c]ontinuously creating and sustaining, God is in all things not as part of their essence but as the innermost source of their being, power, and action."[7]

A good example of this indwelling can be seen in the Book of Job, specifically chapter 38 and following, where God speaks of entering into the spring of the sea, and walking in the recesses of the deep; putting wisdom in the "inward parts" and numbering the clouds; birthing the ice and the hoarfrost of heaven; providing prey for the raven when its young cry to God for food. God's intimate knowledge of the mountain goat, the wild ass, the ostrich, the horse and the hawk is described in almost shocking detail. Near, indeed, is God to creation, not only generally and universally, but also individually and particularly.

Second, this metaphor affirms the inherent goodness of our physical bodies, and, by extension, the physical world. The material creation is not simply disposable temporary housing for the true jewel, the spiritual creation. Instead, God created the physical world from God's very self and called good every aspect of our bodies and every aspect of the physical body of the world as well. From the moment of creation onward, God has continued faithfully to watch over this material world with care and attention.

Finally, using the metaphor of mother to describe the Triune God—who is in and of Godself inherently relational—opens up the possibility of seeing humanity's own practice of "cooperative mothering" as another way in which we embody the *imago Dei*. In her book *Mothers and Others*, Sarah Blaffer Hrdy argues that the cooperation that humans show in mothering—allowing others (called "alloparents") to participate in the rearing of

---

[6] Elizabeth Johnson, "Heaven and Earth are Filled with Your Glory," in Michael J. Himes and Stephen J. Pope (eds), *Finding God in All Things* (New York: Crossroad Publishing Company, 1996), p. 91.

[7] Ibid., p. 92.

children—is one of the key evolutionary developments that has allowed humans to become the species we are today. She writes:

> [A] long, long time ago, at some unknown point in our evolutionary history but before the evolution of 1,350 cc sapient brains (the hallmark of *anatomically* modern humans) and before such distinctively human traits as language (the hallmark of *behaviorally* modern humans), there emerged in Africa a line of apes that began to be interested in the mental and subjective lives—the thoughts and feelings—of others, interested in understanding them.[8]

It was this development that led to the cooperative breeding practices that characterize human societies still today, where aunts and uncles, grandmothers and grandfathers, godparents, friends and neighbors all lend a hand in helping mothers and fathers care for their children. From a Christian perspective, can we not also think about this behavior as another way in which humans mirror the mothering activity of God, in which all three of the persons of the Trinity participate in the work of creating, redeeming and sanctifying God's creation?

These descriptions point to the fact that imaging the creative God as a birthing mother allows us to affirm that when God creates the cosmos, God creates a relationship: one that is enduring, continuing as a part of God's very being, affecting both God and creation and testifying to the reality that God will not be without us.

God is in relationship with all

In the claim that God is in relationship with all creation, Christians affirm that God is present in all of God's creation—even and perhaps especially in the darkest, most tragic places, in the same way that a mother gives particular attention and care to her children who are in danger, at risk, or marginalized in any way. This relationship crosses religious boundaries and includes those who not only are believers in another religious tradition but even those who have no religious affiliation at all. In examining how this relationship is experienced in the boundaries of human life, I want to start with a specifically Christian articulation of this relationship, and then suggest a possible way to envision how such a relationship might be understood in the context of non-Christians and/or non-believers.

---

[8] Sarah Blaffer Hrdy, *Mothers and Others* (Cambridge, MA: Harvard University Press, 2009), pp. 30–31.

Many Christians describe their ongoing relationship with God first and foremost through a theology of baptism. God's relationship with humanity is made visible primarily in the transformative journey each person undertakes from baptism to the kingdom, a journey in which baptism is not only the starting point, but the touchstone as well. In her book, *A World According to God,* Marty Stortz writes that

> baptism removes the infant from its family of origin and adopts it into a new one. The most important name conferred in baptism is not the family name [. . .] but the name "Child of God." With baptism, we receive a new identity, an identity that does not come with passport or ID card but with relationships. Within the horizon of baptism, *who* we are depends decisively on *whose* we are, and baptism signals new relationships of belonging to God and to Christ.[9]

She notes further how Luther "made baptism the site of pilgrimage" and counseled a "daily return to baptism because baptism was the hostel pilgrims sought, a safe haven where Christians would daily be nourished, comforted, and reoriented."[10]

Surprisingly, this theology of baptism has fascinating resonances with work being done in a relatively new area of Christian theology, typically included under the rubric of "queer theology." Mindy Roll, one of many scholars doing work in this area, has done some interesting research on the topic of theology and transgender persons,[11] and the way in which their own transformation echoes the Christian theology of baptism. She writes:

> [O]ne gift of the transgender community to the church, seen most explicitly in the life of transsexuals, is the personification of certain theological concepts like transformation and journey [. . .]. Transformation and rebirth are enfleshed particularly in the life of one who is "born-again" into a new gender.[12]

She cites Matt Kailey, who writes a first-person account of a transsexual journey in his book, *Just Add Hormones.* Describing that experience, he

---

[9] Marty Stortz, *A World According to God* (San Francisco: Jossey-Bass, 2004), p. 40.

[10] Ibid., 39.

[11] A person who identifies with or expresses a gender identity that differs from the one which corresponds to the person's sex at birth.

[12] Mindy Roll, unpublished paper, Lutheran Theological Seminary at Gettysburg, Gettysburg, PA, fall 2008.

remarks that "[g]oing through a gender transition is a bit like being born [. . .]. You can literally start your life over."[13]

Kailey also notes that an important part of the process is choosing one's own name, which, on the surface, seems quite opposite to what happens in baptism, where Christians profess that we receive, rather than choose, our "true name," the name that signifies who we have been created to be and who we are at our core. However, some parallels remain, as, for Kailey, the whole point of choosing a name is that the new name is the "name that should have been, and that's what makes it right."[14] In his experience, Kailey's new name reflects his true identity, the man he was created to be. In this way, we see similarities to the gifting of the baptized with the name, "child of God," which also reflects the person we were created to be.

Roll notes that this tie to new birth and a new name have the potential to bear rich theological fruit. She refers to Kailey again, who talks about the experience of transgender people ("transpeople") as a "rebirth." He writes:

> Transpeople, more than any other life-form, are allowed the opportunity to be reborn. We can literally start new lives at twenty, thirty, forty, or seventy [. . .]. Transpeople are change personified. We can, and do, reinvent ourselves, physically and otherwise. And the best thing about reinvention is that we don't have to be stuck where we were before. We can create entirely new beings out of the ashes of our former selves.[15]

I recognize that there is another important difference here in terms of agency. Christians would affirm the work of the Holy Spirit in bringing about this transformation, rather than assuming it is work we are capable of doing on our own. Nonetheless, Roll posits that there are "startling parallels" with Christian baptismal beliefs. She notes, "[Kailey] writes of change as a positive process, a moving forward from the ashes (death) of one's former self. Is this not what Christians believe happens in baptism?"[16] Certainly, there is enough here to warrant further dialogue and reflection. Perhaps we might even consider the possibility that the lives of transgender persons, and their experience of transformation given and received in the ongoing grace and love of a relationship with God, might be lifted up and celebrated by the church.

---

[13] Matt Kailey, *Just Add Hormones* (Boston: Beacon Press, 2005), p. 25.

[14] Ibid., p. 26.

[15] Ibid., 122.

[16] Roll, op. cit. (note 12).

But what about others who are not Christian? While, for Christians, baptism exemplifies well one's transformative relationship with God, what type of experience might we point to for those outside the church, for whom the symbol of baptism has no meaning? How might we reflect upon this continuing relationship with God on behalf of believers in other religious traditions who either do or do not experience something of the God revealed in Jesus Christ? While I would not presume to name others' experience, I feel confident in speaking about God's end of that relationship. From that end, there is something that can be asserted about God's nature that offers some insight into the relationship God has with those outside the church.

Given the birthing mother metaphor for God that I suggested above, we can see the series of parables Jesus tells in Luke 15 as various manifestations of this same model of God: the shepherd and the lost sheep; the woman and the lost coin; the father and the lost son. In all three of these images, we are given a vision of a very persistent God, a God who is not satisfied with a few, but wants all; a God who is both patient and determined, who refuses to give up or walk away; a God who chooses to be in relationship with everyone, even the lost and reluctant, in spite of all obstacles and all difficulties. Certainly, such a God would not simply turn Her back on Her children in other religious traditions, for the simple fact that God has revealed Godself to be One who does not abandon or give up on anyone, but persists always in seeking, looking and waiting.

Another way of interpreting this image can be found in the play *W;t*, which tells the story of a terminally ill cancer patient, Vivian Bearing, a renowned professor of English. At the end of the play, when Vivian is near death, her mentor, Evelyn Ashford, comes to visit her in the hospital. She offers to recite some John Donne poetry, Vivian's area of expertise, but Vivian is too sick, too weak and too exhausted for this. Instead, Ashford takes out a children's book, *The Runaway Bunny*, and begins to read:

> Once there was a little bunny who wanted to run away. So he said to his mother, "I am running away." "If you run away," said his mother, "I will run after you. For you are my little bunny." The little bunny persists: "If you run after me," said the little bunny, "I will become a fish in a trout stream and I will swim away from you.'" "If you become a fish in a trout stream," said his mother, "I will become a fisherman and I will fish for you."

At this point in the play, Ashford stops and says, "Look at that. A little allegory of the soul. No matter where it hides, God will find it. See, Vivian?"[17]

---

[17] Margaret Edson, *W;t* (New York: Faber and Faber, 1993), pp. 79–80.

This, too, is an insightful, accurate image of our God, who continually seeks all God's children in love, in many forms, under many guises.

In pointing to these two images, I am arguing that because the claim about God's desire to be in relationship with the whole of creation is a claim about God's nature, this relationship is an objective reality, not dependent on our subjective realization of it, and certainly not dependent on our choosing the "right" religious affiliation. It is not that one's active participation in this relationship makes no difference in one's life—it certainly does—but God's relationship with humanity does not depend on our actualizing it or claiming it for ourselves.

This relationship does not end at death

This leads to my final conclusion: this relationship with God does not end with our death. Instead, the very fact of God's relationship with creation is salvific; and to the degree that final annihilation and/or damnation can be equated with God-forgottenness, God-forsakenness, and the absolute, final absence of God, all creation is already and eternally saved by being in a permanent, ongoing relationship with God. To support this argument, I make two claims. First, I challenge the Christian understanding of hell as an eternal destination of utter godforsakenness. Second, I posit that because Jesus "harrowed" hell with his presence, he has destroyed it forever.

It almost goes without saying that for Christians, their relationship with God does not end with death. The metaphor of heaven points to the belief that upon death, the perfect relationship with God, which Christians have longed for, finally will be achieved: God will be seen face-to-face and believers will rejoice in the fullness of God's presence. But what happens to non-Christians upon death? Historically, many Christians have consigned non-believers to hell, which I consider to be absolute and never-ending godlessness, an everlasting "casting away from God's presence." But in light of the description of God as a birthing mother, who unceasingly and eternally loves and cares for her children, the theological description of hell as a timeless place of either divine punishment or divine abandonment is untenable. In other words, if it exists at all, hell must be temporal, not eternal.

One of the classic arguments, used by different theologians through the centuries to explain the final abolition of hell, is based on the scriptural witness promising that, in the end, God will be all and all. Two primary passages in Scripture have been used to defend this position: Philippians 2:10–11, "[. . .]

at the name of Jesus every knee should bend, in heaven and on earth and under the earth, and every tongue should confess that Jesus Christ is Lord, to the glory of God the Father," and 1 Corinthians 15:22–28,

> [. . .] as all die in Adam, so all will be made alive in Christ. But each in his own order: Christ the first fruits, then at his coming those who belong to Christ. Then comes the end, when he hands over the kingdom to God the Father, after he has destroyed every ruler and every authority and power. For he must reign until he has put all his enemies under his feet [. . .]. When all things are subjected to him, then the Son himself will also be subjected to the one who put all things in subjection under him, so that God may be all in all.

It is believed that Clement of Alexandria was the first Christian writer to suggest, albeit hesitantly, that the fires of hell would, eventually, be extinguished. Clement used the Philippians passage quoted above, among others, to argue that in Christ, God has saved the whole world, and, ultimately, the whole world will come to serve God and worship God, including those in hell. Thus, for Clement, the whole purpose of hell was for purification; once that is complete, hell will come to an end. He used medical imagery to explicate his argument and compared the "discerning fire" of eschatological punishment with various types of curative surgery performed on a diseased arm or leg, such as amputation and the removal of diseased tissue by a surgeon.[18]

Another line of argumentation for the ultimate demise of hell comes not from God's lordship, but rather from God's love, making it the more fitting argument for the case I am making here. Romans 8:38–39 reads, "For I am convinced that neither death, nor life, nor angels, nor rulers, no things present, nor things to come, nor powers, nor height, nor depth, or anything else in all creation, will be able to separate us from the love of God in Christ Jesus our Lord." Although many theologians do not interpret the "anything else in all creation" as including hell and/or Satan, there does seem to be warrant for considering the possibility that Paul did intend to be genuinely all-inclusive.

---

[18] Certainly Clement was not the only one to make this argument. Most famously, perhaps, it is found in the writings of Origen, who focused on the 1 Corinthians text cited above, and reasoned from those verses that ultimately, all God's enemies would be subjected to God and worship God. For Origen, evil—and consequently hell—ultimately would be excluded from God's harmonious universe. Gregory of Nyssa should also be mentioned here, as he, too, argued for the final destruction of hell, but using a different logic. For Gregory, evil did not have true existence; only what comes from God's hand has permanent, genuine existence—evil lives only as a parasite on the good. Thus, God had no part in either creating or willing the existence of evil [and, by extension, hell]. Gregory, too, believed in the purification process inherent in punishment; and argued that once the evil was burned off, the individual would be left with a purely good will, and would, then, freely choose to be with God. Over time, everyone who needed it would go through this process, and thus hell would cease to exist.

Read this way, this passage (and others like it) points to the reality that separation from God is never permanent; because God is eternal and it is in God's nature to reach out to humanity, so also is God's hand everlastingly extended in love and grace. Continually and eternally, God reaches out across every gap that would separate humanity from God, and, ultimately, God's loving desire for all creation will be accomplished.

This leads to my final point, which is based on a particular theological analysis of Christ's descent into hell. I argue that this was not a onetime event but has everlasting significance. It is a key aspect of the crucifixion/resurrection event that forever defines God's relationship with humanity and the world. While many have not interpreted the "harrowing of hell" as comprehensive, it is certainly possible to see this act of love by Jesus Christ as filling the most godforsaken place one could ever imagine or inhabit, thereby destroying it forever.

John Chrysostom points to this idea in his Easter homily on the resurrection:

> [Jesus] destroyed Hades when he descended into it. He put it into an uproar even as it tasted of his flesh [. . .]. It was in an uproar because it was done away with. It was in an uproar because it is mocked. It was in an uproar, for it is destroyed. It is in an uproar, for it is now made captive. Hell took a body, and discovered God. It took earth, and encountered Heaven. It took what it saw, and was overcome by what it did not see [. . .]. Christ is Risen, and life is liberated.[19]

On this point, I give the final word to Hans Urs von Balthasar, who writes that, in the end, it is impossible to know definitively whether or not all people will be reconciled to God and hell finally abolished. It is only God who judges and only God who knows. Nonetheless, von Balthasar argues that Christians should not be indifferent to this matter; it is incumbent upon them to desire a positive outcome for all. He says, "[L]ove *hopes all things* (1 Cor 13:7). It cannot do otherwise than to hope for the reconciliation of all men in Christ. Such unlimited hope is, from the Christian standpoint, not only permitted, but *commanded*."[20] He goes on to quote Catherine of Sienna, who wrote,

> How could I ever reconcile myself, Lord, to the prospect that a single one of those whom, like me, you have created in your image and likeness should

---

[19] John Chrysostom, "The Resurrection," as quoted in *Spirituality,* vol. 15, no. 83 (March–April 2009), p. 128.

[20] Hans Urs von Balthasar, *Dare We Hope "That All Men Be Saved"?,* transl. by David Kipp (San Francisco: Ignatius Press, 1988), p. 213, author's own italics.

> become lost and slip from your hands? No, in absolutely no case do I want to
> see a single one of my brethren meet with ruin, not a single one of those, who,
> through their like birth, are one with me by nature and by grace. I want them
> all to be wrested from the grasp of the ancient enemy, so that they all become
> yours to the honor and great glorification of your name.[21]

Ultimately, judging from the history of God with God's people, it seems fair to say that God chooses repeatedly to err on the side of grace, rather than on the side of judgment. This is my preference as well. Regardless of the persuasive doctrines we articulate together as a church, I am confident that we will be wonderfully delighted and greatly surprised at who is seated around the great messianic banquet table.

Concluding hopes for transformation

Theology is always performed in service to the church. Thus, I conclude by suggesting how this line of thought might be transformative in the life of the church. First, the practice of using a much greater range of metaphors for God creates the possibility of envisioning God and relating to God in a wide variety of ways. This serves to deepen our understanding of who God reveals Godself to be, and how God has chosen to be in relationship to the world. This, in turn, creates a fresh openness to seeing the presence and work of God in new ways in and among God's people.

Second, this can serve as an impetus for both starting and continuing dialogue with believers in other religious traditions. If God is in relationship with non-Christians, and is at work in those religious traditions themselves, then surely Christians have something to learn about God through a deeper knowledge of non-Christian religions, and a deeper appreciation of the beliefs and practices of faithful Buddhists, Muslims, Hindus, etc.

Finally, I have proposed a vision for the future in which the concept of hell does not play an enduring or dominant role. Such a vision enables love, not fear, to serve as the primary motivation both for discipleship in the world and for spreading the gospel. It empowers Christians to think creatively and positively about the role their brothers and sisters of other faith traditions might have in God's economy of salvation. It is my belief that such transformative practices will serve the church well in facing the global challenges posed in our twenty-first century contexts.

---

[21] Ibid., pp. 214–5.

Pluriform Unity in Christ: Lutheran Ecclesiology and the Challenges of Religious Pluralism

Eva Harasta

The challenges of religious pluralism for Lutheran ecclesiology

Religious pluralism presents a host of challenges for today's churches. Both in theory and in practice, the situation is confusing and highly complex.[1] Yet, one basic theological implication of this confusing situation is quite obvious: the contextual quality of all religious truth claims calls for theological multiperspectivity. How can the witness to Christ be combined with a truly open invitation to learn from other religious witnesses? I suggest that ecclesiology is a promising starting point for responding to religious pluralism in a theologically constructive way.

In ecclesiology, the theological challenge and contextual inspiration of religious pluralism come together. While all ecclesiologies speak within and for their immediate contexts, Protestant ecclesiologies particularly make a point of critically reflecting upon their context (*ecclesia semper reformanda*). This practice of establishing critical distance without ignoring contextuality is apparent when inquiring ecumenically about the "truth" of the church, that is, when comparing or even confronting other ecclesiologies. Here I will interpret the religious "truth" that has been challenged by pluralism as a "communal truth," that is, as the truth of a (denominational) community of faith, as a living and testified truth.

However, ecclesiology is not an obvious starting point for responding to religious pluralism. Other theological points of departure might be (1) problematizing religious truth claims as such (religious pluralism as a challenge to exclusivism);[2]

---

[1] For an analysis from a German Lutheran perspective, cf. Dorothea Wendebourg and Reinhard Brandt (eds), *Traditionsaufbruch* (Hannover: Lutherisches Verlagshaus, 2001), esp. pp. 47–88.

[2] Or, in Alan Race's influential terminology: the exclusivist and pluralist approaches, Alan Race, *Christians and Religious Pluralism* (London: SCM Press, 1983).

and (2) reinterpreting the doctrine of God (religious pluralism as a challenge to an established understanding of God).

From the exclusivist perspective, religious pluralism appears to relativize religious truth claims,[3] and is responded to either with defensiveness or by downplaying the differences between truth claims. This approach to religious pluralism presupposes that it is possible to look at religious pluralism from the perspective of a neutral observer who can judge religious truth claims "objectively." This is also the case for the defensive stance, in which one particular truth claim is regarded as the absolute and "objective" truth for all reality. However, the premise of an "objective" evaluation of religious truth claims is not persuasive, because it contradicts the contextuality of all religious thinking as well as Luther's concept of freedom.

From the perspective of the doctrine of God, religious pluralism testifies to the ambiguity of God's being and actions.[4] God reveals Godself in various ways, and since all of them are equally true, the unity of reality cannot be assumed. Different religions live in different worlds, all of them true with regard to their particular reality.[5] In theory, this may lead to a peaceful coexistence of religions and a theology that works toward the secularization of society. But, from the ecclesiological perspective, this approach does not seem realistic because it represents a systematic separation of religious doctrines from their carriers—actual human communities. The contextuality of theology and religious practice here is elevated to an ontological principle, sacrificing the possibility of real dialogue between different revelatory traditions.

Both of these approaches see the contextuality of religion as a problem rather than an inspiration. In contrast, the ecclesiological perspective can illuminate the opportunities of multireligiosity. Ever since the Reformation, religious pluralism has been discussed as an issue concerning the truth and

---

[3] Alvin Plantinga proposed an elegant and thought-provoking defense of religious exclusivism, but concentrates on the perspective of the individual (and does not refer to relational ontology). Alvin Plantinga, "Pluralism: A Defense of Religious Exclusivism," in Thomas D. Senor (ed.), *The Rationality of Belief and the Plurality of Faith* (Ithaca, London: Cornell UP, 1995), pp. 191–215.

[4] A prominent proponent of this approach is John Hick. John Hick, "Trinity and Incarnation in the Light of Religious Pluralism," in John Hick (ed.), *Three Faiths—One God* (Houndmills/London: Macmillan, 1989), pp. 197–210.

[5] On this basis, George I. Mavrodes argues for descriptive (if not cultic) polytheism, which he (provocatively) views as compatible with Christianity. George I. Mavrodes, "Polytheism," in Thomas D. Senor (ed.), *The Rationality of Belief and the Plurality of Faith* (Ithaca, London: Cornell UP, 1995), pp. 261–86. But he does not take ecclesiology or Trinitarian theology into account. Troubling, but probably in the end to be refuted by Trinitarian theology, is Laurel C. Schneider's defense of "divine multiplicity"; she claims it can be grounded in Christology. Cf. Laurel C. Schneider, *Beyond Monotheism: A Theology of Multiplicity* (London/New York: Routledge, 2008), esp. pp. 153–63.

unity of the church. Additionally, ecclesiology focuses on the bearers of re-ligion, the communities of faith. It does so by raising up the visible form of Christ's universal claim, while simultaneously reminding us that no earthly institution can be directly identified with the kingdom of God. This poses a much more profound challenge of relativization than does any external claim by rivaling religious convictions and communities. At the same time, it does not deny the binding character of revelation. Third, if the church is a community of proclamation, revelation can be defined as revelation that is witnessed; testifying to revelation depends on God's verification. The question is not whether but how this testimony can be given under conditions of pluralism. Fourth, ecclesiology poses the question about the identity of the community of faith in relation to the world around it. Thus, it seeks to establish criteria for the critical treatment of religious pluralism.

On this basis, I will sketch four pluralistic challenges for ecclesiology, using the four attributes of the church as an hermeneutical guideline. From the perspective of the church's universality, religious pluralism leads into the question of how we can interpret the all-encompassing claim of Christ's revelation in a way that allows for a pluriformity of this one truth without compromising its binding character. I will approach this challenge by referring to Luther's concept of relational reality and Bonhoeffer's concept of Christ-reality. From the perspective of the unity of the church, religious pluralism compels ecclesiology to focus on the church as a particular, contextual unity. In approaching this challenge, I will take up Bonhoeffer's concept of the mandates. With regard to the church's apostolicity, the challenge of religious pluralism is how we can conceive of the church's proclamation in a way that respects the proclamation of other religions—but without denying our own identity. Here, I will make use of Luther's distinction between law and gospel and Bonhoeffer's thoughts on preparing Christ's way. Finally, the challenge of religious pluralism to the sanctity of the church is finding criteria for critically examining religious pluralism, while also maintaining a truly pluralist spirit. I will approach this challenge through Luther's notion of *simul iustus et peccator* and Bonhoeffer's interpretation of the church's confession of guilt.

The disruptive challenge: religious pluralism and the universality of the true church

How can we conceive of Christ's universal claim in a way that allows for the pluriformity of reality under his rule? Dietrich Bonhoeffer's *Ethics* fragments grapple with this question. In developing his concept of reality, Bonhoeffer draws on Luther's relational ontology (justification *sola fide*) and updates it for his context. Hence, I will briefly touch on Luther's anthropology before turning to Bonhoeffer's concept of Christ-reality.

The foundations of Luther's reality concept can easily be accessed in his treatise "On the Freedom of a Christian,"[6] in which he describes justification through faith as the root of individual freedom.[7] True freedom is kenotic freedom, because believers receive it from the crucified and resurrected Christ, and are called to give up their own freedom accordingly, in love for the neighbor. Faith is the form of Christ's freedom between the justified and God: Christ's righteousness is their righteousness.[8] Luther's claim is universal and absolute; there is no human freedom except in Christ's justification.[9]

Luther furthermore distinguishes between the church and the world as two different ways of Christ's universal rule (or two forms of Christian freedom in action) by differentiating between Christ as "Head" and "Lord."[10] Christ's role as Head imbues the members of his body with life.[11] As sovereign Lord, his authority encompasses the whole of creation, believers and non-believers alike. With his distinction between Head and Lord, Luther prepares to open up the uniform Christ-reality into a plurality of relationships with Christ. But he does not carry this out. His later ecclesiology, where he tends toward identifying the true church with "his" church—not to mention his disparaging statements about Judaism—attest to the fact that he was not a pluralist theologian. Yet, his insight into the fundamentally relational character of reality paves the way for a reality concept in which the *solus Christus* and a plurality of religions are not mutually exclusive.

In the *Ethics* fragments, Bonhoeffer attempts to develop such a pluriform understanding of how Christ relates to his reality. Rather than downplaying ecclesiology, Bonhoeffer ascribes a fundamental role to the church within Christ's pluriform reality: "Ethics as formation is possible only on the basis of

---

[6] *WA* 7, 20–38 (German), 39–73 (Latin).

[7] *WA* 7, 27.56.

[8] From the beginning of the tractate about freedom, Luther ascribes both the royal freedom and the priestly ministry of all believers to Christ's justifying work (*WA* 7, 26f. 56). Cf. Gerhard Ebeling, "Die königlich-priesterliche Freiheit," in Gerhard Ebeling, *Lutherstudien*, vol. 3 (Tübingen: Mohr, 1985), pp. 157–80, here p. 174.

[9] *Definitio hominis breviter est hominem iustificari fide: WA* 39/1, 176 (*Disputatio de homine*, 1536).

[10] Martin Luther, "Von dem Papsttum zu Rom wider den hochberühmten Romanisten zu Leipzig, 1520," in *WA* 6, 285–324, cf. esp. 297f.

[11] *WA* 6, 298.

the form of Jesus Christ present in Christ's church."[12] Bonhoeffer emphasizes that in Christ's world reconciliation is already present as a reality (*Wirklichkeit*), not merely as a possibility. Those who knowingly partake of reconciliation recognize the truth about the reality of the world, as already accepted into the Christ-reality.[13] The emphasis on actual reconciliation follows from a Christological focus on the resurrection: Christ's resurrection is viewed as the realization par excellence of fulfilled reality. Christ claims the whole of creation for himself; his resurrection announces and initiates the re-creation of the whole world. Here, Bonhoeffer's concept of Christ-reality seems almost like a blind approval of pluralism. Does he forfeit all differentiations within the world *coram Deo*? Not at all. Bonhoeffer stresses that it is Christ alone who identifies "world reality" with "Christ-reality." Christ's verifying work does not stop with this identification, but leads into a diversified unity.

The diversification of the one reality is not a matter of neatly distinguishable "parts" that combine into one "unity." Instead, it pertains to the multitude of ways in which Christ relates to reality as a whole. Here Bonhoeffer adapts and radicalizes Luther's differentiation between Christ as Head and Christ as Lord. Bonhoeffer makes it very clear that the different "relational modes" are not an hierarchy. They are Christ's ways of relating to reality as a whole that correspond to different aspects of his person and his work. The unity of reality has its only root in its reconciled relationship with Christ. But Christ is a living person, not a principle. Christ shapes the world as God incarnate, as the crucified and resurrected one.[14] While Christ realizes his form in all of world reality, the church is the place in which he manifests himself "vicariously and representatively as a model for all human beings."[15] This is how

---

[12] Dietrich Bonhoeffer, *Ethics*, transl. by Reinhard Krauss, Douglas W. Stott and Charles C. West; Clifford Green (ed.), *Dietrich Bonhoeffer Works*, vol. 6 (*DBWE* 6) (Minneapolis: Fortress, 2004), p. 102. German original: Dietrich Bonhoeffer, *Ethik*, ed. by Ilse Tödt, Heinz E. Tödt; Ernst Feil and Clifford Green (eds), *Dietrich Bonhoeffer Werke*, vol. 6, 2nd edition (*DBW* 6) (Gütersloh: Gütersloher Verlagshaus, 1998), p. 90. In the following, most references are given with page numbers of both editions; however, the English translation cites the page numbers of the German edition *Dietrich Bonhoeffer Werke*, so even where (occasionally) the English page numbers are not given, the references are easily located.

[13] *DBW* 6, pp. 39–40. "There is no explaining the mystery that only a part of humanity recognizes the form of its savior." (*DBWE* 6, p. 96/*DBW* 6, pp. 83–84). But this "mystery" also has positive implications, as Peter M. Scott argues: "The theological task is therefore not to apply the mystery of reconciliation to the doctrine of creation but to attempt to rediscover and relearn the dynamics of reconciliation in creation." Peter Manley Scott, "Postnatural Humanity? Bonhoeffer, Creaturely Freedom and the Mystery of Reconciliation in Creation," in Kirsten Busch Nielsen, Ulrik Nissen and Christiane Tietz (eds), *Mysteries in the Theology of Dietrich Bonhoeffer* (Göttingen: Vandenhoek & Ruprecht, 2007), pp. 111–34.

[14] *DBW* 6, pp. 81–83.

[15] *DBWE* 6, p. 97 (*DBW* 6, p. 84).

Bonhoeffer strikes a balance between the universal claim of reconciliation in Christ and the particular role of the church.

In the tradition of Luther, Bonhoeffer focuses on the cross and the resurrection, but he places more emphasis on the resurrection than does Luther. Also, following Luther, Bonhoeffer does not conceive of Christ's ascension and *status exaltationis* as the Christological "form." Thus, when Bonhoeffer describes the relationship between Christ and the believer, he does not reflect on the mediation of this relationship by the Holy Spirit, but only focuses on Christ's formative action. In contrast, the state of exaltation refers to Christ's (specific) withdrawal after his ascension, by taking a seat at the Father's right hand. In this way, the ascension points to the "cooperation" of the Holy Spirit with Christ—to a truly Trinitarian ontology.

The absence of the ascension as a Christological criterion forecloses viewing Christ as relating to and influencing the world precisely through an involved withdrawal. As the exalted, Christ is the implicit form of his reality, gently at work, perhaps even wondering himself about how human beings relate to the truth of reality in divine love. This can be helpful when trying to come to terms with religious pluralism from the point of view of Christ's claim on the world.

From Bonhoeffer's perspective, such an "involved withdrawal" can at least be approached through the incarnation, as the incarnation reveals that Christ is present even in places where the cross and the resurrection have not been proclaimed explicitly. The church also has to take note of this implicit type of formation, because it belongs to world reality, just as world reality belongs to the church.[16] The Christ-reality is a diversified, yet undivided reality; it leads human beings not into conflict, but into agreement. Here Bonhoeffer may point towards a "community of mutuality" that "recognize[s] need as a gift that makes us kenotically open toward others."[17] The church owes its Christ-conformity to Christ's creative acts alone, not to its own endeavors. It testifies to an ontological need that can only be fulfilled by Christ, and yet is full of trust in Christ.

---

[16] The following idea of Bonhoeffer's from one of his prison letters also needs to be read in this context: "God is beyond in the midst of our life. The church stands, not at the boundaries where human powers give out, but in the middle of the village." Dietrich Bonhoeffer, *Letters and Papers from Prison,* ed. by Eberhard Bethge and transl. by Reginald Fuller & others (New York: Macmillan, 1972), p. 282. Although Bonhoeffer here refers to "God," that does not mean he distances himself from the Christocentricity that characterizes his theology as Rebekka A. Klein maintains. Rebekka A. Klein, "Der Andere und der Liebende," in Andreas Klein and Matthias Geist (eds), "Bonhoeffer weiterdenken…." (Münster et al.: LIT, 2007), pp. 72–73.

[17] Allen G. Jorgenson, "Mutuality, Kenosis and Spirited Hope in the Face of Empire," in Karen L. Bloomquist (ed.), *Being the Church in the Midst of Empire,* Theology in the Life of the Church series, vol. 1 (Geneva/Minneapolis: The Lutheran World Federation/Lutheran University Press, 2007), p. 163.

Thus, Bonhoeffer suggests a Lutheran concept of reality from a thoroughly Christological perspective. The "Lutheran" quality of his ontology comes to the fore by how he asserts the true and real presence of Christ in the world without equating this presence with specific institutions.[18] How Bonhoeffer identifies world reality with Christ-reality may be criticized as a dangerous blurring of the distinction between church and world. But, conversely, it may also be seen as a trailblazing step toward an ecclesiology friendly toward pluralism. Bonhoeffer shows that (religious) pluralism does not necessarily mean the disintegration of the one reality into "parts" that are irreconcilable or alien to one another. But, does Christianity misappropriate and co-opt other religions in this way? Or might the church here be in danger of losing its own space?

The visible challenge: religious pluralism and the unity of the church

From the perspective of the unity of the church, religious pluralism provokes ecclesiology to focus on the church as a particular, contextual unity, correlated with the overall unity of Christ's reality. Here, Luther is not of help. His intention was not to find truth in strange places (like Rome), but to overcome misguided forms of the church. Yet, his polemical approach can serve as a warning against suspending the truth question or overlooking interdenominational (or even interreligious) differences.

If we interpret the church as one specific manifestation of Christ's relationship to the world as a whole, then its specific unity follows from its universality. The churches represent peculiar crystallizations of how Christ relates to reality as a whole. But how can we comprehend their unity in the face of denominational and religious pluralism? From a Lutheran perspective, it is impossible to identify one specific institution with the one true church. Then, what remains of the visibility of this unity?

Notwithstanding his critical stance toward dividing reality into sacred and profane,[19] Bonhoeffer indicates that there is a specific "space" (or "realm")

---

[18] Elsewhere as well Bonhoeffer is mainly interested in the relation between church and state—for contextual reasons; e.g., Dietrich Bonhoeffer, "Theologisches Gutachten: Staat und Kirche," in Jørgen Glenthøj, Ulrich Kabitz and Wolf Krötke (eds), *Dietrich Bonhoeffer Werke*, vol. 16 (*DBW* 16) (Gütersloh: Gütersloher Verlagshaus, 1996), pp. 506–35. English: Dietrich Bonhoeffer, "A Theological Position Paper on State and Church," in Mark S. Brocker (ed.), *Dietrich Bonhoeffer Works*, vol. 16, transl. by Lisa E. Dahill and Douglas W. Stott (*DBWE* 16) (Minneapolis: Fortress, 2006), pp. 502–28.

[19] *DBW* 6, pp. 41–43.

of the church within Christ-reality.[20] His starting point is the form of Christ incarnate. Christ has accepted humankind by becoming a specific human being. Precisely because he already has reconciled the whole of reality with God, Christ can also claim a specific, particular space within his reality.[21]

Bonhoeffer describes the particular, specific form of the church by viewing it as one of four divine "mandates" (church, family, work/culture and authority). The mandates can be understood as customs in the relationship between the world and Christ; Bonhoeffer here sketches the appropriate creaturely responses to Christ's formative work.[22] Entirely in keeping with Luther (and Article VII of the Augsburg Confession), he states that it is the church's mandate to proclaim Christ.[23] Yet, for Bonhoeffer, the reverse is also true: wherever Christ is proclaimed, there is the church. The church exists for its mission to convey the message of reconciliation to other people and to address them as participants in Christ's reality. Nevertheless, the church is also an end in itself.[24]

As one of the four mandates, the church is interrelated with the other mandates in a matrix of "with-one-another," "for-one-another" and "over-against-one-another."[25] Bonhoeffer has not elaborated on the interrelationships between the mandates. But the three terms can help develop a concept of the church's unity that deals constructively with denominational

---

[20] *DBWE* 6, p. 62 (*DBW* 6, p. 48).

[21] *DBW* 6, p. 49.

[22] Already Karl Barth criticized Bonhoeffer's selection of the mandates as arbitrary but he did not elaborate on what part of reality he found missing. Karl Barth, *Die Kirchliche Dogmatik,* vol. III/4 (Zürich: Evangelischer Verlag, 1951), p. 22. Bonhoeffer himself reflected on friendship as a possible fifth mandate in a prison letter, finally deciding that friendship belonged to the mandates like the cornflower belongs to a field of wheat. Dietrich Bonhoeffer, *Widerstand und Ergebung: Briefe und Aufzeichnungen aus der Haft*; Christian Gremmels, Eberhard Bethge. Renate Bethge and Ilse Tödt (eds), *Dietrich Bonhoeffer Werke,* vol. 8 (*DBW* 8) (Gütersloh: Gütersloher Verlagshaus, 1998), p. 292, no. 102: letter dated 23 January 1944. In the same letter, he differentiates "culture" and "work" (ibid., p. 291). In *Ethics*, work and culture seem to function as synonyms (compare *DBW* 6, pp. 54, 57 with *DBW* 6, p. 392).

[23] *DBW* 6, p. 59. Cf. *DBWE* 6, p. 396, "The mandate of the church is the divine word" (*DBW* 6, p. 399).

[24] Cf. Dietrich Bonhoeffer, *Sanctorum Communio: Eine dogmatische Untersuchung zur Soziologie der Kirche*; Joachim von Soosten (ed.), *Dietrich Bonhoeffer Werke,* vol. 1, second edition (*DBW* 1) (Gütersloh: Gütersloher Verlagshaus, 2005), pp. 176–7. English: Dietrich Bonhoeffer, *Sanctorum Communio: A Theological Study of the Sociology of the Church*, transl. by Reinhard Krauss and Nancy Lukens; Clifford J. Green (ed.), *Dietrich Bonhoeffer Works* vol. 1 (*DBWE* 1) (Minneapolis: Fortress, 1998), pp. 115–6.

[25] *DBWE* 6, p. 393 (*DBW* 6, p. 397). In his dissertation, Bonhoeffer proposed an understanding of "community of Spirit" that combines a relation of "with-each-other" between church community and church member and relations of "active being-for-each-other" between the individual church members (*DBWE* 1, pp. 177–92, here p. 178; *DBW* 1, pp. 117–28). The concept of the mandates seems to expand these ecclesiological principles by describing them as principles of all reality (as Christ-reality).

and religious pluralism. Going beyond Bonhoeffer's original meaning, it could be suggested that the different Christian denominations function as manifestations of the different aspects of Christ's explicit relationship to his reality—"with-one-another," "for-one-another" and "over-against-each-other." This is their common ministry of proclamation, even when they ostensibly stand "over-against-each-other." The Christian denominations have in common that they are places where Christ's relational acts are explicitly proclaimed. In this, they differ from non-Christian religions. Yet, the Christian denominations cannot be described as qualitatively superior to other religions because all reality depends on receiving its truth from Christ. With these thoughts, however, we have moved quite far from Luther's completely "non-pluralistic" definition of churchly unity.[26]

The competitive challenge: Religious pluralism and the apostolicity of the church

How can we conceive of the church's proclamation in a way that respects the proclamation of other religions—without denying our own identity, and without leveling the difference between interreligious and ecumenical dialogue? The church proclaims Christ's justifying grace. Is it therefore a community of contrast, calling on the sinful world to repent, or should proclamation first and foremost focus on inner-ecclesial communication? While Luther certainly stresses both of these functions, he delineates a positive understanding of how the church relates to the world as well, because Christian freedom leads to responsibility for changing our circumstances, as well as changing the church itself in order to prepare the way for Christ. Faith releases an hermeneutical competence for distinguishing between gospel and law.[27]

According to Luther, the community is responsible for granting or refusing forgiveness in the name of Christ.[28] This is the priestly responsibility of the church, and is vital for the community.[29] If this key ministry (in its twofold form) is performed faithfully—that is, relying solely on God's grace—then

---

[26] Martin Luther, "Contra Henricum Regem Angliae, 1522," defines the unity of the church as "*idem sapere, idem iudicare, idem cognoscere, idem probare, idem docere, idem confiteri, idem sequi,*" in *WA* 10/2, 219.

[27] Martin Luther, "*De servo arbitrio, 1525,*" in *WA* 18, 677.

[28] Martin Luther, "Treatise on the Keys, 1530," in *WA* 30/2, 465–507, esp. 498.

[29] *WA* 30/2, 502.

it is a public manifestation of Christ's work.[30] The community has no authority of its own as a community of salvation; it thrives on Christ's grace
and justice. With regard to the Word of God beyond the church, Luther
sets forth the distinction between the "two kingdoms."

Luther narrows down the functions of political decision makers for church
reform by discussing the position of the church as an institution within the
social and political hierarchies, and by asking about the limit of authority for
individual Christians within the church.[31] The secular authority does God's
good work by exerting force and pressure, that is, by subduing evil with the
law.[32] Thus, Luther grants secular authority its own type of proclamation, but
clearly limits it to interpersonal relationships. The secular authority must not
interfere with people's relationship to God. Nonetheless, the church has a
public ministry in the secular realm: proclaiming justification has political
implications even as it shows the kenotic character of Christ's kingdom—he
reigns not by force, but by justifying grace.[33] Of course, this is also important
for the interpretation of the ministry of mission,[34] and has implications for
interreligious dialogue. An emphasis on kenosis for interreligious relations
may safeguard an inclusive Lutheran approach to multireligiosity against
presuming superiority over the other partners in the dialogue.

Bonhoeffer refers to Luther's distinction between the two forms of
Christ's rule, but emphasizes their unity: the proclamation of the resurrected Christ leads to insights about penultimate life, where we await the
ultimate. Christ's resurrection is the absolute ultimate; "the penultimate
becomes what it is only through the ultimate."[35] Nevertheless, the penultimate must be respected and protected as such.[36] Bonhoeffer does not

---

[30] Luther emphasizes the public character of the keys especially with regard to the binding key, *WA*
30/2, 503.

[31] Martin Luther, "Secular Authority: To What Extent it Should be Obeyed, 1523," in *WA* 11, 245–81.
Regarding Christian individuals, *WA* 11, 246.

[32] *WA* 11, 251. Here, Luther treats the relation of church and state as an instance of individual discipleship (*WA* 11, 258.264 as in "To the Christian Nobility of the German Nation, 1520"). Accordingly,
Bornkamm identifies a perspective of pastoral care in Luther's political theology as Luther rather speaks
as a councilor than as a proponent of systems theory. Heinrich Bornkamm, "Der Christ und die zwei
Reiche," in Heinrich Bornkamm, *Luther* (Gütersloh: Gütersloher Verlag, 1975), pp. 255–66.

[33] *WA* 11, 271.

[34] Cf. Bloomquist, op. cit. (note 17), p. 18.

[35] *DBWE* 6, p. 159 (*DBW* 6, p. 151). Ernst Feil underlines that there is no way from the penultimate to
the ultimate, but only from the ultimate to the penultimate. Ernst Feil, *Die Theologie Dietrich Bonhoeffers*,
5th edition (Münster et al.: LIT, 2005), p. 297, fn. 35.

[36] *DBW* 6, p. 152.

confuse the reality of the eschaton with the situation under the conditions of sin, but calls upon believers to take the world reality seriously as a locus of Christ's grace. The church's mandate is to prepare the way for the ultimate, for Christ. This preparation is "a commission of immeasurable responsibility given to all who know about the coming of Jesus Christ."[37] Yet, "preparing the way for Christ" is an act of Christ himself in which he makes use of the church.[38] The reality outside of the church also belongs to the already emerging Christ-reality and must be made aware of this fact. But, belonging to the Christ-reality is not limited to the church. It has many, but not infinite or arbitrary forms. This interpretation of world reality is certainly very friendly toward pluralism, but critics may fear that it leads to a justification of the status quo and may overlook the critical potential of churchly proclamation.

The pure challenge: Religious pluralism and the sanctity of the church

How can we find criteria for critically examining religious pluralism while maintaining a truly pluralist spirit?

The immediate relationship with God brought about by justification correlates with the priesthood of all believers.[39] Still, as their deeds continue to convict them, believers continuously depend on justification by Christ's grace (*simul iustus et peccator*).[40] But the priesthood of the justified also represents a mission for the believers. In Christ's discipleship, they are to see themselves and their interpersonal relationships *coram Deo*.[41] Luther pointedly calls the community of believers a priestly community,[42] which means that communal freedom follows the same principles as individual freedom. The church as a community also falls under the conditions of the *simul iustus et peccator*. This aspect, however, gradually fades into the

---

[37] *DBWE* 6, p. 163 (*DBW* 6, p. 155).

[38] *DBW* 6, p. 154.

[39] *WA* 7, 27.56.

[40] *WA* 7, 54.25.

[41] *WA* 7, 27. Cf. ibid., 38.69.

[42] Luther discusses the priesthood of all believers in his paragraph about the (Roman) sacrament of ordination and defines it as an immediate implication of being baptized. (Martin Luther, "*De captivitate Babylonica ecclesiae praeludium*," 1520," in *WA* 6, 564.566).

background of Luther's ecclesiology as he tends to identify the emerging Protestant church with the true church of apostolic times,[43] and tends to lessen the difference between the visible church and God's kingdom. Yet, it is only by emphasizing the difference between the church and God's kingdom that space is created for honoring other ways Christ and his reality are related—and thus for a constructive ecclesiological response to pluralism.

Bonhoeffer takes up Luther's emphasis on the effective quality of justification, and on the continuing dependency of the believers on Christ: "Christian life means being human in the power of Christ's becoming human, being judged and pardoned in the power of the cross, living a new life in the power of resurrection. No one of these is without the others."[44] Yet, Bonhoeffer strongly emphasizes *simul iustus et peccator* as an ecclesiological criterion, and even begins to expand it to encompass the whole of world reality.

Bonhoeffer defines the church's "sanctity" in terms of the crucified Christ, that is, in terms of the judgment of grace. The form of the crucified Christ is the form of the judged sinner. When the church is conformed to this form of Christ, it takes the place of the rightfully condemned in which Christ has placed himself to reconcile the fallen world reality with God. In facing the reconciled form of the crucified and resurrected Christ, the sinner's eyes are opened to what being a sinner means. Acknowledging one's own guilt is only possible because we have already been reconciled with God.[45]

The church is "the place where this acknowledgement of guilt becomes real;" it is the place where this acknowledged guilt of all fallen reality is confessed before God.[46] But the subsequent salvation is rooted not in the church but in Christ's grace, which is the basis of the church's dignity or sanctity. The church as the place where guilt is acknowledged and confessed means that the church, due to Christ's grace through the resurrection, is also the place of rebirth and renewal.[47] Christ's cross and resurrection are inseparable, which is also evident in the church: "Only [!] as drawn into

---

[43] Martin Luther, "Wider Hans Worst, 1541," in *WA* 51, 469–572.

[44] *DBWE* 6, p. 159 (*DBW* 6, p. 150).

[45] *DBW* 6, p. 125.

[46] *DBW* 6, p. 126. For Bonhoeffer, penitence is the fundamental aspect of justifying faith, the visible form of the *simul iustus et peccator*—individually as well as communally. Against Gregory L. Jones, who thinks Bonhoeffer deemphasizes the communal confession of guilt; Gregory L. Jones, "The Cost of Forgiveness: Grace, Christian Community and the Politics of Worldly Discipleship," in Wayne W. Floyd and Charles Marsh (eds), *Theology and the Practice of Responsibility* (Valley Forge: Trinity Press International, 1994), pp. 149–69, here p. 155.

[47] *DBW* 6, p. 126.

the shame of the cross, the public death of the sinner, is the church—and the individual in it—received into the community of glory of the one who was awakened to new righteousness and new life."[48]

Just as the guilt of the whole world falls upon the church when it is led to confess, so does the revivification of the church in turn affect the whole of world reality.[49] The church must be aware of itself as a part and an expression of the communal, political, economic and social conditions surrounding it. It is called to repent of the sin of the world, which as one indivisible whole stands in its opposition to Christ (explicitly or implicitly). Bonhoeffer himself suggests such a confession by the church.[50]

Insisting that the church should first confess its own sin is a distinctively Lutheran interpretation of the church's sanctity, consistent with *simul iustus et peccator*. What would such a confession by the church look like today? How are Lutheran churches guilty in their present interactions with other religions?

Christ taking form "among us today and here"[51] amid religious pluralism

Luther's relational ontology leads to an interpretation of reality in which the *solus Christus* and religious plurality are not in contradiction. Bonhoeffer has taken decisive steps toward such an interpretation, preparing the way for a positive appraisal of concurrent religious claims and communities. But further differentiation is needed. The ability to honor the plurality of religions theologically may be a sign of progress, but it leads to the pragmatic question of what this means for our proclamation as a particular faith community.

Christ unifies his reality by relating to it as a living person. He does so in specific, idiosyncratic ways, both in– and outside the church. Bonhoeffer

---

[48] *DBWE* 6, p. 142 (*DBW* 6, p. 133).

[49] Bonhoeffer speaks of a hoped-for renewal of the "occident" (*Abendland; DBW* 6, p. 133). This confinement to the West (Bonhoeffer refers to Europe and the USA: *DBW* 6, pp. 88f.) does not agree with Bonhoeffer's emphasis on the universality of Christ's claim. Yet it is anachronistic to hold this against Bonhoeffer—he intended a widening of the horizon of the German regional churches (*Landeskirchen*) by reminding them that their context was broader than the German state borders. Cf. Dietrich Bonhoeffer, "Die Bekennende Kirche und Ökumene," in Otto Dudzus, Jürgen Henkys, Sabine Bobert-Stützel, Dirk Schulz and Ilse Tödt (eds), *Dietrich Bonhoeffer Werke*, vol. 14 (*DBW* 14) (Gütersloh: Gütersloher Verlagshaus, 1996), pp. 378–99; here: pp. 379–80.

[50] *DBW* 6, pp. 129–33.

[51] *DBWE* 6, p. 99 (*DBW* 6, p. 87).

insists that Christ has also accepted the penultimate—the world outside of his explicit proclamation. The first option, then, would be to gather divergent religious claims under the umbrella of the penultimate and to define the church's proclamation in this space as the "call for the ultimate," that is, exclusively as a law sermon in the sense of the *usus politicus legis*. Drawing attention to the relevance of God's laws for political coexistence certainly is an important task for the church. Yet it is the first of two steps in dealing with other religions in pluralist contexts. Good political relations with other religious groups are essential, but they do not express how one's own proclamation—because of the universality of Christ's claim—actually may depend on the testimony of other religions. Truly engaging with religious pluralism within the Christ-reality implies proclaiming in a way that respects otherness. Such proclamation seeks to find Christ's grace in otherness. From this perspective, the various religious testimonies depend on each other because they depend on the unity of Christ's reality—which, of course, is not theirs to control but lies in Christ's hands alone.

Bonhoeffer's notion that the mandates are interrelated in "with-each-other, for-each-other, over-against-each-other" is his way of describing the diversification of reality from the perspective of the world. With this notion, he expands on Luther's distinction of the two forms of Christ's rule. Bonhoeffer's mandates were not conceived for the sake of interreligious dialogue, but for examining the relationship between church and state. Thus, I am adapting his notion of the mandates when I use them as a model for Christ's personal, living and relational truth.

"With-each-other" implies that it is an essential task of the church to engage with other religious communities. That the church engages in this interaction solely for the sake of Christ does not mean it misappropriates its counterparts as being anonymous Christians. The interaction with each other occurs in proclamation, the proclamation of law and gospel. It also occurs in the form of a question—of vulnerable openness—because it emulates the kenosis of Christ. The church must expect to find the gospel of Christ in unexpected places, in the testimony of other religions, such as in the testimony of the Muslim immigrant in whom Christ may reveal himself to the Christian.[52] Keeping a truly open mind and a truly open heart,

---

[52] In order to describe neighborly love, Karl Barth interprets the parable of the Good Samaritan (Lk 10:29–37; Karl Barth, *Die Kirchliche Dogmatik* vol. I/2 (Zürich: Evangelischer Verlag, 1948), pp. 460–2. Could this be viewed as a prefiguration of Christian relationships to other religions? It may be no coincidence that it is a religiously different person—a Samaritan—who acts here as the good neighbor.

takes considerable strength—a strength that the community of believers receives through the Holy Spirit.

"Over-against-each-other" means engaging with other religious communities without leaving behind critical thought, much less denying our own bond to Christ. But this opposition, this "over-against-each-other," is not a clash of religious cultures, because above all, the church's repentance acknowledges its own guilt. The church is guilty of having rejected its own truth, Christ's grace. Thus, the "over-against-each-other" is a trace of the *simul iustus et peccator*, Christ's judgment of reality. True judgment remains Christ's prerogative. Yet, the call for repentance is part of the church's ministry because within Christ's reality, community implies responsibility for each other, and the knowledge that every act of repentance follows from Christ's forgiveness.

"For-each-other" calls for seeing oneself as standing immediately before God along with other religious communities. It means interceding for each other and trusting in the anticipated new creation. Obviously, this is not a mission that the religious communities can accomplish on their own strength. It leads us to the plea for the Holy Spirit. It also calls individual believers to pray and to witness, each in their own way, each out of the particular situation of their individual existence.

I have argued, on Lutheran grounds, for an inclusive perspective. From the perspective of other religions, there of course are different angles to the question of truth and pluralism. For the Lutheran churches, it would amount to self-denial to engage with other religions while ignoring Christ. Yet—and this is the kenotic point—on the basis of the Lutheran heritage, interacting with other religions is not about being right. Rather, it is about trusting Christ's actions and being his witnesses, about getting to know Christ, perhaps in surprising, new ways. Backed by the strength of the resurrection, this endeavor is not dispirited, bashful, or desperate—it is an endeavor filled with hope and trust.

On the Art of Properly Distinguishing Law from Law

Allen G. Jorgenson

God speaks but one Word. To be sure, it is variously heard: here as law, there as gospel. In either event, it is the one Word, spoken by the Father and borne by the Spirit who births hearers through both creation and redemption. This is the starting point from which this chapter proceeds. What does it mean to confess the unity of the divine Word even while admitting the various modes in which that Word is heard? Moreover, what might this mean when students of the Reformation pause to ponder the dialectic of law/gospel as further illumined by the equally significant, although less acknowledged, paradox that law itself is twofold in nature.[1] In sum, this paper will argue that although attention to the art of properly distinguishing law and gospel is foundational for Lutheran parlance, Lutherans ignore the task of distinguishing the first and second uses of the law at their peril. This article will propose that this is an especially pressing project today in light of the ecological crisis as well as the crisis of meaning.

I first revisit the very nature of the law/gospel dialectic, underscoring the Wittenberg theologian's insistence on that particular taxonomy and its significance for a Lutheran soteriology. I next examine the two uses of the law, exploring the latent possibilities for a theology of creation in closer attention to the nature of the first use of the law. In the final part of the chapter, I examine how this first use of the law provides resources for rethinking the gift of diversity as it bears upon both creation and redemption.

---

[1] Here I will not pursue the question of the third use of the law insofar as it was not favored by Luther. Moreover, its treatment in confessional documents does not suggest its significance for the following discussion. Cf. Timothy J. Wengert, *A Formula for Parish Practice: Using the Formula of Concord in Congregations* (Grand Rapids: William B. Eerdmans, 2006), p. 91: "As we shall see, for the concordists, the third use of the law was nothing but first and second uses applied to Christians." The author gratefully acknowledges that financial support for research related to this work was received from a grant funded partly by the Wilfrid Laurier University operating fund and partly the Social Sciences and Human Research Council Institutional Grant awarded to Wilfrid Laurier University.

On the art of distinguishing and ordering law and gospel

From the outset, I affirm the critical and indispensable nature of the task of distinguishing law and gospel: it is, in fact, the *sine qua non* for the possibility of distinguishing law from law. Moreover, like all arts, this is one that takes a lifetime to master. But, as I hope to demonstrate below, distinguishing law from law itself sharpens the tools for the task of distinguishing law and gospel. I begin by clarifying the Lutheran insistence on the particular taxonomy of first law, then gospel.

The Lutheran Reformers understood well that the question of whether to begin with law or gospel was of profound import. The possibilities and perils of the various answers to this question are written into the Formula of Concord; within certain Lutheran circles, the law–gospel order was first reversed and in some instances reduced to gospel alone. [2] The Confessors did not allow this possibility, asserting that the sinner experiences first the terror of law before the release of gospel. This is not an insignificant insight, yet it intuits a deeper theological affirmation. It suggests that repentance itself is under the aegis of grace, since both law and gospel are instances of God's self-communication. Yet the primacy of grace is often equated with the primacy of the gospel via a theological paradigm that, under the influence of Karl Barth, has become decisive for many theologies.

Among the many places in which Barth addresses this theme, the second volume of his doctrine of the Word of God is especially important.[3] Barth here ponders the relationship of law to gospel in light of the human call to praise God, especially in light of the actual reality of the neighbor. Barth teases out a provocative phenomenology of the neighbor. Strong reminders of Luther's treatment of the law are evoked here as Barth notes that the neighbor holds a mirror before us; they remind us of our precarious position in life, and before God. Law functions as a mirror. Law is also something of a hammer, driving home the difficulty of living well with the neighbor and so summoning us to our knees. Yet, Barth also writes that the neighbor acquires a sacramental sign for us,[4] summoning us afresh to the love of God. "If we were not forgiven, our neighbor has nothing at

---

[2] Cf. "The Epitome—Article V: Law and Gospel" and "The Solid Declaration—Article V: Law and Gospel," in Robert Kolb and Timothy J. Wengert (eds), *The Book of Concord: The Confessions of the Evangelical Lutheran Church* (Minneapolis: Fortress Press, 2000), pp. 500ff. and pp. 581ff.

[3] For what follows, cf. Karl Barth, *Church Dogmatics: The Doctrine of the Word of God,* vol. 1, part 2, ed, by G.W. Bromiley and T. F. Torrance, transl. by G. T. Thomson and Harold Knight (Edinburgh: T&T Clark, 1956), pp. 434–40.

[4] Ibid., p. 437.

all to say to us when he exemplifies our sin and misery. Our meeting with him can only lead to another act in the great revolt of Adam."[5]

Yet Christians know their neighbor as "a sacramental sign" precisely because the neighbor is finally known in Christ. And so,

> [f]or the one who not only knows the need, but also the help in need, a very definite obligation to his neighbor arises out of the fellowship which he has with him in need. Note that only now, even from the standpoint of the Law, can we speak meaningfully and seriously about the claim of our neighbor and our responsibility to him. His claim and our responsibility are a direct result of the fact that he has done us a service and a benefit as a living sign of the grace of God. In relation to our neighbor, then, the road does not lead, as we are often told, from Law to Gospel—there is no road that way—but from Gospel to Law.[6]

Theologians respond in various ways to Barth's reversal of the Lutheran taxonomy. Gustaf Wingren is especially important in this regard.[7] He reads Luther through the twin lens of historical enquiry and theological sensitivity. He continually balances the need to locate Luther's passion for a center in the midst of the vicissitudes of history. In considering the event of salvation, this makes him a useful interpreter of Luther's treatment of law and gospel.

Luther shared with the medieval thinkers, who he otherwise disparaged, the assumption that knowing and being are convertible. Knowing and being advance and retreat hand in hand. Who I am changes as I learn, and, as I change, my learning changes. For this reason, Luther can talk about a new kind of knowing that accompanies the hearing of the gospel. When we have been made new, our knowing too begins to be renewed. This is made clear in Luther's commentary on Genesis:

> In this manner this image of the new creature begins to be restored by the Gospel in this life, but it will not be finished in this life. But when it is finished in the kingdom of the Father, then the will will be truly free and good, the mind truly enlightened, and the memory persistent.[8]

---

[5] Ibid., p. 435.

[6] Ibid., pp. 437, 438.

[7] Cf. Gustaf Wingren, *The Living Word*, transl. by Victor C. Pogue (Philadelphia: Muhlenberg Press, 1960); Gustaf Wingren, *Creation and Law*, transl. by Ross Mckenzie (Philadelphia: Muhlenberg Press, 1961); Gustaf Wingren, *Creation and Gospel* (Toronto: The Edwin Mellen Press, 1979).

[8] Martin Luther, "Lectures on Genesis, Chapters 1–5," in Jaroslav Pelikan (ed.), *Luther's Works*, vol. 1 (Saint Louis: Concordia Publishing House, 1958), p. 65.

Luther, in fact, was a radical and ingenious thinker, who worked with the intellectual tools at hand, the convertibility of knowing and being among the most significant. This medieval presupposition, borrowed from Aristotle, is upended in modernity. Under Kant's tutelage, questions of being are bracketed and human thinking comes to the fore. Barth, of course, was not thoroughly Kantian yet like Luther he worked with the philosophical tools at hand. Not surprising then, when he talks of revelation it is largely explicated in terms of knowing. This is because Barth does not equate being saved with knowing it. Wingren asserts that, for Barth, being saved and knowing it to be so are disparate *theologomena* (theological themes). Revelation is a knowing event centered on the Christ who reveals himself to those who are known without knowing it.[9] For this reason, Barth is more interested in the order of knowing than in the taxonomy of the creed.[10]

Here Wingren finds Barth least helpful, in fact, problematic. Wingren invites us to bracket Enlightenment assumptions when pondering the biblical narrative. The Bible does not move from knowing to being, but from creation to *eschaton.* And so, Wingren asserts that both the Scriptures and the creeds narrate a movement from creation to Fall to redemption, a narration that begins with law insofar as it was with humanity from the beginning. Law, in the first instance, is gift without condemnation. The Fall, of course, changes all of that. Yet, even with the second use of the law, something of the first use is resident. In our condition of fallenness we know of God's demand. Insofar as we know God's demand we know God's gift, in a world in which law is the condition for the possibility of life ordered for the good of all. As Wingren asserts, by judging human works, the law valorizes them.[11] Yet, it not only judges human works, but reminds us that the law makes such human work possible.

On the art of distinguishing between different uses of the law

It is important, first of all, to recognize how pervasively Luther affirms creation. His sacramental theology confirms the human need to know sensually; his affirmation of the common priesthood celebrates the ordinary;[12]

---

[9] *Creation and Gospel*, op. cit. (note 7), p. 40.

[10] Ibid., p. 41.

[11] Ibid., p. 98. n. 36.

[12] Charles Taylor, *A Secular Age* (Cambridge: Harvard University Press, 2007), p. 179.

his treatment of the two reigns proposes the validity of what is considered secular. Continually we see Luther asserting that created reality is good in spite of our abuse of this most precious gift from God. Wingren considers the first use of the law to be a corollary of a doctrine of creation.

It could be objected that Wingren and others make a drastic mistake in linking the first use of the law too closely with Luther's doctrine of creation. After all, did not the human community in Eden consist of church and family, and expand only after the Fall to include government? Did Luther not follow Augustine in seeing government as what God provided only after the Fall? Although here Luther followed Augustine, the following points to an important dimension in Luther's lectures on Genesis:

> After the church has been established, the household government is also set up, when Eve is added to Adam as his companion. Thus the temple is earlier than the home, and it is also better this way. Moreover, there was no government of the state before sin, for there was no need of it. Civil government is a remedy required by our corrupted nature.[13]

Two points are worth noting. First, the church precedes family and civil government follows sin. Note also how Luther describes the family as "the household government." Of course, one does not usually speak of households as governments, yet here Luther does precisely that because civil and household government both exist by the gift of order. Moreover, our propensity to think first of civil government when we hear of law is a betrayal of the development as narrated by Luther. Household government comes first; civil government is added after the Fall, when "households" threaten the destruction of the human race.

Further, in his discussion of the Fourth Commandment, Luther underscores that civil government depends on the family:

> Thus all who are called masters stand in the place of parents and must derive from them their power and authority to govern. They are all called fathers in the Scripture because in their sphere of authority they have been commissioned as fathers and ought to have fatherly hearts toward their people.[14]

---

[13] Luther, op. cit. (note 8), pp. 103, 104.

[14] "The Large Catechism—The Ten Commandments," in Kolb and Wengert, op. cit. (note 2), p. 406.

Luther helps us to see that civil government is a derived and secondary manifestation of government. In the first instance, it is the family that provides order in human society. Order names here what we otherwise call the gift of the law. If we forget this, we misconstrue the relationship between the first and second uses of the law, as well as the relationship between law and gospel.

The first use of the law points to God's intention for order in human life. Order does not, of course, mean mindless conformity to extraneous rules. Luther here simply shares in the thought of his intellectual forebears who lived with a worldview that presumed meaning was to be found in the universe because it was fittingly and lovingly ordered by a Creator. Meaning was deemed to be immanent in the cosmos.[15] Moreover, order resided both in the church (Adam and Eve at the Tree of Life) and in the family (Adam and Even in relationship). After the Fall, order is given as a gift to restrain human sin, which is named by Luther as the civil use of the law. Yet the first use of the law bears a broader connotation than the manifest laws of the land:

> [God] has established [marriage] before all others as the first of all institutions, and he created man and woman differently (as is evident) not for indecency but to be true to each other, to be fruitful, to beget children, and to nurture and bring them up to the glory of God. [. . .] Married life is no matter for jest or idle curiosity, but it is a glorious institution and an object of God's serious concern.[16]

In pairing civil law with the governance over marriage, Luther reminds us that the first use of the law points to the gift of order in creation, granted for our good. Lack of clarity about this leads to confusion in understanding the relationships between world, self and society. Lutherans have a tendency to speak so frequently of the theological use of the law that we forget about its first use. Reading Luther can guard against this, even though certain readings of the Confessions can contribute to this, because they primarily speak of law in theological terms. The problem arises when, in reading Luther and the Confessions, we transfer the condemnatory character of theological use of the law to the civil use of the law. This is most easily done because we commonly think of law in terms that point

---

15 Taylor, op. cit. (note 12), pp. 459, 60.

16 "The Large Catechism—The Ten Commandments," op. cit. (note 14), p. 414.

to laws that are broken, instead of as laws that make the good ordering of life possible. Then law becomes primarily God's condemnatory word in relation to the human project, and we forget that Luther believed law to be already present in Eden. In commenting on 1 Timothy 1:9–10 in light of Genesis 2:16, 17, Luther writes:

> From this there follows nothing else than that Paul is speaking about that Law which was given after sin, and not about this Law which the Lord gave when Adam was still guiltless and righteous.[17]

Law also speaks of the order granted Adam and Eve in the Garden of Eden before the Fall, an echo of that order fashioning both our words and our world, that deep and penetrating harmony regularly reminding us that what is clarified in Christ was not unknown before.[18] This is law, in the first instance, as a primordial reality. This law is of a piece with creation.[19] The passing of time in Genesis 1 speaks to the divine will for the grammar that makes poetics possible. Law is in this guise a gift, as is law ordered to the gospel, which is also a gift. Gifts here abound, but how are they to be related?

God speaks but one word—law and gospel. The same words are variously heard according to the situation of the hearer. It is the same word, in one instance doing this, in another instance doing something altogether different. But we can and must distinguish how God variously uses this word. Law and gospel both reveal the nature of God and so our nature. The second use of the law reveals what God demands of us, while the gospel reveals God's promise to us. The two uses of the law share God's intent to see human life ordered for human good. But the first use of the law can be distinguished from the second use, because the former points to God's original mode of promise in ordering, while the latter points to God subsequent demand in the face of disorder. The focus on promise, then, relates the first use of the law with the gospel. Yet, these two are not collapsed because the first use of the law points us to the gift of creation, while the gospel points us to the gift of redemption. Moreover, the gospel reveals God's mode of promise in the first use of the law. But it is precisely this

---

[17] Luther, op.cit. (note 8), p. 106.

[18] *Creation and Law*, op. cit. (note 7), p. 61.

[19] *The Living Word*, op. cit. (note 7), p. 146, "The law binds us to the earth."

promise in creation that seems under assault today, which is why I turn now to consider this promise in light of the above distinctions.

Creation and promise

In general, the modern history of the Christian tradition has been a venture in playing off creation against redemption. The Bible has often been made into an unwilling ally in this all too common denigration of creation, which is of a piece with redemption.[20] Too easily, creation becomes a foil over against redemption, replete with reference to the "worldly" in such a manner that it becomes synonymous with evil. This identification of "world" and "evil" is not surprising insofar as it indicates a habit of theological thought: we read the second use of the law into the first. Consequently, we understand the first use of the law wholly in light of a post-Fall (postlapsarian) perspective. Law becomes wholly identified with God's condemnation of human disorder. In the first instance, it is the disorder of the individual (read the second use of the law) that is condemned and in the second instance, the disorder of human community (read the first use of the law). Law is arrested from its noble vocation of referring to God's promise of creation.

It is necessary to reclaim the theological significance of creation in light of the global realities that bear upon us. As the world shrinks, we find ourselves shoulder to shoulder with those who share our passion for creation and who provide us with insights to wed to Luther's. Lamin Sanneh, an African theologian, invites us to ponder more carefully our relationship to creation by first imagining God's estimation of human culture and the languages that bear it. These latter are God's particular gifts to us, who are part of creation.[21] Sanneh writes:

> The characteristic pattern of Christianity's engagement with the languages and cultures of the world has God at the center of the universe of cultures, implying equality among cultures and the necessarily relative status of cultures vis-à-vis the truth of God. No culture is so advanced and so superior that it might claim exclusive access or advantage to the truth of God, and not so marginal and remote that it can be excluded. [. . .] The relationship of

---

[20] *Creation and Law*, op. cit. (note 7), p. 30.

[21] Further to this, cf. Per Lønning, *Creation—An Ecumenical Challenge?* (Macon GA: Mercer University Press, 1989), p. 62.

> the Christian movement to culture was shaped by the fact that Christianity is a translated—and translating—religion, and a translated Christianity is an interpreted Christianity, pure and simple. "Original" Christianity is nothing more than a construction.[22]

Elsewhere Sanneh has underscored the significance of this theological pattern as an affirmation of human culture.[23] Affirmation of creation and affirmation of culture go hand in hand. What is culture if not the gift of human life together given by the Creator to the created? Creation's gift to humanity is culture, borne by language. It is no surprise that Luther, with a strong theology of creation, insisted on the need to translate the Bible into the vernacular. He was equally insistent that preachers be masters of the biblical languages.[24] To think theologically is to attend to language precisely because it points in two directions: to the material foundation of human thought and to the manner in which culture shifts and slips. The first reminds us that we cannot think without recourse to our sensual nature—we cannot think of redemption in abstraction from creation. The second reminds us that we cannot speak without failure—we cannot embrace creation apart from finitude. In short, being able to speak of the gospel in the face of the radical diversity of creation and culture is to speak of God's miraculous presence in the midst of languages. Luther celebrated the gifts that languages bring to theology. We, too, can consider the plurality of languages as a gift, one wholly in accord with what the Bible says about creation. Diversity is a gift. Both biologists and the Bible teach us this. The metaphor of the body of Christ builds upon such an affirmation, yet the church too readily forgets this lesson from creation, preferring sameness over diversity. Thus, creation assaults our sensibilities, disarms our comfort by reminding us that difference is written into the very grammar of life. This is precisely what can both terrorize and comfort us, depending on our posture in life.

For those who tend to see creation as a foe, its vicissitudes evoke an anxiety that leads to attempts to keep the world out of the church. Yet this

---

[22] Lamin Sanneh, *Disciples of All Nations* (Oxford: Oxford University Press, 2008), p. 25.

[23] Cf. Lamin Sanneh, *Translating the Message: The Missionary Impact on Culture* (Maryknoll: Orbis Books, 1993), p. 27, "For all of us pluralism can be a rock of stumbling, but for God it is the cornerstone of the universal design."

[24] Martin Luther, "To the Councilmen of All Cities in Germany That They Establish and Maintain Christian Schools, 1524," in Walther I. Brandt (ed.), *Luther's Works*, vol. 45 (Philadelphia: Fortress Press, 1962), pp. 360–7.

is impossible to do. Insofar as the human is made of water and minerals, as well as the warp and woof of the language that is a piece of the culture, the world is assuredly present in the church—precisely in our being there.[25] We bear the world with us into the church, and, by God's grace, we bear the church into the world. But our desire to bracket world and church is a sign of our discomfort with the fundamental fact of our existence: we are as dependent upon God in creation as we are in redemption. Both point unequivocally to our need to live in a mode of receptivity and gratitude.[26] Perhaps this is what we finally wish to eschew in our uneasiness with creation. If we are saved by grace in redemption then perhaps we still hope to make something of ourselves in creation. If creation is raw material that is ready at hand, then at least we can feign mastery over this aspect of our lives. Perhaps this is our real discomfort with bringing the world into the church. When the world becomes that place where I assert self-mastery, then I want to keep it as far as possible from the church. At least this bit of my life can be untouched by the stark reminder that I am in need.

Creation, in fact, is an astounding gift. Sin, however, drives us to make creation into material for our self-projection. Sin also entices us to separate creation from redemption, by imagining the former to be profane and the latter sacred. Thankfully, this ruse is undone by the gospel, the power of God for salvation, which calls us to repentance. To confess Christ is to love the world that groans in labor pains (cf. Rom 1:16; 8:22). In fact, insofar as we are creation, to love the world is to love the world we are, which God so loves and saves.

Salvation, of course, is an eternal category—the presence of God, ever present and present everywhere to save what is lost.[27] Yet, it is not enough to assert the eternity of redemption. Creation is also an eternal category. Thomas wrote that creation, properly speaking, is neither a motion nor a change.[28] There is something assaulting in how Thomas puts this. With our propensity to speak of co-creation, we imagine creation to be a temporal "manu-facture" (work of the hand). Yet, as assuredly as redemption, creation is temporal only by analogy. It is, in fact, the condition for the possibility

---

[25] *Creation and Gospel*, op. cit. (note 7), p. 106, "The gospel is a *yes* to the body."

[26] Cf. Kathryn Tanner, *Jesus, Humanity and the Trinity: A Brief Systematic Theology* (Minneapolis: Fortress Press, 2001), p. 42.

[27] And so the verb "to save" is variously found in past, present and future tenses in the New Testament. Cf. Ephesians 2:8; 1 Corinthians 15:2; Romans 5:10.

[28] St Thomas Aquinas, *Summa Contra Gentiles, Book Two: Creation*, transl. by James F. Anderson (London: University of Notre Dame Press, 1975), p. 54.

of time and space. Creation is a divine, eternal, act. Just as redemption touches time and space in such a fashion that we return each day to the font, creation too touches space and time in such a way that every moment is the Genesis narrative anew. It is precisely this eternal recurrence of creation that allows us to receive diversity as the gift it is. Genesis is what it means to be human. Change is our being, which entails diversity. This fact of creation is sustained by the promise of salvation: out of chaos God brings order. Here the first use of the law and the gospel echo one another. *Creatio ex nihilo* and new creation share a promissory character.[29] Herein lies a challenge for the church: will we ponder creation after redemption?

It is interesting to read pre-modern sermons and commentaries on Genesis. At a first glance, it is rather amusing: ancient theories of creation and science seem quaint to sophisticated ears. But, on second glance, we realize that these preachers of old were engaging the best scientific thought of their time in conversation with theological insights. They demonstrate a decided interest in the cosmos. They anticipate that the cosmos—as read through the lens of the gospel—will be an open book to them, revealing something of the nature of the God who gives the divine self in and with creation. Consider Luther:

> For here we see how the Father has given himself with all creation and has abundantly provided for us in this life, apart from the fact that he also showered us with inexpressible eternal blessings through his Son and the Holy Spirit, as we shall hear.[30]

Such a perspective has revolutionary potential. What would happen if the baptized coming from the font were as passionate about the water that washed their flesh as there were about the words which washed their soul? What would happen if creation itself were perceived as the locus of the self-giving of God? How might this order priorities in the church differently? How might ecclesiology, soteriology, hamartiology, missiology, etc., be reframed if we understand creation to be a peer of redemption? These are significant and pressing questions for a church in the midst of modern paradigms that threaten a too easy peace between the church and world; a peace that is, in fact, no peace at all, but a divorce.

---

[29] It is beyond the scope of this paper to deal with Catherine Keller's provocative thesis that the Bible narrates a *creatio ex profundis* rather than a *creatio ex nihilo*. Cf. Catherine Keller, *Face of the Deep: A Theology of Becoming* (London: Routledge, 2003).

[30] "The Large Catechism—The Ten Commandments," op. cit. (note 14), p. 389.

Conclusion

I have explored the too easily forgotten distinction in Luther's thought between the civil and theological use of the law. In so doing, I revisited Gustaf
Wingren's observation that Luther's insistence on a taxonomy of law/gospel
emerged from his theological affirmation of the biblical and creedal pattern of beginning with creation. In exploring the significance of creation
for Luther, I underscored a Lutheran propensity to project the theological
tenor of condemnation from the second use of the law onto the first use. In
so doing, we too readily set up a way of doing theology, which undermines
and undervalues the dynamic nature of creation and human community as
narrated in Scripture and understood by the tradition: creation as an eternal
category, which is a peer of redemption. I proposed, finally, that reclaiming
this insight awakens us to the promissory character of creation.

In conclusion, it should be noted that such a reclamation has astounding
potential for Christian thought and praxis. Creation itself bespeaks the
value of plurality and invites us to revisit our propensity to supplant diversity
by homogeneity. Moreover, creation reminds us of the divine self-giving
that makes of creation a cause for doxology and expectation. In a time of
ecological crisis, when strident atheists speak eloquently of the inspirational
potency of nature, a theology that fails to address this potency of creation
risks a thorough and well-deserved indifference. Moreover, I have traced
the manner in which Luther's theology itself invites a more robust and
intentional theological attentiveness to the self-giving of God. Those with
such an expectation cannot but help to make common cause with those of
every faith, or no faith, to adore the world in a fashion consonant with the
One who so adores both humans and the world in which they live.

Deep Incarnation: The Logos Became Flesh

Niels Henrik Gregersen

Quicquid ab aeterno nascitur, semper nascitur
What is born from eternity, is born every moment[1]

Introduction

The English crime writer, Dorothy L. Sayers, once said the Christian dogma of incarnation is unique by claiming that God has not only created the framework of the world, but also has a "date" within it.[2] This intertwining of Creator and creature—"without separation, without confusion" (Council of Chalcedon 451 CE)—is without parallel in other world religions.

What Christians say about God's eternal Word, the *logos,* becoming body and flesh in Jesus and dwelling amongst us (Jn 1:14) exceeds what a Jew would say about Isaiah, or a Muslim about Mohammad. Jesus Christ is more than a teacher (bringing information about God) and more than a prophet speaking on behalf of God (bringing information from God). Rather, Jesus Christ embodies in himself the divine pattern of information (*logos*), and offers human beings a share in divine life and truth. So we also read in the Pauline tradition: "For in him all the fullness of God was pleased to dwell, and through him God was pleased to reconcile to himself all things, whether on earth or in heaven, by making peace through the blood of his cross" (Col 1:19–20). Moreover, this radical view of divine incarnation exceeds the otherwise admirable notion of *avatars* in Hinduism and Pure Land Buddhism. It is God who is present in divine fullness on earth.

God having a "date" with human beings is particular to the Christian faith. This helps to explain why the Christian tradition has privileged time and history, whether in terms of certain temporal events (the *kairoi,* as in the theology of Paul Tillich) or in terms of the universal history of

---

[1] *WA* 39/II, 293.

[2] Dorothy L. Sayers, "The Shattering Dogmas of the Christian Tradition," in Dorothy L. Sayers, *Christian Letters to a Post-Christian World* (Grand Rapids: Wm. B. Eerdmans, 1969), p. 14. "Date" here refers to both a location in time-space and an appointment.

humanity (*Universalgeschichte*, as in the theology of Wolfhart Pannenberg). Furthermore, it is understandable that the Christian tradition has given priority to humanity when speaking of salvation, since we are obviously creatures in need of conversion, unlike grass, sparrows and dolphins.

The problem with such a focus on time and human history, however, has been the corresponding neglect of space and nature as the sustaining structures of existence. By forgetting place and "bodiliness," however, Christian self-reflection loses scope and becomes "chronocentric." Even though Christians routinely speak of incarnation (*in-carnatio* literally means "going into flesh"), theologians prefer to speak of God "becoming human." Christology's cosmic dimensions then tend to be overlooked. Accordingly, the Johannine statement that God became "flesh" (*sarx*), and the Pauline statement that God through Christ reconciles "all things (*ta panta*), whether on earth or in heaven," recede into the background, if the cosmic dimensions are not denied outright. Yet, paradoxically, we dwarf ourselves by elevating ourselves above space and place, and become less than human by claiming to be human in an autonomous way, separated from the web of creation.

The argument

In order to overcome the exclusive emphasis on time and human history, the fields of eco-theology and of theology and science have drawn attention to the idea of creation in the biblical traditions. In what follows, I presuppose the important work done in both fields, and as a proponent of Scandinavian creation theology (K. E. Løgstrup and Gustaf Wingren), I fully affirm the fundamental role of the First Article in a theology of nature. In what follows, however, I want to show in addition how the Second and Third Articles, on Christ and the Spirit, constitute rich but relatively untapped resources for an ecological sensitivity in the life of the churches. My main goal is further to develop, and exegetically to strengthen, the concept of deep incarnation that I have earlier proposed in discussing Darwinism and Christology.[3]

My proposal is that the divine *logos* (translated as "Word," "pattern," or "formative principle") has assumed not only humanity, but the whole malleable matrix of materiality. By becoming "flesh" in Jesus, God's eternal

---

[3] Niels Henrik Gregersen, "The Cross of Christ in an Evolutionary World," in *Dialog: A Journal of Theology* vol. 40:3 (2001), pp. 192–207. Further developed in the context of the climate crisis, in "Fra skabelsesteologi til dybdeinkarnation. Om klimaforandringens økologi og teologi," in Mogens Mogensen (ed.), *Klimakrisen—hvad ved vi, hvad tror vi, og hvad gør vi?*, Ny Mission 16 (Frederiksberg: Unitas 2009), pp. 14–40.

logos entered into all dimensions of God's world of creation. "He came to what was his own" (Jn 1:11), just as "[a]ll things came into being through him" (Jn 1:3). In Greek, *sarx* primarily denotes particular bodies (in Jn 1:14 the blood and body of Jesus), with the special connotation of the frailty and vulnerability that is always attached to being a particular body living in a particular habitat, susceptible to growth and decay. In ancient Greek thinking, however, bodies were understood as being part of a whole flux of material beings, and thus always in contact with one another. Hence, *sarx* also meant all that was composed of the basic elements of earth, water, air and fire (in the sublunary world). In a modern sense, *sarx* would cover the whole realm of the material world from quarks to atoms and molecules, in their combinations and transformations throughout chemical and biological evolution. Speaking in biblical language, my proposal of deep incarnation suggests that God's own *logos* unites itself with the body of Jesus, with his person and life story. So, the divine *logos* became a human being, but by implication also entered a bodily world filled with fields, foxes and sparrows, conjoined in its destiny even with the growing and withering grass. Indeed, the *logos* became earth in Jesus. Jesus did not "belong to the world" (Jn 17:14), i.e., the human world of sin, but he certainly was fully connected with the material world.

This concept of deep incarnation was inspired by the concept of "deep ecology," a term coined by the Norwegian philosopher Arne Næss.[4] According to Næss, the sciences of ecology should be supplemented by an "ecosophy," that is, an experientially based understanding of oneself as a part of a rich natural nexus that far exceeds that of humanity. Thus, nature must never be used merely as a means for humans' self-serving purposes. This is an extension of the ethical principle outlined by Immanuel Kant, who stated that one must never make use of another person as a mere means but always regard the other as intrinsically valuable.[5] In theological terms, nature itself should be seen as our neighbor. And since we as embodied persons are part of nature, we have to care for ourselves and others within our ecological settings.

Deep ecology is associated with bio-centric or eco-centric perspectives. From an ecosophic ethical perspective, the long-term flourishing of living systems is of central concern; life cannot flourish without being sustained

---

[4] Arne Næss, "The Shallow and the Deep: Long Range Ecology Movement," in *Inquiry* 16 (1973), pp. 95–100; this was later developed in Arne Næss, *Ecology, Community and Lifestyle: Outline of an Ecosophy*, transl. by D. Rothenberg (Cambridge: Cambridge University Press, 1989). See overview in Bron Taylor and Michael E. Zimmermann, "Deep Ecology," in Bron Taylor (ed.), *Encyclopedia of Religion and Nature*, vol. 1 (London: Continuum International, 2005), pp. 456–60.

[5] Næss, ibid., p. 174.

by ecosystems as a whole, including mountains, soil, water and weather systems. According to deep ecologists, this is better served by re-sacralizing nature, as indigenous religions usually do, or by adopting east or south Asian religions such as Taoism, Hinduism and Buddhism. Occidental religions such as Christianity are critiqued for being too anthropocentric.

Although I share Næss's and other deep ecologists' concern about such anthropocentrism, I concur with most scholars of religion that there are ample biblical resources for understanding humanity in the context of nature. At the same time, however, I am skeptical about adopting an eco-centric view that does not allow for distinguishing between different levels of nature. In the first thesis of the 1974 *Deep Ecology Platform*, Næss and his colleagues stated that "human and nonhuman life *alike* have intrinsic value."[6] This view neglects the dirty biological fact that all life is lived at the expense of other life, and that some "higher" or more complex life forms should be valued more highly than some "lower" forms of life.[7] I would argue that in practical life we cannot, and should not, avoid making distinctions within nature. We need to combine a systemic view of nature (at lower or more general levels) with a special regard for individual creatures, especially creatures with highly sensitive sensory organs that allow these creatures to develop complex repertoires of awareness and even self-awareness. We humans are among such creatures, but we are not the only sensitive beings on our planet.

Global warming shows us how an ecological crisis has worldwide consequences, even though the effects will hurt particular life forms and communities living in lowland areas and in the areas around the poles and the equator. Thus, even though I begin from the idea of deep ecology when addressing the themes of deep incarnation, I do not subscribe to the purely systemic view of nature propagated by the movement of deep ecology.

The Stoic background of logos Christology

The cosmic *logos* Christology in the prologue to the Gospel of John is a piece of creation theology. The early patristic exegesis of its first verse ("In the beginning was the Word") indicates that early Christianity was not conceptualized within a Platonic framework, but reflected Jewish Wisdom and Stoic thinking. Unlike

---

[6] See the full list in Taylor and Zimmermann, op. cit. (note 4), p. 457, author's own italics.

[7] "Whenever we celebrate something, we slaughter something," as Ramathate Dolamo pointed out in the discussion of this paper at Augsburg 2009.

Platonism, Stoic physics was basically materialist but retained space for rational aspects of the material world. Today, most New Testament scholars agree that the Gospel of John should not be seen as a religious text explaining the meaning of the Jesus story in "plain personal" terms (as Adolf von Harnack argued), nor as a type of Gnostic redeemer myth (as Rudolf Bultmann argued).[8]

A new school of thought argues that Stoic anthropology and physics influenced not only the ethics, but also the cosmology of both Paul and John. This opens up new theological possibilities for understanding the way in which the writings of Paul and John presuppose a synthesis of Stoic and Jewish ideas, common to many of their contemporaries.[9] Hence, God and matter are not simply divided into two separate realms, as in Platonism and Gnosticism, nor is the meaning of the gospel explained in purely anthropological terms, divorced from a cosmological perspective. According to this new perspective, early Christian thinking may have more in common with contemporary scientific questions than with existentialist interpretations that presuppose that both God and humanity are divorced from nature.

The prologue to the Gospel of John (Jn 1:1–14) begins by placing the significance of the historical figure of Jesus in a cosmic perspective. The divine *logos* is seen as the creative and formative principle of the universe "in the beginning" (Jn 1:1–5), and as the revealer for all humanity since the dawn of humanity (Jn 1:9). It is this universally active divine *logos* that became "flesh" (*sarx*) in the life of Jesus of Nazareth (Jn 1:14).

The divine *logos* is said to be "in the beginning" (*en archē*). The Greek term *archē*, denoting a continuous foundation, signifies what we might call ultimate reality: *logos* is the beginning from which all other beginnings come. *Logos* was therefore also "in God" (*en theōi*). Being "in the beginning" and being "in God" are correlatives, insofar as God is the generative matrix of all that was, is and will be. *Logos* is not said be identical with God in the substantive sense, but *logos* is God in the predicative sense of being divine (*theos*).[10] *Logos* belongs to God and is God, but although *logos* is one with the Father in a mutual relation (being-in-one-another, Jn 14:10; 17:21), *logos* and the Father are not identical, since the Father is "greater" than Jesus (Jn 17:28).

[8] See Adolf von Harnack, "Über das Verhältniss des Prologs des vierten Evangeliums zum ganzen Werk," in *Zeitschrift für Theologie und Kirche* 2:3 (1892), pp. 189–231; Rudolf Bultmann, *The Gospel of John: A Commentary* [German original, 1941] (Philadelphia, PA: Westminster Press, 1971).

[9] As developed within the Copenhagen School of New Testament scholarship by Troels Engberg-Pedersen and Gitte Buch-Hansen, who I thank for their inspiration and clarification.

[10] C. K. Barrett, *The Gospel According to St. John* [1955] (London: SPCK, 1972), p. 130, "*Theos*, without the article, is predicative and describes the nature of the Word."

Logos is most often translated as "Word." However, Tertullian did not even consider this translation, but rather pointed out that *logos* in Latin could be rendered both as *ratio* (rationality) and as *sermo* (speech). Yet, he found it inconceivable to think of God as "speaking" in eternity, before the beginning of time. Rather, *logos* denotes the divine rationality or mind (*ratio*), perhaps an inner dialogue (*sermo*), which is not expressed outwardly until the creation of the world, when there are creatures with whom to dialogue.[11]

Tertullian here presupposes the Stoic distinction between the "inherent *logos* in God" (*logos endiathetos*) and the "outgoing divine *logos*" (*logos prophorikos*). The Greek Church Fathers such as Theophilus of Antioch (writing around 190) explicitly use this Stoic distinction[12]—again indicating that Stoic distinctions were well known among Christian writers during the Roman Empire. These early interpretations of John testify that Stoicism influenced early Christian thinking, thus making a strong link between God's "inner" nature and God's "external" creativity.

This interpretation finds support in the prologue of John: "All things came into being through him [*logos*], and without him not one thing came into being" (Jn 1:3). Here, *logos* is identified as the divine informational resource, or the informational matrix for the concrete forms that have emerged and will emerge in the world of creation. Using the models of divine creativity in Genesis 1, which forms a subtext for John 1, the divine *logos* is creative by setting distinctions in the world (carving out "this" and "that"), while also bringing informational patterns into motion (combining "this" and "that").[13]

In Stoic thinking, there is no gulf between God and world as in the Platonic tradition. *Logos* is all pervasive as the outgoing structuring principle of the universe. *Logos* thus expresses itself in the harmonious order of the universe as well as in the rational capacities of human beings. Accordingly, the Prologue of John states: "in him [*logos*] was life, and the life was the light of all people" (Jn 1:4). Here "people" and "everyone" do not refer to specific religious groups, but to any human being born into the world: "The true light, which enlightens everyone, was coming into the world" (Jn 1:9).

---

[11] Tertullian, *Adversus Praxeas* 5, *"non sermonalis a principio, sed rationalis Deus etiam ante principium"* (text in *Patrologia Latina*, ed. Migne, vol. 2, p. 160).

[12] Theophilus of Antioch, *Ad Autolycum* II,10 (text *in Patrologia Graeca*, ed. Migne, vol. 6, p. 1064).

[13] I have elaborated on the similarities between "cutting information" that creates differences, and "shaping information," in "God, Matter, and Information: Towards a Stoicizing Logos Christology," in Paul Davies & Niels Henrik Gregersen (eds), *Information and the Nature of Reality: From Physics to Metaphysics* (Cambridge: Cambridge University Press, forthcoming 2010).

I am not claiming that the Johannine concept of *logos* is derived exclusively from the Stoic tradition, for it is semantically flexible and has Jewish, Stoic and Middle Platonic connotations. On the other hand, it seems inappropriate to associate the Gospel of John exclusively with Platonism or Gnosticism. In the Gospel of John there is no division (Plato: *chōrismos*), between God's eternal *logos* and the *logos* working in creation within the one field of physical differentiations, biological life and human enlightenment. "He was in the world, and the world came into being through him; yet the world did not know him. He came to what was his own, and his own people did not accept him" (Jn 1:10–11). The *logos* is obviously "at home in the universe" prior to the incarnation. The problem is not that there should be a distance between God and world, but humans failing to be aware that the *logos* came into this world.

Christians departed from the Stoics in insisting on the pre-material status of the divine *logos*. Stoic ideas were more easily appropriated in the domain of cosmology than in that of theology itself. John seems to have understood *logos* as being immaterial in its primordial state in God (Jn 1:1–2), even though from the beginning *logos* was oriented towards the world of creation (Jn 1:3) and the incarnation in time and space (Jn 1:14). If so, the later Alexandrian distinction between the immaterial *logos* "in the beginning" (*logos asarkos*) and the incarnate *logos* "in the midst of time" (*logos ensarkos*) is well supported by the logic of the text itself.[14] Here the Christian tradition has retained a Jewish sense of God's transcendence, while balancing this Platonizing element with a strong Stoic influence on the doctrine of the incarnated *logos*: "And the Word [*logos*] became flesh and [*sarx*]" (Jn 1:14).

Divine logos assumes the depths of materiality (Jn 1:14)

Like the idea of *logos*, the term "flesh" is also semantically flexible: s*arx* can mean simply "body and flesh" in referring to the historical person of Jesus. But *sarx* can also mean "sinful flesh" (cf. Jn 3:6), thereby implying that the incarnation of *logos* as Jesus Christ already anticipates the death of Jesus for all humankind. "It is finished!" are Jesus' final words in the Gospel of John (Jn 19:30). Flesh can also refer to the realm of materiality in general, with a sense of frailty and transitoriness. This is also presupposed in John,

---

[14] For a classical reference of this distinction, see Athanasius, *De Incarnatione Verbi* VIII.1.

when considered as a philosophical as well as theological text in the first centuries by apologists such as Justin Martyr who viewed Christianity as the "true philosophy."

From this deep incarnation perspective in John 1:14, the divine *logos* became incarnate not only in a particular human person, "the blood and flesh" of Jesus, but the incarnation extends also into Jesus becoming an example of humanity, in whom the "frail flesh" of biological creatures is instantiated. With the cosmological background in mind, we can now also say that in the incarnation the divine *logos* is united with the very basic physical matter of creation. In other words, the flesh that is assumed in Jesus of Nazareth, is not only the man Jesus, but also the entire realm of humanity, animal and plant life, even the soil itself.

The highest (eternal thought and power of God) and the lowest (flesh which comes into being and decays) are united in the process of incarnation. Incarnation signifies coming-into-flesh, so that God, the Creator, and the world of the flesh are conjoined in Jesus Christ. God connects with all vulnerable creatures, with the sparrows in their flight as well as in their fall (cf. Mt 10:29), indeed, with all the grass that comes into being one day and fades the next day. In Christ, God is conjoining all creatures and enters into the biological tissue of creation itself in order to share the fate of biological existence. God becomes Jesus, and in him God becomes human, and (by implication) foxes and sparrows, grass and soil.

This notion of deep incarnation has been taken up by theologians who are prepared to rethink the Christian tradition in its biological scope.[15] *Celebrating Christ with Creation—A Theology of Worship for the Season of Creation*, by Norman Habel, David Rhoads and Paul Santmire, features a chapter on "A Theology of Deep Incarnation and Reconciliation," in which they propose that if we recognize the earth as a living organism, should we then not say that God became "incarnate" in the earth? Does Jesus, as a creature, represent the whole earth? They argue that Jesus, dust taken from the earth and given life, is that piece of earth where the presence of God is concentrated during incarnation. In Jesus, "God becomes flesh, soil, Earth."[16]

---

[15] Such as Denis Edwards, *Ecology at the Heart of Faith* (Maryknoll, NY: Orbis, 2006), pp. 52–60; Christopher Southgate, *The Groaning of Creation: God, Evolution, and the Problem of Evil* (Louisville: Westminster John Knox Press, 2008), pp. 75–77; Celia Deane-Drummond, *Christ and Evolution: Wonder and Wisdom* (Philadelphia: Fortress Press, 2009), p. 107; pp. 178–80; pp. 128–59.

[16] See **www.seasonofcreation.com/theology**, accessed December 2009.

Synoptic and Pauline parallels to deep incarnation

This interpretation becomes even more meaningful when considering the synoptic Jesus traditions as well as the Pauline traditions. The connection between Jesus and earth persists in the Jesus tradition. In his preaching, Jesus compares the growth of God's kingdom to the growth of a mustard seed (Mt 13:31–32, Mk 4:30–32; Lk 13:18–19); he tells the disciples to be as carefree as the birds of the air and the lilies of the field (cf. Mt 6:25–34; Lk 12:22–31); he teaches them to pray, "Your will be done, on earth as it is in heaven" (Mt 6:10; cf. Lk 11:2). The disciples, moreover, are required to become the "salt of the earth" (Mt 5:13; cf. Mk 9:50; Lk 14:34–35). To the people who were not part of the inner circle of the disciples Jesus says, "Blessed are the meek, for they will inherit the earth" (Mt 5:5; cf. Lk 6:20). First and foremost, Jesus referred to himself as the Son of Man, in Aramaic most likely *bar 'ænash* corresponding to the *ben adam* in Hebrew. Thus, Jesus has come as the "son of Adam" who himself was the "son of the earth" (earth, in Hebrew, is *adamah*). In this sense, Jesus was the son of the son of earth. Paul considers this connection between Adam and Christ by seeing Jesus as the second Adam, the new earthling (Romans 5).

In the Pauline tradition, the idea of incarnation is spelled out in dimensions of both depth and length. The important image of the church as the body of Christ (1 Cor 12–13), indicates a continuing process of incarnation (often called "inhabitation" or "indwelling"). Jesus is the head of the body, while the church constitutes the members of the body of Christ. Also, the bread and wine of the Eucharist are the body and blood of Christ (1 Cor 11), which as communicants receive, circulates in them and thus facilitates the social fluidity of the communion. Finally, Paul sees the individual body as the dwelling place of the Holy Spirit, and asks, "Do you not know that your bodies are members of Christ?" and "do you not know that your body is a temple of the Holy Spirit within you [. . .]?" (1 Cor 6:15; 19).

The depth dimension is also present in Paul, the theologian of the cross: "For I am convinced that neither death, nor life, nor angels, nor rulers, nor things present, nor things to come, nor powers, nor height, nor depth, nor anything else in all creation, will be able to separate us from the love of God in Christ Jesus our Lord" (Rom 8: 38–39).

The crux of the interpretation lies in two questions: (1) Who is the "us" that Paul speaks about? (2) How can nothing in creation separate us from the love of Christ? I propose, first, that the "us" is anything and anybody within the world of creation that through the spirit is "groaning in labor pains," while "we wait for adoption, the redemption of our bodies" in order to become united with the love of Christ. Thus, also here salvation has both a temporal length and spatial depth dimension (Rom 8:22–25). Second, how does salvation come into being? Not by Jesus transporting bodies out of this world, but by bringing their bodies into the bond of God's love in Christ, who is present both in life and death, in the heights as well as in the depths of creation. This is what one might call the Pauline version of deep incarnation.

As we sing in the popular Danish hymn by N. F. S. Grundtvig (1783–1872), "Hail you Savior and Reconciler," Christ is truly the "deep connection." "Let me love the world in you, so that my heart beats for you alone, so that you are the deep connection."[17] There is no contrast between my love of Christ and my love of this world, though there is an established order of priority, since Christ is the everlasting bond of love between all things. Expressed in Johannine terms, Christ is the all-comprehensive *logos* pattern of love that sustains all things and redeems the labor pains of creation.

From cave to tomb

Paul was painfully aware that the material world in which we live is a vulnerable world. Also in John, the scope of "flesh" involves the frailty of existence. Consequently, there is a close connection between the incarnation of the Son of God and the cross of Christ. From this perspective, the incarnation of the Son of God is not only an event associated with the birth of Jesus, but rather a process that extends through Jesus' life story and ends in his death. Many of the Eastern Christian icons depict the birth of Jesus in a cave, carved out of the earth and anticipating the tomb at the end of his life: Jesus emerged out of the earth, and returns to the earth, from which he is raised again.

Thus, Jesus is not only the second Adam who assumed flesh but also the second Job who assumed pain. The Son of God follows his creatures, in fellowship with human beings, sparrows and grass, even into the processes of decay, so that no creature shall ever be left alone in death. "Are not two sparrows sold for a penny? Yet not one of them will fall to the ground apart from your Father," said Jesus (Mt 10:29). After Christ's crucifixion, it could be added that no sparrow dies without the Son of God, sent by the

---

[17] Author's own translation from the Danish.

heavenly Father into the very biological tissue of life and death. To God, the dirty earth is as close as are the heavens. In Christ, "high" and "low" communicate with one another.

In this sense, God has not only created a world capable of generating ever more complex forms of life, but God the Son also carries the costs of complexity by being present in "the least of these who are members of my family" (Mt 25). Here the thinking of deep ecology is corrected. In the depths of incarnation, God not only joins with the ecosystem of Gaia, but also with individual and vulnerable creatures. In Christ, God intertwines life and death for the benefit of all those creatures, who in their own bodies experience life's blossoming as well as suffering, even the untimely ending of life.

Such a biophysical interpretation of incarnation has significant consequences for understanding the relation between God and the material world at large, and biological existence in particular. The divine *logos* is not only present in the body of the church but at the very core of material existence. From the perspective of deep incarnation, the death of Jesus fulfills the self-divesting nature of the divine *logos* for all sentient and suffering beings, human or animal. *Logos* becomes the light not only for every human being entering the world (Jn 1:9), but also the "light of the world" and "light of life" (Jn 8:12).

Such a cosmic interpretation of the gospel is possible already against the background of the Jewish idea of God making God's "home" (*shechinah*) in the midst of the world. But this interpretation becomes even more plausible in relation to the Stoic background of John's prologue. *Logos* is affirmed as the living bond between the ultimate reality of God and the penultimate reality of the world. Hence, the two concepts of corresponding extension, *logos ensarkos* and *sarx*, are brought together in John 1:14.[18]

Nevertheless, I am not claiming that the Gospel of John elaborates a soteriology that is universal in scope. In John, salvation is so closely connected with the proper (re)cognition of Christ, and with the corresponding new praxis, that we do not find in John sustained reflections on the eschatological fate of nature. My point is that there is a strong emphasis on the conjunction between God's own *logos* and the material world in John,

---

[18] This interpretation is based on the Johannine position that the truth and the way still need to be re-enacted by the Holy Spirit in human beings. It is necessary for Jesus Christ, as the personified *logos*, to leave his disciples, for otherwise the Spirit is without a place to energize the disciples, and to "guide you into all the truth" (Jn 16:13).

which is open to the possibility of a transformation of the very world of
matter: that which is touched by Christ will not remain unaltered.

"What has not been assumed has not been healed"

Gregory Nazianzus famously stated the principle, "That which he has
not assumed (*aproslēpton*) he has not healed (*atherapeuton*), but that which
is united to his Godhead (*ho de hēnōtai tōi theōi*) is also saved (*sōzetai*)."[19]
Gregory's concern was that the divine *logos* should not supplant human
rationality. The *logos* adopted a fully human nature, including a human
body, human soul and human mind. Thus, Gregory argued, if Jesus Christ
had not been endowed with a rational mind, how then could he have
been fully human? Gregory's point was that the divine *logos* ("Word" or
"Thought") lives comfortably together with human rationality, without the
one excluding the other. God does not exclude humanity, just as humanity
does not exclude God. "Keep, then, the whole man (*anthropon hólon*), and
mingle Godhead (*mixon tēn theotēta*) therewith that you may benefit me
in my completeness (*teléōs*)."[20]

Martin Luther was certainly familiar with Gregory's principle. He refers
to the catholic faith (*fides catholica*) of Chalcedon, and reminds his readers of
the doctrine of the "communication of attributes" (*communicatio idiomatum*)
between the characteristics of the divine and human natures in the one
person of Jesus Christ. In this context he proposes a distinction between
the "old language," in which God and creature are defined in contrast to
one another, and the "new language" (*nova lingua*) of the gospel.

> Thesis 20. Nonetheless it is certain that with regard to Christ (*in Christo*) all
> words receive a new signification, though the thing signified is the same.

> Thesis 21. For "creature" in the old usage of language (*veteris linguae usu*) and
> in other subjects signifies a thing separated from divinity by infinite degrees
> (*infinitis modis*).

---

[19] Greek text in Grégoire de Nazianze, *Lettres Théologiques*, Sources Chrétiennes 208, ed. by Paul Gallay
(Paris: Éditions du Cerf, 1974), p. 50. English translation in Edward Rochie Hardy (ed.), *Christology of
the Later Fathers*, The Library of Christian Classics (Westminster Press: Philadelphia, 1954), p. 218.

[20] Gregory Nazianzen, *Epistola* 101.36, text in ibid., p. 52; English translation in ibid, p. 219.

> Thesis 22. In the new use of language it signifies a thing inseparably joined with divinity in the same person in an ineffable way (*ineffabilibus modis*).[21]

In his explanations to thesis 20, Luther is addressing the counterargument that "the same thing cannot be predicated of God and man." His response is that only from a philosophical (that is, an Aristotelian) perspective could one treat divine and human issues as having no inner relationship and no mutual communication. Luther continues, "But we not only establish a relation, but a union (*unio*) of the finite and the infinite. Aristotle, if he had heard or read of this, would never have been made a Christian, for he would not have conceded this position that the same relation belongs to the finite and the infinite."[22]

According to Luther, a Christian who is familiar with the "new language" of the Bible should be fully prepared to acknowledge the infinite God within the framework of the finite creation. For God stretches from the highest to the lowliest, while finitude itself is capable of giving room to the infinite: *finitum capax infiniti*.

John 1:14 was one of Luther's favorite texts, on which he already preached on Christmas Day 1514.[23] In 1537, Luther addressed its meaning, following Gregory's principle of the relation between divine assumption and divine healing. He too was wary of Apollinarius, who taught that the divine *logos* was a substitute for the human mind. Luther says "no" because in German "the word 'body' does not denote a corpse; it denotes a living person in possession of body and soul."[24] Hence, a body also possesses human mental

---

[21] Martin Luther, *Disputation on the Divinity and Humanity of Christ*, translated from the Latin text (*WA* 39/2, 92–121) by Christopher B. Brown, available at **www.iclnet.org/pub/resources/text**.

[22] Here it should be noted that Luther remained an Aristotelian in all philosophical matters, as evidenced in detail by Theodor Dieter, *Der junge Luther und Aristoteles. Eine historisch-systematische Untersuchung zum Verhältnis von Theologie und Philosophie*, Theologische Bibliothek Töpelmann, 105 (Berlin: de Gruyter, 2001). Let me pose a counterfactual question, What would have happened, had Luther been a philosophical Stoic, rather than an Aristotelian? With regard to the *communicatio idiomatum*, for Luther there can be no communication of attributes between divine nature as such and human nature as such. If Luther had presupposed the Stoic concept of substance, only one substance would exist, namely the original unity of God–and–world. In this case one would not be able—as Luther actually does (cf. *Disputatio* 1540, theses 5–8, *WA* 39/2, 92)—to distinguish so firmly between the divine and human predicates, when taken *in abstractis* (referring to natures), although they belong together *in concreto* (that is, when referring to the personal union of Jesus Christ). This problem raises the issue as to whether a Christian theology is bound to follow a particular philosophical scheme when conceiving of Jesus Christ as both divine and human.

[23] In Luther's sermon of 25 December 1514, "In Natali Christi, A. 1515," in *WA* 1, 20–29.

[24] Martin Luther, "Sermons on the Gospel of St. John Chapters 1–4," in Jaroslav Pelikan (ed.), *Luther's Works,* vol. 22 (Saint Louis: Concordia Publishing House, 1957), p. 111.

capacities. In this sense, Luther argues against "those stupid asses," who take the word of flesh "to mean the kind of flesh dogs and wolves have."[25] For Luther, the important thing is to retain Jesus' full humanity. Therefore, he resists identifying the flesh of Jesus Christ with just an animal body, or a corpse, to which the life-giving divine *logos* could then be added (as in Apollinarianism). Jesus Christ is not a chimera, half human flesh, half divine *logos*.

In explaining the meaning of flesh, Luther is acutely aware that Scripture does so "to point out its weakness and its mortality." This approximates the observations made above on the meanings of *sarx* in Paul and John. In contrast to the view of deep incarnation as developed above, Luther shows no interest in the relationship between human and non-human nature. His interest lies exclusively in the relationship between human and divine nature. So, when speaking of weakness and mortality, Luther refers only to human sin as the cause of weakness and mortality: "For Christ took on the human nature, which was mortal and subject to the terrible wrath and judgment of God because of the sins of the human race. And this anger was felt by the weak and mortal flesh of Christ."[26]

In short, there is neither in Luther nor in Gregory Nazianzus any expressed concern for the aspects of "flesh" that are common to human and non-human nature. The natural nexus of human life simply was not at the center of his interest. This does not mean that the natural conditions were systematically excluded by Luther and his contemporaries. Rather, the natural conditions of life were not seen to be of relevance. Today, however, the cosmic dimensions of incarnation stand in need of theological re-articulation. Otherwise, we continue to stay within chronocentric interpretations of Christianity, which leave behind the spatial and bodily character of God's self-revelation in Christ, and thus cannot express the universal scope of Christology, which extends from the historical into the material basis of the human condition. This basis we share with other creatures on planet earth (and perhaps beyond our planet).

What I have proposed here is that we attend to the full dimension of the gospel: "And the Word became flesh." Just as *logos* has the connotations of the divine Word and the creative informative principle of creation, so also *sarx* includes the meanings of "body and blood," frail and sinful nature and the material world *in extenso*.

---

[25] Ibid.

[26] Ibid.

Conclusion

I have argued that the "flesh" assumed by *logos* denotes the person and body of Jesus, yet also signifies the whole dimension of materiality, especially the aspects of complex matter related to weakness and disintegration. Complexity is costly; what is unique and precious is bound to disintegrate in the end. Accordingly, when God in Christ became human, the Son of God entered the realm of material life, in which human beings die, sparrows fly and fall to the ground and grass grows and withers away. It is as natural for God to dwell in the world of dirt and waste, as it is for God to reign in the heavenly stars.

I have proposed a concept of "deep incarnation" in order to formulate the mystery of salvation in such away that incarnation stretches into the depths of our planet's conditions for life. This view is developed in critical interaction with the idea of "deep ecology," which seeks to overcome anthropocentrism. All expressions of life have intrinsic value apart from their utility for human beings; accordingly, the ecosystem as a whole must be affirmed as fundamental to planetary life. I have argued, however, that a Christology of deep incarnation cannot rest content with a systemic view of the ecological order as proposed by deep ecology. The holistic notion of the interconnectedness of all things must be balanced by a sense of the frailty of individuality: of the uniqueness of human life, of the singularity of each sparrow and of the particular beauties of lilies, of grass and of weeds.[27]

[27] I thank Professor Allen G. Jorgensen for helpful comments on a draft of this paper, and to my colleagues Troels Engberg-Pedersen, Tilde Bak Halvgaard, Frederik Mortensen, René Rosfort, Stena Nordgard Svendsen, Johanne Stubbe Teglbjærg and Runar Thorsteinsson.

Speaking for the Church— Speaking to the Church

Vítor Westhelle

Who speaks on behalf the church?

Augsburg 2009 marked an historical event in the life of the Department for Theology and Studies (DTS) of the Lutheran World Federation (LWF). This consultation, the closing one in a series of seminars held throughout the world, brought together theologians from around the world, from various socioeconomic, religio-political, cultural, ethnic and gender realities to reflect on how different faith experiences and theological perspectives can become an enabling and transformative Lutheran theology in the twenty-first century. It is the apex of a process that formally began in 1995, when the Council of the LWF, meeting in Namibia, received the "Ten Theses on the Role of Theology in the LWF," drafted by the Program Committee for Theology and Studies. This seminal document stated that, unlike the way in which theology had hitherto been practiced in the LWF (with DTS producing and disseminating theology), the times called for theology to be done by way of connecting local theological knowledge, produced throughout the whole of the communion, (a) to give expression to theology in the life of the churches and (b) to offer guidance that could orient and correct the ministry of the church as it carried out its missions. As theses 6 and 7 succinctly state:

> 6. In the history of the LWF as a communion of diverse churches, the awareness of the tension between the gospel that hold us together, and the diversity with which we express it, grew as a creative challenge for both the self-understanding of the LWF as a communion and its theological practice.

> 7. This challenge offers new opportunities for the exercise of theology in the LWF through which the communion will be promoted if, and only if, these characteristics of a theological practice are followed: a) the LWF offers itself as a place for different articulations of diverse experiences; b) as a catalyst for innovation within theologies in different contexts; and

c) as a guarantor of both the diversity and of the necessity of expressing commonalities.[1]

What was envisioned at the time was to continue carrying out theological studies in the LWF despite the substantially reduced availability of financial and human resources. This situation offered the possibility to reimagine theological formation in and for the life of the churches. The culmination of this process, as witnessed in the 2009 Augsburg consultation and the earlier events that had led up to it, evinced a tension that the churches of the Reformation inherited from their inception: the Reformation was not about reforming theology, but about "re-forming" (in sense of reshaping) the church, for sake of a renewed formation. Theology is a function of this re-forming.

Exercising this function implies certain questions of power. Who speaks for the church? Who holds the authority to "present" it in the public sphere? Who "authors" its claims of legitimacy? Speaking for the church implies: to speak as church, as the authoritative voice of the church, as *ecclesia docens*, the teaching church, and to speak to the church, addressing it and correcting it, as *ecclesia discens*, the learning church.[2]

Communion takes place in this tension between the teaching church that speaks and the learning church that is spoken to, but only as far as this tension is maintained. In other words, communion is the event that takes place in the actual interface between the teachings of the church (its dogmatic function) and its mission (its receptive function). If teaching means being faithful to the apostolic witness, mission means listening to the other and speaking back to the church.

An example here may be helpful. When Paul uses *koinonia* in Galatians 2,[3] the pillars of the church of Jerusalem (Cephas, John and James) were speaking as the church, but Paul, because of his mission to the uncircumcised, was speaking to the church. In that tense meeting, *koinonia* happened even without settling the differences in theological or dogmatic convictions. The pillars spoke as the church; Paul, from a mission perspective, spoke to the church for the sake of the people. The one feature that kept the communion

---

[1] The theses were formulated by the Program Committee for Theology and Studies at its meeting in 1995 and were reproduced, in Wolfgang Greive (ed.), *Between Vision and Reality: Lutheran Churches in Transition*, LWF Documentation 47/2001 (Geneva: The Lutheran World Federation, 2001), pp. 497–8. They are also available at **www.lutheranworld.org/What_We_Do/Dts/DTS-Welcome.html**.

[2] See Vítor Westhelle, *The Church Event: Call and Challenge of a Church Protestant* (Minneapolis: Fortress Press, 2010), p. 56.

[3] See the chapter by Barbara Rossing, in this publication, pp. 39ff.

together was that they agreed to remember those who were considered the least, those who had the face and the wounds of Jesus.[4]

We are truly inheritors of the Reformation not only because of our theological formulations, but above all, because the audacious spirit with which we speak as and speak to. In that sense, we become points of intersection. In this crossing, the feeble, unstable and weak (re)formation of the community of the cross happens. Tension, conflict and strife are not transitional moments in the process of finding new stable ground and settling there. The Reformation itself survives insofar as this audacious spirit keeps on breathing life into the church. In the spirit of the Reformation, there is no guaranteed stable ground for the church to be church, but it is on this unstable ground between the church and challenges of its mission that communion ensues. This is precisely what is meant by the expression *ecclesia reformata semper reformanda est* (the reformed church is always to be reformed), which was coined later.

How did this come about? It came about at the moment when those who spoke as church, its magisterium, had to be spoken to; they had to be held accountable on the basis of the foundation of their legitimacy, the very apostolic witness which they claimed as the very basis for speaking as church. The theological voices of protest were raised by those who experienced in their lives the transforming power of God's Word (this is all that *sola scriptura* means). Experience, indeed, makes a theologian, as Luther pointed out. Certainly, the Reformation did not separate speaking as from speaking to, much less cancel the former. One cannot exist without the other: the teaching church needs simultaneously to be a learning church. Speaking to is already speaking as and vice versa. Nevertheless, the distinction is important because one of these "voices" at any given moment takes the commanding tone; there is a time to teach and a time to learn.

The picture and the proxy

Over the second half of the millennium times changed. Today, hardly a theologian, church representative, or office in the tradition of the Reformation would claim to be speaking as the church. Yet, the same attitude, grounded in a claim to an entitled voice, was present among the participants

---

[4] Barbara Rossing, "Models of *Koinonia* in the new Testament and Early Church," in Heinrich Holze (ed.) *The Church as Communion: Lutheran Contributions to Ecclesiology*, LWF Documentation 42/1997 (Geneva: The Lutheran World Federation, 1997), pp. 65–80.

at Augsburg 2009. It is recognizable when the commanding, magisterial tone of theological discourse presents a case in the same way that a picture purports to describe something. The "picture" is framed by what supports its claim to the truth, such as Luther's writings, the confessions, ecumenical agreements, a tradition, a liturgical practice, a philosophical foundation, an epiphany and so forth. It can be quite impressive and elaborate, very inclusive and sophisticated, detailed and clearly to the point. If one accepts what is portrayed in it, there may be no dispute as to its representational accuracy. However, the frame always excludes something, cutting off that which is deemed unimportant or irrelevant. In speaking to, there is always also a speaking for, on behalf of that which the frame leaves outside the picture.

The other theological voice comes through those who represent or are a proxy for something or someone, standing in for those realities the frame excludes. This voice claims the right for inclusion, or at least contests the hegemonic function of the portrait. When this happens, we have the spirit of reform at work and the tension that (re)forms community. When these two are unhinged, and the picture is impermeable to anything else, we have fundamentalism and all other forms of authoritarianism. When we have only the proxy attitude, without any claim to a place in the picture, we have anarchy. If the proxy voice frames an alternative picture, then we have sectarianism. But when the two are in a tensile relation then we have disputation, controversy, revolt or, hopefully, a conversation, which means "to keep company with," "to turn about with."

This conversation, which may include revolt, controversy or protest, is what was evident in the texture being woven at Augsburg 2009 and the communion that took place there. Distinct voices could be heard in the discussions after the lectures, in the seminars, group discussion and personal exchanges. While the lectures were attempts to hold the hinges in place, with an emphasis either on the "picture" or on the "proxy" side, occasional interventions lifted up the distinct tonalities of the two voices that I refer to as the conversational parties that make Reformation a living event.

The axes of conversation

This conversation runs along different axes in which we can identify elements of the tensile polarity between speaking as and speaking to the church for sake of the people:

Methodological axis: This is about the operational principle at work: text versus context; acculturation versus inculturation; academic versus practical; center versus margin; proclamation versus dialogue; theory versus praxis; one versus many; unity versus diversity; the solid versus the fluid; stability versus instability; disciplinary versus interdisciplinarity; and so on.

Thematic axis: The topic or theme here is Ariadne's thread: purity versus hybridity; dissemination versus networking; confessionalism versus ecumenism; colonialism versus postcolonialism; orthodoxy versus orthopraxis; outreach versus indigenization; Luther scholars versus biblical scholars; systematic versus pastoral theology; anthropocentrism versus environmentalism; straight versus gay; liturgical rigor versus spontaneity; biblical literalism versus secularism; formalism versus event; and so on.

Geographical axis: Here the topics reflect the emerging awareness of the planetary dimensions of Lutheranism. Topics included: West versus East; North versus South; global versus local; cosmopolitan versus parochial; and so on.

Institutional axis: Tensions here are between hierarchy versus egalitarianism; academia versus community; church versus society; conservative versus liberal; liberalism versus liberation.

These poles that carry the position of the picture and the proxy happen at different levels. This is something that is commonly observed at international meetings as well as in local contexts, very much like the dynamics in a family, or even in one's own personal experience, when we have cognitive dissonance, the process by which our mind keeps changing, evincing that we are still alive.

The opposing sides in these pairings in the four axes identified above are not static, but unstable and full of tensions. The forms of representation—whether picture or proxy—slide as on a slippery slope, and, depending on the context, the sides might be changed. For example, in some contexts, literalism may be the picture (as for some Evangelicalism in the USA), while secular liberalism carries the voice of the proxy; while in others it is the reverse (for many mainline Protestants in the USA).

"To each tribe its scribe" conveys the contextually bound character of this equation between the two forms of representation. Within these contexts, there is relative stability—because no context is hermetic and globalization has made them ever more porous. Within these "tribal" contexts, conversation is also relatively stable. Contexts can be defined, among other things, by the fact that they administer dissent. Complications occur when contexts of relative stability encounter other contexts in which the picture and the proxy are different. Then, what in one context might be the picture turns into the proxy and vice versa. This is what happened at Augsburg 2009, where people from every corner of the world came together.

Hegemonic overdeterminations

Who spoke as and who spoke to, and how was that decided in this multi-contextual meeting? The first set of factors is related to entitlement. One of these is the official language utilized, English, which entitles some to a better command of the discursive practice. Other factors of entitlement are symbolic and carry genealogical weight, in this case, the historic city of Augsburg, Germany, the birthplace of the most acclaimed confessional document of world Lutheranism. Genealogies establish birthrights which, in turn, generate entitlement (e.g., in the references to "our Luther") and lay claim to a preferential tradition (five hundred years on the European continent—which, admittedly, is significantly more than in any other part of the world). A further entitlement is the control over disciplinary borders (e.g., what is allowed and demanded by what is called "Luther research," history, biblical exegesis, etc.). This set of entitlement factors interfaces with power—political, economic and ideological resources—which was amassed by the North Atlantic world during and through the colonial enterprise. In summary, if we put these elements together, we have hegemony, i.e., power linked to entitlement. This produces overdetermination, in which one pole overrules the opposing pole, regardless of its intrinsic claim to legitimacy. The first term in the above axes is likely to define the contours of the hegemonic position to the extent that the categories fit. The second term is likely to define those who have limited power and little claim to entitlement. So, in a multi-contextual environment, those who identify with the second set of terms are likely to speak to hegemony on behalf of the communities they represent. Even back home they are probably the ones who hold the "picture" and set the frame. In other words, a hegemonic position at home might turn into a subaltern one abroad.

The good news is that this intercontextual conversation is happening in the midst of and because of our differences. This superb example of communion is happening for at least three reasons. First, when challenged to expand its picture of what is Lutheran, the very hegemonic center came to realize that what it had was indeed an idiosyncratic picture bound to a given context and framed by its limits. This is European theology becoming aware of its own contextuality.

The second reason is the mirror image of the first. To a certain extent, those who are the theological subalterns of European (and later North American) Lutheranism are eager to learn it, because this knowledge gives them leverage in addressing hegemony. Postcolonial studies have shown that the subalterns are more adroit at reading the entrails of hegemony, than the hegemons are at reading the subaltern.

However, the third reason is more pertinent: the voices that speak to and for have become more audible. If half a century ago, the Lutheran presence outside the North Atlantic axis was all but negligible, today at least forty percent are already outside Europe and North America—and they are growing at a fast pace. When we celebrate the 500th anniversary of the Reformation, the majority of those who can claim a legitimate invitation to the banquet probably will be outside of the traditional axis of Lutheranism. Lutheranism is migrating *en masse*, and the father of the German language is now speaking many tongues. Luther's figure is being transfigured. Catchwords of the Reformation assume new meanings, with theological as well as social, economic and political overtones (e.g., "Here I stand!"). This is what DTS recognized more than a decade ago. It has responded to the challenge, which resulted in the Augsburg 2009, with a panoply of people and voices. Here the networking that was envisioned happened; here the tapestry into which we are woven produced new and beautiful patterns.

What did not happen? Deficits

The hypothesis laid out at the beginning of this summary is that the intercontextual conversation happening in the midst of and because of our differences is imbued with the very spirit of the Reformation. This spirit was described as the tense encounter between the voice that speaks as church and the one that speaks to church and for the people, breathing life into the body of the communion. As times have changed, the content of the debates over the centuries, the tonality of the voices represented and the tension into which they are inscribed testify to the same spirit and indeed the spirit of restlessness that enlivens.

By its very nature, true conversation is always and by definition an event that ends in a deficit, and in this deficit lies the key to what still needs to be talked about. Some of them became evident and remain on the agenda to be pursued as we continue to converse. For example, there is a need to deepen and broaden our eschatology to other questions. Probably we need to move into such questions as, Where is/are the *eschaton/eschata*? Where are the dead? Where is hell? There was also a certain amount of uneasiness with regard to probing more deeply into the question of sexuality. Further, the ecological challenge requires reexamination so as not to be cast primarily as a so-called First World agenda. What is a so-called Third World agenda for understanding how humans relate to the rest of creation? A similar issue that often cuts across latitudinal lines is the dialogue with people of other faiths. This dialogue will increasingly be a challenge. Consider the upcoming scenario: not only are increasing numbers of Lutherans migrating to traditionally non-Lutheran parts of the planet, but the majority of Lutherans in the global South will be members of churches in places where they are small minorities in relation to other faiths, particularly in Asia and parts of Africa. If communion happens in the tension between church teachings and the challenges of mission, what will communion mean in these contexts? What was also surprising was the absence of a discussion about Lutheran theology and economy, particularly in this crucial crisis of unprecedented global scope. While the last day was dedicated to topics related to church and state, theology and society, little attention was given to the relationship between the church and political regimes, particularly in the context of Islamic states (which is related to the upcoming majority-minority challenge). There was also deficit in the discussion of theology and its relation to church structure. Is it enough (*satis est*) to call upon Article VII of the Augsburg Confession to settle the issues pertaining to church structure, ministry and practices?

These deficits are symptoms signaling emerging challenges that invite us to further conversations, even if it is to revision old, unsettled disputes. Conversation that evinces the life-giving spirit that animated and continues to animate the Reformation movement here and now, breathes life into the body communion.

Trajectories: Where from here?

I called the Augsburg 2009 an apex or culmination of a process begun more than a decade ago. But culminations are not terminations. They resemble a summit in a mountain range. Once one is climbed, it is time to go down and to plan for the next, maybe even higher peak. What counts is the hiking and the climbing. The conversation needs to be ongoing.

If the practice of communion and spirit of the Reformation are to keep on giving life to the people of God, the task ahead is to take heed of what has been accomplished, make a note of what has not been addressed satisfactorily, and be attentive to the signs of the time and places where tensions arise and the promise of community abides. When and where we meet to keep the conversation going, the labor is in weaving the tapestry until all strands are woven together. In what has been accomplished we realize how much more is left to be done. The lack of good communication or the exasperation at not having someone agree with us on what seems an obvious point can easily bring the conversation to a halt. Not allowing that to happen is the challenge to which we all are called.

John 20, recounts the well-known story of doubting Thomas, a person for whom I have deep sympathy. He was not there when the disciples were gathered and Jesus came into their midst. He had not seen what the others had already seen. Asking for evidence of a claim that is rather unlikely is not too much to ask. He probably thought that his friends were delusional, were trying to fool him, or were simply nuts. This would be the perfect reason for him to keep some distance to those less than reliable people. But the text continues: "A week later his disciples were again in the house, and Thomas was with them." This is the center of the Thomas story. No matter how much in disagreement he was with his comrades, he did not give up the conversation. Thus a communion was born.

Lutheran Theology in the Future?

Karen L. Bloomquist

Significant shifts in the profile of theological work in the Lutheran World Federation

Christian theology reflects on the God we know in Jesus Christ through the power of the Holy Spirit, and how this God relates to the whole of creation at all times and in all places. It draws upon theological formulas and doctrines of the past, but more is involved than simply repeating them. Good theology is characterized by a spirit of meditation, reflection and inquiry, rather than only by the answers it might provide. Theology is continually asking, What does this mean—today? The value of theology is in terms of the questions it raises, and the new space it opens up for confessing and living out the faith in current contexts. It ought to be a critical accompaniment to all that the church says and does, thereby provoking the ongoing reformation of the church, its structures and practices. Theology should challenge churches to consider new questions and horizons of faithfulness today, in light of the biblical and confessional heritage we share. These are understandings that have undergirded the work of the Department for Theology and Studies (DTS) of the Lutheran World Federation (LWF), especially over the past decade.

The shifts in how theology has been viewed and pursued in recent years can be contrasted with how theological work in the LWF was described in the 1990s, under the subtitle "theology in an era of fragmentation."[1] In that discussion, this theological work was characterized in terms of seven tensions or antinomies:

- Consensus versus controversy
- Global Lutheran identity versus regional differentiation
- Confessional identity versus ecumenical openness

---

[1] Jens Holger Schjørring, Prasanna Kumari and Norman A. Hjelm (eds), *From Federation to Communion* (Minneapolis: Fortress, 1997), pp. 200–202.

- Academic discourse versus the common and popularly expressed concerns of the churches
- Classical theology versus a theology of modern reference
- Tradition versus renewal
- Central leadership versus grassroots initiatives.

Even if these tensions were descriptively accurate when this was written, which itself may be questionable, since then significant attempts have been made to move beyond these dichotomized ways of viewing theological work in the LWF.

The 1997 subtitle, "theology in an age of fragmentation," is itself revealing, implying that the emergence of different voices and perspectives was "fragmenting" a normative Lutheran theology. However, what was assumed to be a consensual normative theology has actually has been pervasively Eurocentric and male-dominated in its assumptions and approaches, which a number of the articles in this Theology in the Life of the Church (TLC) series counter. Labeling what is occurring as "fragmentation" presupposes that there would still be one homogenous theology if only these other voices and perspectives had not arisen, or at least had remained complicit with the theology that the missionaries had bestowed on them. Historically, however, similar kinds of diversity have been present since the beginning of the church, and certainly also in how Lutheran theology has developed in different contexts. Increasingly, we are realizing that diversity is constitutive of what it means to be a global communion, not something that needs to be overcome or homogenized.

Yet, affirming the differences among us, although important, is not sufficient. In Acts 2, Pentecost involves more than that. The work of the Spirit is not only to celebrate diversity but also to further understandings amid these differences, and ultimately reconciliation. The many voices begin to be heard and included, such that what has been the center expands so that ultimately there will no longer be margins.[2] Furthermore, God's gift through the Spirit, which enables understanding across the differences, transforms the lives of people, communities and structures. It may be difficult to trust this transformational work of the Spirit, especially when it threatens what we thought was a settled consensus, but was it really a settled consensus anyway?

Contesting what is assumed to be theological consensus is never without some controversy, especially because of the power disparities that inevitably are

---

[2] Letty M. Russell, *Just Hospitality: God's Welcome in a World of Difference* (Louisville: Westminster John Knox, 2009), pp. 60f.

involved, but typically covered over, while those who do not concur with the consensus are silenced or marginalized. This is compounded when there are such huge disparities between the amount of time and money for theological training, research and argumentation that theologians enjoy, for example, in Europe and North America, compared to those in other parts of the world. How then can the latter contest the consensus that has been arrived at through years of careful refinement in relation to questions and sensitivities that are not theirs, and which have only begun to be recognized in recent decades, and still are not taken that seriously in much of theological discourse today?

An assumption reflected in the above characterizations from the 1990s, is that Lutheran identity runs counter to contextualization. Today, however, it is increasingly apparent that there is no "essential" or unchanging Lutheran identity but that from the beginning of church history through the Reformation and certainly today, all theology has been contextual and dynamic. Identity itself is contextual. The only difference is between those who acknowledge such and those who presume that their theology and theological identity can be applied universally to or speak for all. Particularities, such as regional differences, are constitutive of what it means to be Lutheran in theology and practice.

To be Lutheran is also to be deeply ecumenical. A set-apart confessionalism is contradictory to the spirit and intent of Lutheran theology. Increasingly, theological work is pursued with the intention of bringing Lutheran theological nuances into the ecumenical and public arena, and in dialogue with other theological and faith traditions.

Although academic theological work often still operates in ways and places that are far removed from the real concerns of common people, a central purpose of the LWF Theology in the Life of the Church program has been to encourage academic theological work that engages with the actual challenges people in churches and their societies are facing. This is grounded in Luther's own theological approach, which focused on concrete struggles for the sake of the gospel in the context of church and society in the sixteenth century. Rather than abstract, detached theology that is more accountable to academic discourses, it was intended to be helpful to common people in the church. Not only was the latter the point of reference for Luther's own theological thinking, but furthermore, if a theology of the cross has increasingly come to be seen as what distinguishes Lutheran theology, then it is not those who are learned and "higher up" but the lowly and overlooked who should be the point of reference for an authentically Lutheran theology. It perhaps is no accident that Lutheranism is growing and spreading in a number of contexts where this is occurring.

Also, the distinction from the 1990s between classical theology and theology with "modern reference" no longer makes much sense. Instead, more interdisciplinary approaches are essential today, not only across the traditional theological disciplines, but certainly also with other disciplines—if theology is to engage the real questions and issues that haunt our world today.

Tradition versus renewal is also a false dichotomy. Renewal in theology, worship and church life does not simply mean going back to "tradition," but it involves retrieving, revising, recasting or transfiguring what has been received. In other words, drawing upon a tradition is a crucial aspect of what occurs in renewal, even though it may not be readily recognizable afterwards.

Finally, if central leadership in a global communion is to be effective, it cannot do so if it does not encourage, build capacity and empower decentralized grass-roots initiatives. Centralized versus regionalized is a false dichotomy. Theological work as carried out in more local contexts contributes to and is itself constitutive of the necessary global theological work, rather than a diversion from or in competition with it. The LWF is not what is done in and through a central office but in and through a multitude of places and venues around the world, as part of a global communion.

In other words, there have been significant changes in assumptions, understandings and approaches of theological work that call into serious question the above antinomies used in the 1990s to characterize theological work within the LWF. Much of this has been related to a growing sense of what being a communion of churches implies theologically. These antinomies have largely been transformed from being oppositions into being mutually complementary dimensions of the kind of critical, relevant theological work needed in the twenty-first century.

Pursuing theology today in a Lutheran communion

Theology is necessarily contextual. Universal theological categories that presume to speak with the same meaning to people in very different situations are appropriately viewed with suspicion, especially when they become only platitudes. Contextual perspectives have been raised up, in part, as a protest against dominant theological discourses that have rendered many invisible and silent. But contextual theology involves far more than describing, analyzing and dwelling on the differences. The power and historical factors connected with those differences must be dealt with, but furthermore, addressed theologically: how is the Triune God, to whom Scripture witnesses, active in the midst of this? How might resurrected hope be embodied and enacted amid the emptiness, pathos, and suffering in our realities? How does God's liberating, reconciling work become incarnate in the many contexts in which Lutheran churches today seek to live out the Christian faith?

The challenge is actually to do theology in the midst of a diverse Lutheran communion—especially at those points when the power inequities, tensions and differences seem to divide rather than unite us. The temptation is to walk away from one another at those points—because the "others" are not like "us," or because from our perspective we judge their positions to be unbiblical or un-Christian (e.g., on some matters of sexuality). The secular criteria for what unites the church then become homogeneity or an opinion poll of what people agree or disagree with—typically on grounds that are not explicitly biblical or theological but rooted in culture. In contrast, in the transformative gospel Jesus embodied and proclaimed, he continually was questioning categories by which people judged others, challenging their biases and ways of setting themselves off from others, and bringing about reconciliation.

In 2004—2005, an LWF study team, of nine theologians and ethicists from Brazil, China, Germany, Hungary, South Africa, Sweden and the US, whose contexts and issues initially seem so different, at first were hardly able to converse with one another without significant amounts of suspicion, but as they talked together gradually were able to discover commonalities—through a kind of Lutheran "grammar"—and began to break through some of the cultural barriers of reserve in order to challenge one another.

The faith conviction that the world with all its diversities is God's is what shifted the group's focus from the "many worlds" of postmodernity to insisting, nevertheless, that is it God's one world. What holds us together despite our differences, and empowers us to deliberate in the midst of them, is a resilient conviction of faith in a God who creates, redeems and promises to transform us and our world.[3]

Some of this occurred on a much larger scale at Augsburg 2009, in hundreds of interactions and conversations each day—a coming together not through the imposition of universals but dialogically, through our interactions, which is the beginning of trans-contextual theology.

> In meeting with actual persons rather than generalized others. Such encounters
> can provide the basis for ethical commitments and actions, based on moral norms

---

[3] Karen L. Bloomquist (ed.), *Lutheran Ethics at the Intersections of God's One World*, LWF Studies 02/2005 (Geneva: The Lutheran World Federation, 2005), p. 14.

of equity and complementary reciprocity. Out of this may emerge something like an "interactive universalism" (Benhabib)—not moral guides imposed on others, but the emergence of names for continuing relationships in ways that respect differences and lead us to join together with others to challenge unjust practices and structures. In this process, cultures are likely to be transformed, in light of central faith convictions.[4]

But given this interest, the question quickly arises, On whose terms? As one North American participant at Augsburg 2009 remarked, "what most of us consider academic are life and death matters elsewhere!" Between the North Atlantic and the rest of the world, there are significant gaps in assumptions, methodologies, conceptualizations, types of discourse, educational prerequisites and availability of and access to resources for pursuing theological work. Typically, only a few theologians from the global South are included in academic theological meetings. To move beyond this, Augsburg 2009 made the participation of theologians from the global South a priority, so that nearly half of the 120 participants were from Africa, Asia and Latin America. Yet even if a critical mass is present, the table still tends to be set and the conversations dominated by the North, including who has the time and background to pursue in-depth theological research and writing.

Questions still arise as to what it means to be "Lutheran." Does being Lutheran even matter any more in increasingly ecumenical and interfaith settings? Or for churches that for long have had a united Lutheran and Reformed identity, or that have been strongly influenced by evangelical movements? Much higher priority is given instead to what will connect with the realities of people today and the challenges churches face in their witness in the world. But even if that is the focus or point of departure, the question still remains as to how Lutheran perspectives might challenge people's assumptions, as well as being renegotiated in light of these realities, as some of the authors in this book consider. It is important, not to bolster up a narrow Lutheran identity but to bring Lutheran insights into ecumenical and civil society engagements. Such a Lutheran identity cannot be based only on static Lutheran codes, as Hansen reminds us, or historical legacies brought by missions, or on the basis of ethnic, tribal or cultural identities, or on historical accidents. Instead, sifting through, reconceiving and transfiguring Lutheran theology is a dynamic movement in which the grace and promises of God are communicated through words, symbols and

---

[4] Ibid., p. 232.

actions that may look, sound and feel much different, for example, from those in sixteenth-century century Germany or twenty-century America. In that dynamism we may begin to glimpse what truly is authoritative in a global Lutheran communion today.

Toward a theology that is transcontextual, transfigured and transformative

The articles in this book imply pursuing theology in ways that are trans-contextual, trans-figured and transformative. In concluding this six-volume TLC series, we sketch what this might entail for future theological work in the LWF as a global communion of churches.

Genuinely contextual constructive theology is not easy. It is far easier to cite factors at play in a given context, and then apply some recognizable theological formulas without rethinking what they might mean in new contexts. It is important that this rethinking and reconfiguring be done, not separate from, but connected with the yearnings and questions of ordinary people. This began to occur at the first TLC seminar in 2006 in Arusha, where "lament" emerged as pastorally and theologically essential in the midst of poverty related suffering.[5] In the 2008 TLC seminar in Hong Kong, participants insisted that theological reflection was needed, e.g., on material blessings ("why are some blessed but we aren't?") and on the afterlife (especially relationships with ancestors)[6]—in other words, the kinds of matters that academic theologians have mostly ignored or looked down upon.

This necessitates knowing the Bible, theological traditions and understandings well—having a sense for what different figures, biblical texts and themes, doctrines, historical developments or theological approaches are about; being able to read or interpret them deeply, so as to discern which of these emphases are particularly relevant in situations today. This involves continuing dialogue with theological traditions, not standing apart from but engaging them with freedom and creativity, mindful of both the continuities and the discontinuities. It involves reflecting on what will

---

[5] Karen L. Bloomquist and Musa Panti Filibus (eds), *"So the poor have hope, and injustice shuts its mouth"*: *Poverty and the Mission of the Church in Africa*, LWF Studies 01/2007 (Geneva: The Lutheran World Federation, 2007), pp. 19–20.

[6] Karen L. Bloomquist, *Identity, Survival, Witness: Reconfiguring Theological Agendas*, Theology in the Life of Church series, vol. 3 (Geneva: The Lutheran World Federation, 2008), pp. 59–74.

most appropriately speak to what is really at stake here, and in the process, exposing and critiquing what is occurring.

The point is not just to discern what is applicable or generally related, but to discern which biblical narratives, theological symbols and understandings from the past need to be reinterpreted, reconceptualized, or "trans-figured" for the sake of engaging more deeply and thus transforming particular contexts and sets of challenges. It is having the wisdom and courage to say what needs to be said at those very points, as Luther insisted, where the gospel is under attack or "the devil is raging." This is occurring not only out there in the world, but also in the church itself, especially in how power is exercised. Through the much different power of the Spirit, a heightened awareness of our context is what gives the text, when reinterpreted or even trans-figured, its power and wisdom. This is what genuinely contextual theology seeks to do, and what needs to be nurtured, encouraged and supported.

Although genuinely contextual theologies are essential, admittedly, a danger is that these can become too captive to their own setting or realities. Yet, contextually-grounded theologies do create new conditions for trans-contextual interpretations of the Christian faith, for the sake of more extensive validity in a global society of many cultures. What remains the same, despite obvious changes in historical and cultural conditions, is that which has the ability to trans-contextualize itself.[7]

"Trans-contextual" here refers to movement in the present, across spaces or defined contexts. The underpinnings and authorization for this are not only incarnational (contextual), but also Trinitarian, communicative, interactive (across contexts). We dare to cross boundaries and change our perspectives, inspired by the many ways in which Jesus is depicted in the Gospels as continually crossing boundaries, mingling with those he should not have. Most significantly, it is in crossing over from one context to another that we may be graced with intimations of what transcends each of our contexts, glimpses of how the Spirit of God is active between and among us, in ways that go beyond our own most cherished culture-based beliefs and practices.

Trans-contextual theology is the real challenge—and opportunity. This is where liberation or transformation begins to emerge, not in spite of but through the differences. Immersion in particular contextual realities, and how they both inspire and challenge us, provokes the need for theological

---

[7] Sigurd Bergmann, *God in Context: A Survey of Contextual Theology* (Aldershot and Burlington: Ashgate, 2003), pp. 12, 54.

interpretations that can become transformative. We seek to understand the context more deeply, not so that theology can fit, correspond or be relevant to what is going on (although that also is important) but so that we can sense how the transcendent God is active in these realities. This occurs through trans-contextual ways that no one contextual perspective can own, and that can inspire, motivate and energize what needs to be done to change what is in bondage, broken and in need of transformation. It involves an incarnational vulnerability that is inherent in a theology of the cross, a power in interactivity that empowers.[8]

"Transfiguration" as it is being used here, has to do with what happens to traditions that have been passed down through time. It is far more than just translation or application, but involves creative re-envisioning and making new connections. Vítor Westhelle used "transfiguration" at the Hong Kong seminar to refer to how figures rooted in concrete historical circumstances migrate across time and space and emerge in new situations, catalyzing new associations and meanings, through surprising or unexpected connections.[9] Or, we might more think of this in terms of bread shared in the Eucharist that is transfigured into bread shared around the dinner table with the hungry; outcasts as those through whom Christ is known, the royal Jesus becoming the rejected Jesus of the streets, God revealed in hiddeness and lowliness.

"Transformation" has to do with how we individually and our social realities are changed. Theology in and for the life of the church—and the world—is more than an academic exercise. Liberation and liberating practices are key in this spiritual process of transformation. The indwelling God empowers us through different kinds of assumptions, relationships, ways of living and what we attend to theologically. As Luther put it, through the power of God in the Eucharist, we are changed into one another: … "through the interchange of his blessing and our misfortunes, we become one loaf, one bread, one body, one drink, and have all things in common. [...] In this way we are changed into one another and are made into a community

---

[8] Catherine Keller, *On the Mystery* (Minneapolis: Fortress, 2008), p. 85.

[9] Vitor Westhelle, "Transfiguring Lutheranism: Being Lutheran in New Contexts," in Karen L. Bloomquist (ed.), *Identity, Survival, Witness: Reconfiguring Theological Agendas,* Theology in the Life of the Church series, vol. 3 (Geneva: The Lutheran World Federation, 2008), p. 18.

by love."[10] In and with all our diversity, we become the body of Christ in and for the world. Thus, our contexts become shared contexts, not through our efforts, but because of the transcendent power that transforms us all in the interchange. We discover the transformative potential of Lutheran theology "at the intersections of God's one world." There we find not a morass of postmodern relativism, but fragile yet reliant threads that do hold us together—the creating, redeeming and sustaining love of God that holds us together.

In today's world, and especially in a global communion, it is inadequate, and increasingly unacceptable, to pursue theological work in monocultural ways, or only in relation to one's own context. The resultant theology too readily ends up reflecting and becoming captive to what is normative or acceptable in a given context; it loses its critically transcendent aspect. The kind of theology proposed here needs to be pursued interactively with others who are different from us—and open to what they bring to us rather than only preoccupied with our realities. We must not deceive ourselves into assuming that our ways or concepts are absolute, even if they have been passed on to us as if they were. This is not relativism, but involves testing and struggling to find common ground, or what is authoritative (i.e., true and valid) across contexts. Diversity does not compromise but enriches and expands what is considered authoritative.

We see this, for example, in terms of what it means for the Bible with all its diversity to be authoritative: "In the clash of differences, in combination with the continuing work of the Spirit, new and more profound knowledge of God can become available."[11] Diane Jacobson, a participant in the LWF study program on biblical authority, describes this dynamic sense of authority:

> Our imaginations and our lives are transformed, and we understand things more truly. Biblical truth is found in the midst of all this complexity. The Bible stands authoritatively in our lives not by answering all of our questions but by ever deepening our faith. We are driven to our knees in repentance; we are raised up through the word of forgiveness: we are pulled by the Word into service and a passion for justice; and we are enlivened by and lifted into the

---

[10] Martin Luther, "The Blessed Sacrament of the Holy and True Body of Christ, and the Brotherhoods, 1519," in Helmut T. Lehmann (ed.), *Luther's Works*, vol. 35 (Philadelphia: Muhlenberg Press, 1960), p. 58.

[11] Terrence Fretheim and Karlfried Froehlich, *The Bible as Word of God in a Postmodern Age* (Minneapolis: Fortress, 1998), p. 125.

divine promise. Any notion of authority to overly simplify this encounter is finally a betrayal of the gospel that stands at its core.[12]

Similarly, in trans-contextual theological pursuits, through those persons and perspectives we consider to be "other" from us, the One who truly is other, yet also deeply incarnate with us—both transcendent and immanent—breaks into and transforms our assumptions and realities. As this occurs through the power of God's Spirit, we discern what truly is authoritative—not a set body of texts or doctrines that too often have been used to control, discipline or exclude others, but for Luther as for us today, a living relationship that is liberating and transforms the bondage and injustices that hold us and our world captive. This points toward a coming together not through the imposition of universals but dialogically, through our interactions—an incarnational, perichoretic, embodied conversation, which is anchored in basic convictions and insights of the Reformation. Perhaps this is a foretaste of what might unfold during the second 500 years of theological work inspired by the Reformation.

What does this then imply about authoritative teachings in the life of a communion of Lutheran churches? Among Lutherans, there is widespread and justifiable suspicion about drifting toward any kind of magisterium to determine authoritative teachings in the church. The authority of Scripture read through the lenses of the Lutheran Confessions (especially the Augsburg Confession) is considered sufficient. But as the above discussion indicates, such authoritative sources of our faith need to be unpacked and reinterpreted in highly diverse contexts, so that they become living and transformative in their effects today, rather than only static codes of allegiance, or worse yet, being used as weapons against others. "It is the very impact that the Bible can have which exemplifies its actual authority."[13]

If the liberating, transformative impact is key in discerning authoritativeness, then the above kinds of incarnational, perichoretic, embodied, trans-contextual interactions are essential in what needs to occur in a global communion of churches. It is through these means that a communion discerns together what to rule out of bounds, such as when some impose on others what the others do not experience as true, valid or authoritative, or when some threaten to break communion with those with whom they

---

[12] Diane Jacobson, "Reading Strategies in Light of Biblical Diversity" in Reinhard Boettcher (ed.), *Witnessing to God's Faithfulness: Issues of Biblical Authority,* LWF Studies 02/2006 (Geneva: The Lutheran World Federation), p. 57.

[13] Günter Thomas, "The Bible and the Word(s) of God," in Boettcher, ibid., p. 26.

disagree over matters that really are not at the core of what it means to be the church. If communion is not something we make or break, because it is given through God's grace, then being open to how that grace breaks into and transforms a diverse communion must be at the core of what is authoritative.

What still urgently needs to be addressed

If the above kinds of theological work are to occur in a global communion of Lutheran churches, then it is crucial that the following be given significant attention in a renewed LWF:

- The theological capacities of those in the member churches, particularly the leaders but also all the people of God, needs to be further developed. Priority attention and support needs to be given to enhancing the quality and innovative types of theological education at all levels—so that theology can critique and transform practices of the churches when they contradict the heart of the faith to which they claim to bear witness.

- In many churches, there are serious deficits in understanding the Lutheran confessional writings and Lutheran perspectives on biblical interpretation and basic Christian teachings, and beyond that, in how to contextualize these in critically constructive ways in much different situations today.

- How to think and write theologically, rather than only repeating answers others provide, is a skill or art that urgently needs to be developed through more appropriate methodologies and pedagogies.

- As important as contextual approaches continue to be, trans-contextual approaches that are open to being transformed by those from different life experiences, contexts or regions are crucial for the further development of Lutheran theology globally.